Dior

浙江省普通高校“十三五”新形态教材

时尚品牌解析

（双语）

郑喆·编著

ANALYSIS OF FASHION BRANDS

BURBERRY
LONDON
BURBERRY
LONDON ENGLAND

扫一扫

浙江工商大學出版社 | 杭州
ZHEJIANG GONGSHANG UNIVERSITY PRESS

前　言

时尚千变万化，品牌无奇不有。

在中国实现改革开放之后的现今社会，服装市场发展了四十多年。国际品牌蜂拥而入，国内品牌也茁壮成长。

在服饰海洋和品牌世界中，哪些品牌是人们关注较多、又频繁消费的？普通消费者可能对品牌的名称、形象和产品较为感兴趣，然而服装专业的学生对品牌的历史、文化、设计师等需要了解更多，也更需要知道其来龙去脉和经营管理特色。因此，在多年“时装市场案例研究”“时装营销研讨”等课程教学实践的基础上，编者编成了本教材，命名为“时尚品牌解析”。

本教材把服饰市场分为七大板块，分别是奢侈品市场、快时尚市场、运动服饰市场、牛仔装市场、童装市场、内衣市场和配饰品市场。教材的每一章，先是对每个板块进行了市场综述，再选取各个板块下数个具有代表性的品牌，对其发展的历程、设计师的风格、产品的特色、营销的战略与传播的策略等，进行了解析。

为了迎合全球化、国际化趋势下的高等教育教学要求，响应教育部关于全英文教学和双语教学的号召，本教材采用双语编辑，中英文对照，同时考虑学生接受程度，优化课程教学安排，结合时装品牌案例分析，提高课程的教学质量和教学水平，从而激发学生学习兴趣和提高学生专业英语水平，从两方面着手改善教学效果，增加教与学的有效性。

同时，作为浙江省“十三五”高校教材和新形态教材，本书贯彻全国本科教育精神，利用信

Analysis of Fashion Brands

息技术创新教材形态，充分发挥新形态教材在课堂教学改革和创新方面的作用，不断提高课堂和课程教学质量。书中编辑了大量有助于学生了解时尚品牌的音频、视频资料，以及有利于学生进行案例分析的阅读文献和拓展资源，通过移动互联网技术，以嵌入二维码的方式，将各类多媒体教学资源融合到教材中，实现线上线下相结合的教材新模式。

本书一共分为七章，每个章节都图文并茂、重点突出、内容新颖、通俗易懂。高校相关专业教师可以将其作为专业课程教材，选取其中部分板块和案例作为授课资料，在一个学期32—48课时内完成。本书也可以作为服饰行业从业人员的自学用书，以及时尚消费者获取时尚信息与品牌知识的图书。

本书在编写过程中，得到了大量朋友的帮助。从资料的收集、板块的分析，到案例的积累，一点一滴都凝聚了同仁和学生们的心血。我的硕士研究生们都付出了许多精力，其中庄华同学负责了最后的成稿工作，赵婉怡同学为全书绘制了插图。在此，感谢两位学生的付出，也对其他各位的关心帮助与辛勤付出，一并表示感谢。

本书是浙江省普通高校“十三五”第二批新形态教材建设项目的成果，也得到浙江理工大学教材建设项目的资助，在此表示感谢。最后，感谢浙江工商大学出版社的编辑，他们的认真审阅使得本书可以顺利出版。由于作者水平有限，难免有疏漏和错误之处，欢迎各位读者批评指正，以待日后完善。

编者
浙江理工大学国际教育学院
2019年8月

目录

Analysis of Fashion Brands

第一章

奢侈品牌

Luxury Brands

第一节

奢侈品市场分析

Analysis of Luxury Market

在西方作为身份象征与阶层代表的奢侈品，尽管对现如今的普罗大众来说并非遥不可及，但其在现代生活中依旧享有极为特殊的市场和社会地位。奢侈品并不是必需品，却能使消费者在购买中获得更为强烈的愉悦感，而“luxury”（奢侈品）这一英文单词，正是取自原意指“不计成本地放纵感官”的拉丁文“luxus”。

奢侈品品牌得以形成，源自其所服务的奢侈品。现代西方社会一般认为，奢侈品品牌始于以时尚之父克里斯汀·迪奥为代表的一众设计师之手，而曾经奢侈品品牌创造、制造的中心，恰是以生活方式奢靡、浪费的法国宫廷为代表的古老欧洲王室。

从经济学上来说，奢侈品指的是价值与品质关系比值最高的产品，对其需求的增长往往高于收入增长。在国际上则被定义为“一种超出人们生存与发展需要范围的，具有独特、稀缺、珍奇等特点的消费品”，又称为非生活必需品。

综观全球奢侈品市场，不难发现，经历过2015—2016年的低潮期，如今的奢侈品市场正呈现复苏态势。除此之外，奢侈品行业在新兴的全球语境下，也正不断寻求创新与变革上的突破。如今，奢侈品市场发展趋势呈现以下特点：

1. 奢侈品消费群体变更：中国千禧一代消费者将是构成奢侈品购买人群的不容小觑的一部分。

2. 奢侈品加码电商平台：数字化趋势下，奢侈品线上销售额节节攀升，增速远超于奢侈品行业的整体增速。

3. 跨界合作与联名产品：新世代消费者的崛起与消费者消费习惯的转变，呼唤奢侈品品牌进行改革创新以实现品牌年轻化、创意化，形成新的增长点。

Analysis of Luxury Market

Luxury product, as a symbol of identity and hierarchy in the western countries, is within the reach of the common people today. But it still enjoys a very special market and shows social status in some way in our modern life. Luxury goods are not necessities, but they can make consumers have more intense pleasure in their purchases. The English word "luxury" is derived from the Latin word "luxus", which originally meant "indulging the senses regardless of cost".

Luxury brands are from the luxury goods they serve. Modern Western society generally believes that luxury brands started with a group of designers represented by Christian Dior, and the creation and manufacturing center of luxury brand in the past is the old European royal family.

In economics, luxury refers to the product with the highest ratio of value to quality, and its demand growth is often higher than income growth. Internationally, it is defined as "a consumer product that is unique, scarce, and rare, and also beyond the scope of people's needs for survival and development". It is also called non-living necessities.

From the big canvas of global luxury goods market, it is not difficult to find that after the slow tide of 2015—2016; it is showing a recovery trend today. In addition, the luxury goods industry is constantly seeking breakthroughs in innovation and change in the emerging global context. Lately, the development trend of the luxury goods market has the following characteristics:

1. Changes in luxury consumer groups: Chinese millennial consumers will be the growing part of the buying community.

2. Luxury goods focus on e-commerce platform: Under the digital trend, luxury online sales are increasing, the growth rate far exceeds the overall growth rate of the luxury goods industry.

3. Cross-border cooperation and joint products: The rise of new generations of consumers and the transformation of consumer consumption habits call for luxury brands to carry out reform and innovation to achieve brand rejuvenation, creativity, and form new growth points.

第二节

奢侈品牌分析
Analysis of Luxury Brands

博柏利 Burberry

扫一扫

2016年11月1日，博柏利发布了一则以品牌创始人托马斯·博柏利的生活经历和品牌发展历史为叙事基础的短片，使用戏剧性的情节和优美的音乐，让观众在沉浸于品牌故事的同时深入了解品牌基因。1835年出生于英国萨里郡小镇的托马斯·博柏利有着过人的商业头脑、非凡的创造性以及敏锐的洞察力，从户外服装的开发到华达呢面料的创造性发明，他不断扩展业务，使得博柏利发展成为英国最大的服装品牌之一。

品牌简介

BURBERRY
LONDON
BURBERRY
LONDON ENGLAND

图 1–1　博柏利品牌商标

由托马斯·博柏利于1856年创立的博柏利，以专注于开发户外服装为起点，如今发展为极具英国传统风格的奢侈品牌，涉及高级成衣、配饰、香水、太阳镜及美妆产品等众多领域。

1879年，博柏利开发出首款华达呢面料，这种面料具有耐磨、防水且透气的良好性能，成为品牌发展的基石。博柏利因此成为众多户外探险家的首选，它先后为极地探险家罗尔德·阿蒙森（1911年）和欧内斯特·沙克尔顿（1914年）等提供装备。

博柏利在两次世界大战期间成为英国士兵的服装供应商。其标志性防水风衣“trench coat”（战前被称为“Tielocken”）便诞生于第一次世界大战期间——符合战时军事人员在战壕中作战的需要，并于“一战”后开始受到大众的欢迎，博柏利自此成为英国家喻户晓的品牌。

经典的博柏利格纹则诞生于20世纪20年代，以苏格兰格纹呢为设计基础，在米黄底色上穿插黑、红、白三色条纹。起初主要用于其风衣的衬里，经过40多年的发展运用，成为其时尚标识之一。

图 1-2 1912年，博柏利Trench coat的早期雏形——Tielocken军装大衣①

品牌战略

自20世纪60年代以来，博柏利始终呈现出英伦传统与现代风格完美结合的品牌形象。然而，在20世纪90年代中期，采用博柏利经典格纹图案的商品泛滥成灾，成为年轻工人阶级和足球迷的最爱，致使其品牌形象稀释。直到21世纪初，创意总监克里斯托弗·贝利与首席执行官安吉拉·阿伦茨接管后，开始着手巩固品牌声誉，这一局面才得以扭转，博柏利也从英国风衣制造商转变为世界上最知名的奢侈品牌之一。

2006年，新任首席执行官安吉拉·阿伦茨采取的第一步举措便是将博柏利格纹图样从品牌90%的设计中移除，以尽量减少与低端商品的联系。同时，她宣布博柏利将成为世界上第一家全数字化的奢侈品公司。

事实上，数字营销确实成为其在过去十年中的重点领域。于2001年加入博柏利、先后担任创意总监与首席执行官的英国设计师克里斯托弗·贝利，在负责品牌形象、创意营销及其系列产品设计的过程中，就致力于将博柏利重塑为数字化先锋品牌。比如，2013年与街拍摄影师斯科特·斯库曼合作，建立了数码平台“风衣的艺术”，并将其作为宣传工具，邀请来自不同领域的专业人士上传自己穿着品牌经典风衣的照片。博柏利也是最初使用社交软件色拉布（Snapchat）的知名奢侈品牌之一——于时装发布会前一天，在该平台上首发2016年春夏全系列产品。

扫一扫

贝利还充分利用广告重新定位品牌形象，并通过与社会名流合作，恢复品牌的声誉。比如，邀请知名摄影师马里奥·特斯蒂诺执导广告片，参与其中的有卡拉·迪瓦伊等超模和艾玛·沃特森等知名演员。另外，博柏利于2016年9月的伦敦时装周中成为

① 由创始人托马斯·博柏利先生亲手设计创作，采用单一束带和扣环开襟设计，衣领仅有一颗纽扣。

字母斗篷：于2014年秋冬推出，这一设计实现了品牌零售部门销售额的增长。

The monogrammed poncho: Launched in the fall and winter of 2014, it has raised sales in its retail division.

战壕风衣：作为品牌的核心产品，贝利在其传统基础上融入现代元素，使其以更为多元化的形式呈现。

The trench coat: Since it is central to the brand, Bailey used the house's heritage and tradition; he took on the trench in different ways by reworking it to fit into something far more modern.

博柏利格纹：随着都市街头服饰的兴起，贝利正式重启经典格纹。最为大胆的举措是与俄罗斯街头设计师Gosha Rubchinskiy在2018年春夏系列中的合作。

The Burberry check: With the rise of urban streetwear, Bailey officially heralded the return of the Burberry check. The boldest move is the collaboration with Russian street designer Gosha Rubchinskiy in the Sping and Summer 2018 collections.

图1-3 克里斯托弗·贝利在任期间的代表性设计①

扫一扫

① 本书中时装画稿皆由作者手绘，下同。

首家宣布采用“即看即买”模式的奢侈品牌，顾客可于时装秀结束后立即购买走秀系列，这一举措改变了奢侈品零售业传统的供应链模式。

博柏利于2018年任命意大利设计师里卡多·堤西接替克里斯托弗·贝利，成为新一任创意总监。此前，里卡多·堤西自2005年开始在法国时装品牌纪梵希担任创意总监一职，他擅长将街头服饰与高级时装融为一体，这与当今的奢侈品消费者密切相关，也极大程度地与重塑其品牌形象的要求相匹配。

里卡多·堤西作为博柏利创意总监的重大举措之一是与知名艺术家彼得·萨维尔联袂推出全新品牌专属标识，为这个长期保持传统的品牌注入活力。

Burberry

On 1st November, 2016, Burberry released *The Tale of Thomas Burberry*, a short film inspired by Thomas Burberry's life and achievements, using dramatic plots and beautiful music to immerse the audience in the brand as well as understand the brand DNA. Born in 1835 in the small town of Surrey, England, Thomas Burberry has expanded his business with the development of outdoor clothing and the creative invention of gabardine fabrics with his business savvy, extraordinary creativity and keen insight and made Burberry one of the UK's largest apparel brands.

Brand Introduction

Established in 1856 by Thomas Burberry, Burberry has developed into a luxury British brand with a British traditional style, starting with developing outdoor attire. It has been involved in ready-to-wear, accessories, fragrances, sunglasses, cosmetics and many other fields.

In 1879, Burberry introduced in its brand the first gabardine, a hardwearing, water-resistant yet breathable fabric, which has become the cornerstone of its brand development. Therefore, numerous adventurers picked up Burberry on their expeditions as their first choice, such as the polar explorers Roald Amundsen (1911) and Ernest Shackleton (1914).

And Burberry has become the apparel provider for British soldiers during both World Wars. The iconic "trench coat", known as "Tielocken", was born during the First World War—adapted to the needs of wartime military personnel fighting in the trenches, and after the war, it became popular with civilians. Since then, Burberry has become a well-known brand in the UK.

In the 1920s, Burberry created its classic check, a Scottish tartan design with a beige base, accented by black, red and white. Originally, the check was primarily used as a lining in its trench coats. And it took more than forty years for the design to become a fashion state -

ment of its own.

Brand Strategy

Since the 1960s, the Burberry brand has been a unique combination of British tradition and modern flair. However, by the mid-1990s, the check had become a favorite of young working class and football fans. What Burberry had first created as a mark of luxury and innovation now had negative connotations. Until the beginning of the 21st century, creative director Christo - pher Bailey along with CEO Angela Ahrendts took over and began to solidify the brand's repu - tation, and transformed the British trench coat maker into one of the most widely known luxury fashion houses in the world.

A new CEO, Angela Ahrendts, was appointed in 2006, and her first move was to remove the iconic Burberry check pattern from all but 10% of the brand's designs, to minimise the association with hooliganism. She also announced that Burberry would aim to be the world's first fully digital luxury company.

In fact, digital marketing has indeed become a focus area for the past decade. Since joining the company from 2001, Christopher Bailey has helped recast Burberry as a digital pioneer, spearheading innovative digital campaigns in the process of brand image, creative marketing and product design. For example, in 2013, in cooperation with street photographer Scott Schuman, a digital platform "the art of windbreaker" was established, which was used as a promotional tool to invite professionals from different fields to upload their own photos of wearing the brand's classic windbreaker. Burberry is also one of the first well-known luxury brands to use snapchat, the social software, to release the full range of products in SS16 on platform a day before the catwalk show。

Advertising and cooperating with celebrities have played an integral role in Bailey's repositioning of the company. For example, celebrated photographer Mario Testino directs Burberry's campaigns, which have starred models including Cara Delevingneas as well as globally-renowned British actors like Emma Watson. And the heritage brand was also a pioneer of "see now, buy now" in September 2016 at London Fashion Week that has changed the traditional supply chain model of the luxury retail industry.

Burberry has named the Italian Riccardo Tisci as its new creative officer to succeed Christopher Bailey. Previously, Riccardo Tisci began his role as creative director of the French fashion house Givenchy in 2005. He is good at integrating streetwear with high fashion, which is closely related to today's luxury consumers and match the rebranding of the Burberry's image.

Burberry has teamed up with the famous artist Peter Saville to launch a new brand-specific logo as part of a major rebranding measure under Riccardo Tisci to invigorate this long-standing traditional brand.

香奈儿 Chanel

品牌简介

> 时尚可不仅仅体现于着装。时尚在天空中、在街上，时尚和我们的思想、生活方式、正在发生的事情息息相关。
>
> ——可可·香奈儿

图1-4 香奈儿品牌标志

法国高级时装品牌香奈儿由时装设计师可可·香奈儿于1910年创立，从位于巴黎康朋街21号的女帽店开始，发展成以小黑裙、5号香水、斜纹软呢套装和2.55手袋而闻名于世界的奢侈品牌。如今的Chanel S.A.是由阿兰·维德摩尔和热拉尔·维德摩尔（可可·香奈儿早期商业伙伴皮埃尔·维德摩尔的孙子）拥有的私人控股公司，专营高级时装、成衣、美妆、香水和奢华配饰。除此之外，香奈儿还于2002年推出高级手工坊系列，以保存与继承工作坊的传统工艺和技巧。

香奈儿十分擅长“产品隔离”，在保持核心产品高端定位的同时，以价格较低的香水和美妆产品使世界各地的普通消费者购买到香奈儿的生活方式和梦想：从售价高达10万美元的高级定制时装到28美元的指甲油。这种策略现在仍十分奏效——特别是在财富日益增长的中国，催生了中国奢侈品消费的爆炸式增长。

在内容营销上，这个拥有百年历史的品牌在讲述故事方面也具有得天独厚的优势。2013年，香奈儿推出了以内容为中心的微型网站“INSIDE CHANEL”，将其创建者香奈儿女士的生活与品牌历史相结合进行叙述，以高度可视化的风格，让消费者沉浸在其发展背后的故事中。

关键人物[①]

流行易逝，风格永存。

嘉柏丽尔·香奈儿

嘉柏丽尔·香奈儿于1883年出生在法国卢瓦尔河谷的索米尔，12岁时遭遇母亲过世，后被父亲送入了孤儿院。窘迫的童年生活和严格的修道院教育坚定了她掌控自己命运的决心。为人们所熟知的称呼“可可·香奈儿”则出自其短暂的歌手生涯。

作为20世纪的知名设计师之一，嘉柏丽尔成功地利用自己的风格和个人态度——瘦削的身材、标志性短发和健康的肤色，以及积极且独立的生活方式，对现代女性的着装品味与言谈举止产生了持久的影响。

在服装设计上，她不同寻常地选择了平纹针织面料（通常用于男士内衣）。这种织物简约而实用，且具有良好的悬垂性，恰好契合了其设计的特点：常常受到男装的启发，特别是“一战”时期的军装制服，简洁的款式、宽松的线条和变短的裙摆解放了女性的身体，适应了战时女性活动的需要。这些早期设计的关键元素成为日后香奈儿产品的标志。她曾在《时尚芭莎》杂志上这样说道：“简单就是所有真正的优雅的基调。”比如1926年推出的“小黑裙”，装饰以挺括的白色衣领和袖口，严谨与优雅并存，因其以白天和晚上皆可穿着的礼服为概念，成为时尚的基本款式而大受追捧。

嘉柏丽尔女士于1953年重返巴黎，发现洋溢女性气息的“新样式”主导了战后的时尚风潮。但她认为克里斯汀·迪奥的设计既不富有现代气息，也不符合在“二战”中扮演重要角色的女性的特质。在随后

图1-5 嘉柏丽尔·香奈儿

① 本小节人物插画为作者手绘。

推出的三个系列中，她重新设计了经典的斜纹软呢套装——饰有四个口袋，镶以同色或对比色编结滚边，在下摆缝上精美的链饰使之自然垂坠。此外，香奈儿还重新推出了她的手袋、珠宝和鞋子，并再次取得了巨大的成功。

香奈尔的生平多次被改编成舞台剧和电影等。早在1969年，香奈儿的故事就被凯瑟琳·赫本搬上了百老汇的舞台。巴博拉·伯布洛瓦主演的《可可·香奈儿》和奥黛丽·塔图主演的《时尚先锋香奈儿》都是讲述其传奇人生的经典人物传记电影。

时尚，这是一款必须认真对待的游戏。

卡尔·拉格斐

卡尔·拉格斐（1933—2019）不仅仅是一位时尚偶像，更是将高级时装转变为重磅娱乐的流行文化巨匠。他的形象——黑色墨镜，灰白色马尾辫，以及露指皮质手套都极具辨识度。

在长达60年的职业生涯中，他先后为皮埃尔·巴尔曼、让·巴杜、华伦天奴、查尔斯·卓丹以及蔻依工作。随后，是与芬迪、香奈儿的长期合作。在他职业生涯中所扮演过的无数角色中，他对香奈儿的复兴所起的作用无疑是最为深入人心的。回顾于1983年加入沉寂已久的香奈儿时装屋时，他说道：“曾经有一段时间，Chanel被认为是过时的。只有巴黎医生的妻子们仍然会选择穿它。没有人想要它，它是没有希望的……”

图1-6　卡尔·拉格斐

拉格斐为香奈儿创造了一个全新的词“Cocoisms”（可可风格），他将这个词扩展成为一系列经典元素：山茶花、斜纹软呢套装、绗缝手袋、珍珠、金属链、礼帽和珠宝配饰。同时，他将双“C”标志应用于几乎全部的香奈儿系列产品，从冲浪板到回旋镖再到帆布鞋。香奈儿时装发布会在他的创意下成为一个变幻无穷的剧院，他的秀场可以是冰山、瀑布和火箭，也可以是飞机、赌场和超市。

除了是时装设计师，拉格斐还是一名摄影师和电影制作人，并通过电影和影像将香奈儿的传统融入当代生活。他还拍摄并极富创造性地指导了香奈儿的所有广告。

品牌历史[①]

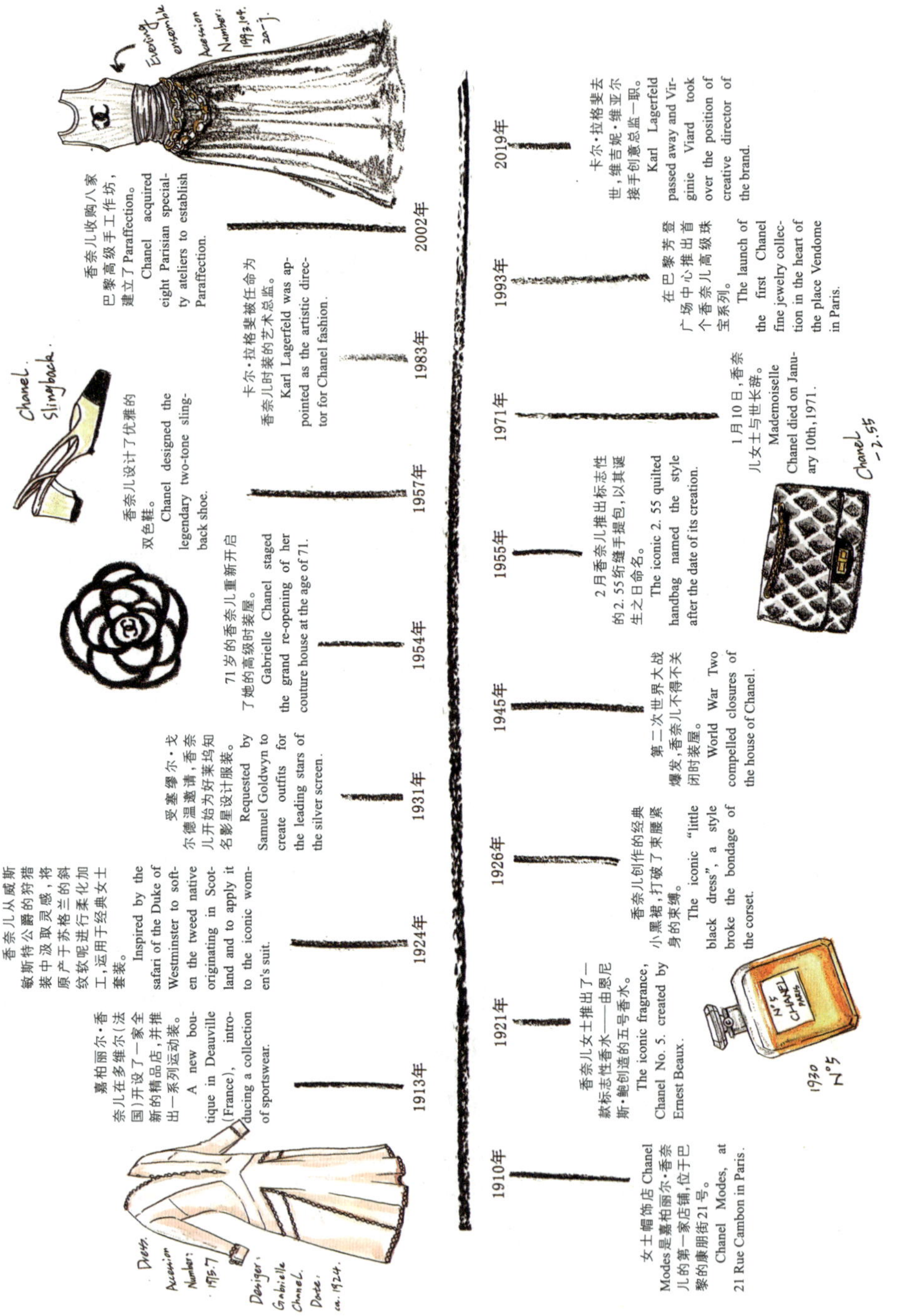

图 1–7　品牌发展时间轴

① 该品牌发展时间轴为作者手绘。

Chanel

Brand Introduction

Fashion is not something that exists in dresses only. Fashion is in the sky, in the street, fashion has to do with ideas, the way we live, what is happening.

——Coco Chanel

The French label Chanel was founded in 1910 by designer Gabrielle "Coco" Chanel. From the women's hat shop at 21 Rue Cambon in Paris, it developed into the world's leading luxury brand famed for the little black dress, No.5 perfume, tweed suits with sloping lines and the 2.55 bag. Today's Chanel S.A. is a privately held company owned by Alain Wertheimer and Gerard Wertheimer, specializing in haute couture, ready-to-wear, beauty, perfume and luxury accessories. Chanel establishes subsidiary company Paraffection in 2002, to preserve the heritage, craft and skill of fashion artisan workshops.

Chanel is quite good at "product isolation". While maintaining the high-end positioning of core products, the cheaper perfumes and beauty products make ordinary consumers around the world buy Chanel's lifestyle and dreams: from haute couture for $100,000 to $28 for nail polish. This strategy is still very effective, especially in China, where wealth is growing. It has spawned explosive growth in Chinese luxury consumption.

In content marketing, this century-old brand also has a unique advantage in telling stories. In 2013, the content-centric microsite "INSIDE CHANEL" was launched to describe the life of its founder, Coco Chanel, in line with the history of the brand. In a highly visual style, consumers are immersed in the story behind its development.

Key Designers

Fashion passes, style remains.

Coco Chanel

Born in Saumur, in the Loire Valley of France in 1883, Gabrielle Chanel was sent to an orphanage by her father at her age of 12 when her mother passed away. Impoverished childhood and strict convent education inspired her to strengthen the control of her own destiny. She acquired the well-known nickname “Coco” from her short singer career.

As one of the key designers in the twentieth century, she made a bold and lasting impression on how modern women should talk, act, and dress by packaging and marketing her own personal attitudes and style. Her own slim boyish figure and cropped hair became an ideal, as did her tanned skin, active lifestyle, and financial independence.

Coco Chanel used jersey cloth since how well it adapted to a simple garment—design which derived from the military uniforms made prevalent by the First World War. Uncluttered styles, with their boxy lines and shortened skirts, allowed women to free their bodies for the practical activities made necessary by the war. Elements of these early designs became hallmarks of Chanel. She once commented on *Harper's Bazaar*, “Simplicity is the keynote of all true elegance.” “The little black dress” of 1926, with the stiff white collar and starched cuffs, whose concept was suitable for day and evening, did gain the universal popularity as a fashion basic.

In 1953, upon returning to France, Coco Chanel found the fashion business enamoured of the “New Look” by Christian Dior. However, Chanel felt his designs were neither modern nor suitable for the women who had survived another war by taking on active roles in society. Within three series, Chanel updated her classic looks, reworking the classic tweed designs—the Chanel suit made of solid or tweed fabric, with collarless jacket trimmed in braid, gold buttons, patch pockets, and—sewn into the hem—a gold-colored chain ensuring it hung properly from the shoulders. Chanel also reintroduced her handbags, jewelry, and shoes with great success.

Chanel's life has been adapted into stage plays and movies. As early as 1969, her story was brought to the stage of Broadway by Catherine Hepburn. Barbora Bobulova's *Coco Chanel* and Audrey Tautou's *Coco Avant Chanel* are classic biographers about her legendary life.

Fashion is a game that has to be played seriously.

Karl Lagerfeld

Karl Lagerfeld (1933—2019) was a giant not just of fashion but of popular culture, who transformed high fashion into blockbuster entertainment. His character with black sunglasses, beige ponytail and the leather gloves with exposed fingers are highly recognizable.

During his sixty-year career, he worked for Pierre Balmain, Jean Patou, Valentino, Charles Jourdan and Chloe. Subsequently, it was a long-term cooperation with Fendi and Chanel. Among the countless roles he has played in his career, his revival of Chanel is undoubtedly the most deeply rooted. Looking back at the long-lost Chanel fashion house in 1983, he said, "For a while, Chanel was considered outdated. Only the wives of the doctors in Paris chose to wear it. No one wanted it, it had no hope..."

Lagerfeld created a new vocabulary for Chanel — "Cocoisms", which he expanded into a series of classic elements: camellia, tweed suits, quilted handbags, pearls, metal chains, hats and jewelry accessories. At the same time, he applied the double "C" logo to nearly all the Chanel collections, from surfboards to boomerangs to canvas shoes.

Lagerfeld supersized the fashion show. He reimagined the catwalk as a theatre that could take many forms. There are icebergs, waterfalls and rockets, as well as a private jet, a casino and supermarket checkouts.

In addition to his design talents, Lagerfeld was also a photographer and film-maker, and brought Chanel's heritage into life through film and imagery; he also shot and creatively directed all of Chanel's advertising.

克里斯汀·迪奥 Christian Dior

品牌简介

Dior

图 1-8　迪奥品牌标志

克里斯汀·迪奥（即迪奥）作为欧洲知名的奢侈品品牌，隶属于世界上最大的奢侈品集团——酩悦·轩尼诗—路易·威登集团（迪奥于20世纪80年代被伯纳德·阿诺特收购）。迪奥时装屋最初由设计师克里斯汀·迪奥于1946年在巴黎蒙田大道30号的“私人住宅”创立，并获得了法国企业家马塞尔·布萨克的资助。有别于今天由高级定制、时尚配饰、香水和美妆产品定义的迪奥，品牌成立之初，迪奥先生着眼于重新定义女性的着装方式，由此引领了一个时代的时装审美。目前，除了主要提供女士产品的主线品牌——克里斯汀·迪奥外，公司还经营男装品牌迪奥·桀傲和童装品牌宝贝迪奥。其产品在全球的零售店及其在线商店进行销售。

迪奥善于借助其传统优势与消费者建立起联系，通过展览推广其经典设计是宣传方式之一，比如其标志性香水迪奥小姐的巡回展览“迪奥精神”，而“迪奥:新形象革新”则展出了1947年至2015年的高级定制时装作品。

扫一扫

此外，迪奥与好莱坞名人及社交媒体的意见领袖建立了牢固的合作关系，以期产生更大的影响，并通过重塑其品牌形象来吸引千禧一代消费者，比如选择詹妮弗·劳伦斯作为迪奥小姐手提包系列的代言人。值得一提的是，迪奥是第一个在中国通过微信平台销售手袋的奢侈品牌。针对中国市场，迪奥在2017年七夕节期间推出了DIORAMOUR系列中国独家限量版Lady Dior手袋，通过超级流量明星的宣传推广，所有产品都在当天售罄。

历任创意总监[1]

1946—1957 克里斯汀·迪奥：初创与开拓

克里斯汀·迪奥于1905年出生在法国诺曼底海岸的海滨小镇格兰维尔。与家人希望他成为外交家的意愿截然不同，迪奥真正想从事的是艺术事业。然而，在其父亲经济支持下开设的画廊，随着家庭变故不得不于1930年关闭。之后，迪奥从出售每张10美分的时装手稿开始，逐渐明确了成为时装设计师的目标，并先后为时装设计师罗伯·贝格和卢西恩·勒隆工作。

1946年，迪奥拒绝了法国企业家马塞尔·布萨克的邀请——为1925年成立的巴黎时装品牌菲利普与加斯东做设计，因为比起复兴一个旧品牌，迪奥更希望以自己的名义创立品牌。最终，在布萨克的支持下，迪奥于1946年12月8日成立了同名高级定制时装屋。

1947年2月12日是注定被载入时尚史册的日子。克里斯汀·迪奥推出的第一个系列恰好迎合了"二战"后女性所渴望的风格——以服装的轮廓强调女性身体的曲线。这种被迪奥称为"花冠型"的新样式设计彻底改变了女性的着装，并在接下来的十年中占据了时尚的主导地位。

同时，迪奥先生是第一位将时装展示搬上T型台的设计师，他也是第一批运用商业炒作的巨大推动力来促进高级定制服装品牌发展，并创造时装版权的设计师。1953年，迪奥开始在全球范围内授权高级定制，并将许可证出售给包括日本在内的不同国家，为高级时装业务创造了一种全新的革命性商业模式。

1957—1960 伊夫·圣·洛朗：短暂的新鲜血液

伊夫·圣·洛朗（1936—2008）出生在法属阿尔及利亚，于17岁时前往巴黎学习时装。在创立其同名时装品牌之前，圣·洛朗从1955年开始加入迪奥时装屋，担任克里斯汀·迪奥的助手，并迅速得到其信任与赏识。迪奥评价圣·洛朗是一个"才华横溢的年轻人"。

1957年，迪奥先生因心脏病离世，21岁的圣·洛朗接掌了迪奥业务，成为世界上最年轻的女装设计师。1958年，伊夫·圣·洛朗于万众期待中，为迪奥呈现了她的第一个系列春夏系列Trapèze。在这个系列中，圣·洛朗尝试着摆脱迪奥传统风格的束缚，设计以简洁的线条、不加强调的腰身、更为明确的肩部以及更短的裙摆为主要风格的时装，并在接下来的系列中逐渐确立了自己标志性的风格——为当时的女性设计有别于20世纪50年代优雅风格的服装。

① 本小节品牌代表性设计与产品插图为作者手绘。

1996—2011 约翰·加利亚诺：华丽的戏剧性

约翰·加利亚诺（1960年11月28日出生）是一位出生于直布罗陀的英国时装设计师，1984年毕业于圣·马丁艺术学院，曾是法国时装公司纪梵希（1995—1996）、克里斯汀·迪奥（1996—2011）及其同名品牌约翰·加利亚诺（1988—2011）的首席设计师。目前，加利亚诺是巴黎时装品牌梅森·马吉拉的创意总监。

1997年，约翰·加利亚诺加入迪奥，为其带来了具有创意性与商业化的重大变化。他的高级定制时装和成衣系列以对戏剧和女性气质的热爱为创作的核心，并通过壮观绮丽的时装秀进行展示——用夸张的比例、极高的鞋跟和超现实的妆容将模特打造成戏剧性人物。除此之外，他与尼克·奈特合作，呈现了极具故事性视觉效果的广告片。这些共同定义了加利亚诺时代的迪奥，并极大推动了迪奥利润的增长。同时，加利亚诺也推出了一系列热门商品，包括于1999年发布的真我香水和2000年推出的广受欢迎的马鞍包。

2012—2015 拉夫·西蒙的极简主义

拉夫·西蒙是一名比利时时装设计师。2012年，他被任命为克里斯汀·迪奥的创意总监，他将自己的目标设定为“回归到我在20世纪90年代所感受到的情绪”，并执行了他所坚信的时尚哲学：时装，包括高级定制在内，应当具有实穿性。这种理念在展现其艺术视野的同时，也强调创新技术以及与艺术家的合作，由此重新塑造了迪奥的形象。

随后，詹妮弗·劳伦斯、蕾哈娜等知名艺人成为品牌形象大使，拉夫的设计在世界各地的红地毯上也频频亮相。迪奥的销售额在其任期内获得了显著的增长。

2016至今 玛丽亚·格拉齐亚·丘里：首位女性创意总监

玛丽亚·格拉齐亚·丘里是一名意大利设计师，在她成为迪奥首位女性艺术总监之前，曾是华伦天奴的联合创意总监。

在丘里的创意指导下，迪奥开始转向渴望个人主义与自我表达的千禧一代消费者——比如成衣系列中增添了标语的T恤。同时，她也延续了品牌丰富的传统，比如再次推出标志性的马鞍包，并借助社交媒体使其在互联网上占据主导地位。丘里认为，她的角色于迪奥来说类似于“策展人”，并说道：“我希望在品牌继承、个人理念以及品牌的未来发展之间找到平衡。”

1946—1957 克里斯汀·迪奥：新样式

左上图为：克里斯汀·迪奥1947年新样式

1957—1960 伊夫·圣·洛朗：Trapèze 系列

右上图：克里斯汀·迪奥1958年 Trapèze 系列（设计师伊夫·圣·洛朗）

1989—1996 詹弗兰科·费雷

右下图：与20世纪50年代迪奥的原创作品相比，费雷设计了一件包裹全身的衣服

1960—1989 马克·博昂：修长风格

左下图：迪奥1963年春夏高级定制（设计师马克·博昂）

图 1-9　迪奥早期部分代表性设计与产品

1997—2011 约翰·加利亚诺：马鞍包、真我香水

左上图：克里斯汀·迪奥1998年春季高级定制（设计师约翰·加利亚诺）

2012—1015 拉夫·西蒙：对Bar外套的重新演绎

右下图：克里斯汀·迪奥2012年秋季高级定制

2016至今　玛丽亚·拉格齐亚·丘里：写有标语的T恤

右下图：2017年春夏“我们都应该是女权主义者”T恤

图1-10　迪奥后期部分代表性设计与产品

Christian Dior

Brand Introduction

Christian Dior (Dior) is a European luxury goods company belonging to LVMH, the world's largest luxury group (Dior was purchased by Bernard Arnault in the 1980s). The House of Dior was established in 1946 in "a private house" at 30 Avenue Montaigne in Paris by designer Christian Dior, which was financially backed by wealthy businessman Marcel Boussac. Different from today's Dior, which is defined by Haute Couture, fashion accessories, perfumes and beauty products, Mr. Dior has focused on redefining the way that women dressed, thus leading the fashion aesthetic of an era. When Christian Dior label remains largely for women's offerings, the company also operates the Dior Homme division and the Baby Dior label. Products are sold throughout its portfolio of retail stores worldwide as well as its online stores.

Dior uses its heritage to connect to consumers. And boosting its classic through exhibitions is one of the propaganda methods. When "Esprit Dior", the travelling exhibition examined the allure of its iconic fragrance Miss Dior, "Dior: The New Look Revolution" Exhibition features Haute Couture pieces from the label dating from 1947 to 2015.

Dior has created strong partnerships with Hollywood celebrities and social media influencers to reach more demographics and re-establish its identity to resonate with millennials, such as Choosing Jennifer Lawrence as the face of their Miss Dior handbag range. It is worth mentioning that Dior is the first luxury brand to sell handbags through WeChat platform in China. For the Chinese market, Dior launched the limited handbag during the Qixi Festival in 2017, and with the promotion of superstars from entertainment industry, all the models of the bag were sold within the duration of the day.

The Creative Director in Different Periods

1946—1957 Christian Dior: Startup and Development

Christian Dior was born in Granville, a seaside town on the coast of Normandy, France, in 1905. Dior's family had hoped he would become a diplomat, but Dior was artistic and wished to be involved in art. However, the gallery opened under the financial support of his father had to close in 1930 with family accidents. Then Dior began to express the goal of becoming a fashion designer after selling his fashion sketches for 10 cents each, and worked for fashion designers Robert Piguet and Lucien Lelong.

In 1946, Marcel Boussac, a successful entrepreneur known as the richest man in France, invited Dior to design for Philippe et Gaston, a Paris fashion house launched in 1925. Dior refused, wishing to make a fresh start under his own name rather than reviving an old brand. On 8 December, 1946, with Boussac's backing, Dior founded his fashion house.

12 February, 1947 is a day etched in the history of fashion. Christian Dior's first collection offers something that the women after World War Two were craving for—highlighting the beauty of the female figure through the silhouette. This "New Look", which Dior called the "corolle", completely changed the women's dress and occupied the dominant position in fashion in the next decade.

At the same time, Dior was the first designer to bring the fashion show to the T-station. He was also the first designer to use the commercial hype to promote the development of Haute Couture clothing brands and create fashion copyrights.

In 1953, Dior started worldwide licensing Couture, selling the licenses to different countries, including Japan, and creating a new revolutionary business model for the business of Haute Couture.

1957—1960 Yves Saint Laurent: An Air of Youthfulness

Yves Saint Laurent (1936—2008) was born in French Algeria. At the age of 17, Saint Laurent moved to Paris and learned about fashion. Prior to founding his eponymous fashion brand, Saint Laurent joined the house of Dior in 1955 as an assistant of Christian Dior and quickly gained his trust and appreciation. Dior evaluated Saint Laurent as a "young, but immense talent".

When Christian Dior died from a heart attack in 1957, Saint Laurent became his successor and the world's youngest couturier at the age of 21. In 1958, Yves Saint Laurent presented his first spring-summer collection for Christian Dior, called Trapèze. In it, he freed himself a little from the influence of Christian Dior's traditional style, and found his own aesthetic voice: clean lines, less focus on the waist, more defined shoulders as well as shorter dresses. In the following collections, his style signature gradually established—a clothing for the women of his generation, which was different from the dictates of 1950s elegance.

1996—2011 John Galliano: Gorgeous Drama

John Galliano (born on 28 November, 1960) is a Gibraltar-born British fashion designer who graduated from Saint Martin's School of Art in 1984. He was the head designer of French fashion companies Givenchy (1995—1996), Christian Dior (1996—2011), and his own label John Galliano (1988—2011). At present, Galliano is the creative director of Paris-based fashion house Maison Margiela.

In 1997, John Galliano joined Dior, bringing significant changes in creativity and commercialization. His Haute Couture and ready-to-wear collections are centered on the love of drama and femininity and are presented through spectacular fashion show—with exaggerated proportions, hyperextended heels and surreal makeup, models dressed as topiaries. The runway shows, together with the narrative images he and Knight created for the ad campaigns, defined the French couture house in the Galliano era and sent profits soaring. At the same time, the designer got down to the business of minting commercial hits at Dior, including the perfume "J'adore" released in 1999 and the wildly popular Saddle bag, introduced in 2000.

2012–2015 The Minimalism of Raf Simons

Raf Simons is a Belgian fashion designer. In 2012, he was announced as the creative director at Christian Dior. Simons said he aims "to bring some emotion back, to what I felt in the nineties." He executed the philosophy that fashion, even Couture, should be wearable, which allowed him to express his own artistic vision and helped to reestablish the codes of Dior through innovative technical work and collaborations with artists.

A cast of cool ambassadors followed (from Jennifer Lawrence to Rihanna) and consequently his designs clocked up miles on the red carpet all over the world. And sales were boosted too under his tenure.

2016 Up to now Maria Grazia Chiuri: The First Female Creative Director

Maria Grazia Chiuri, the Italian designer, who has been co-creative director at Valentino, is the first woman to be the artistic director at the House of Dior.

Under Chiuri's creative direction, Dior has consistently targeted the millennial generation shoppers who yearn for individualism and crave self-expression, such as the slogan T-shirts in ready-to-wear collections. At the same time, she has been managing to stay true to its rich heritage by lifting the iconic Saddle bag from the archives, for example, which dominates the Internet in the way of marketing influence in virtue of social media. Chiuri says that her role at Dior is similar with a curator. "I want to find a balance among the heritage, my point of view, and what I think is relevant for the brand in the future," she says.

古驰 Gucci

品牌简介

古驰是代表意大利顶级工艺的奢侈品牌，专营高端皮具和高级时装，如今以其影响力和创新性成为业界最为热门的品牌之一，重塑了21世纪现代奢侈品牌形象的同时，也推动其母公司开云集团（原名巴黎春天集团，即Pinault-Printemps-Redoute，简称PPR，是1962年由弗朗索瓦·皮诺创立的法国奢侈品集团，于1999年收购古驰）业绩的增长。

图1-11　古驰品牌标志

品牌战略

得益于在各大社交媒体平台上的活跃，包括Facebook，Twitter，Instagram，YouTube，Google，Pinterest和Snapchat等，古驰成功获得了潜在年轻消费群体的青睐，显著的品牌差异性也为其带来了更高的市场份额和销售额。比如旨在推广一系列新产品的国际当代艺术展活动，包括与Instagram meme账户（“meme”通常指以诙谐调侃的语气在网络上传播内容）合作发起话题#TFW Gucci，以流行的互联网艺术形式推广全新腕表系列，试图将对话有效转化为实际销售。

同时，古驰专注于在线购物体验。亚历山德罗·米歇尔的重要举措之一就是重新启动古驰官方网站，以丰富的视觉图像分享设计系列背后的灵感及其思维过程，讲述每个图案和单品所蕴含的故事，与消费者建立起强烈的情感联系与互动。

古驰也与好莱坞名人、社交媒体意见领袖开展合作。比如借助蕾哈娜、布莱克·莱弗利、哈里·斯泰尔斯等现代风格偶像的影响力，试与千禧一代产生共鸣。而社交媒体意见领袖则发挥引导消费者购买行为和决策的作用。

关键人物①

扫一扫

汤姆·福特（1994—2004）

出生于得克萨斯州的设计师汤姆·福特在1994年被任命为古驰的创意总监时，品牌正经历最艰难的阶段——低迷的销售额、缺乏辨识度的产品和毫无噱头的品牌故事。他逐渐着手负责品牌的各个方面，包括成衣系列、视觉营销、包装、室内设计和广告等，并将品牌的重心转移至奢侈品零售，以恢复古驰的声誉与品牌价值。

汤姆·福特为古驰注入了一种当时少见的性感风格，并将其渗透到秀场和广告当中。1995年大胆剪裁的白色紧身连衣裙，以及1996年搭配以低胸丝绸衬衣的女士西服套装，都与20世纪90年代的极简主义流行形成鲜明对比，却完全为消费者所接受。同时，在此期间发布的富有挑衅意味而极具争议的广告，也迅速促成了品牌业绩的快速增长。

汤姆·福特的任期标志着明星设计师、强大的创意总监时代的开始，其责任与影响力远远超过了产品设计和品牌营销本身。

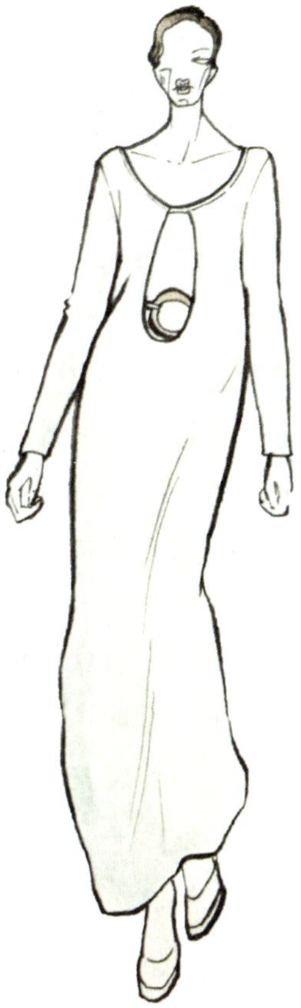

图1-12 白色紧身连衣裙

亚历山德罗·米歇尔（2015— ）

现任创意总监亚历山德罗·米歇尔于2015年接手品牌相关事务，此前他已与品牌合作超过12年。凭借其独特的美学理念和理想的故事叙述，米歇尔创造出一种人们意欲效仿的生活方式，促使品牌业务实现强劲增长。

自2015年首次亮相米兰时装周以来，米歇尔始终将这个意大利品牌的丰富历史与现代性融为一体。他从品牌的档案中汲取灵感，把经典双“G”标志装饰以鲜花或卡通图案，醒目地置于手袋或其他配件上，这样一种轻松幽默的呈现方式成功吸引了年轻消费人群；把流行文化融入服饰之中，运用意大利文艺复兴艺术与东方古典元素图案，加以褶边、印花、层次感与多色彩的极繁主义设计，创造出浪漫复古的品牌形象。

图1-13 女士西服套装

① 该品牌历任设计师标志性产品设计为作者手绘。

品牌历史

扫一扫

年轻的古驰奥·古驰（1881—1953）受启发于酒店客人使用的高品质行李箱，于1921年在家乡佛罗伦萨开设了同名皮具店，销售造型经典的精美皮具。起初，古驰的主要业务是为骑马者制作马鞍等配件，随着品牌的扩张，古驰先后在米兰和罗马开设店铺，开始出售皮革配饰（包袋、皮鞋），以及丝巾和针织品。

图1–14　波士顿包 THE BOSTON BAG

作为高端品质象征的双“G”字样标识诞生于1933年。古驰奥·古驰的长子阿尔多·古驰进入家族企业后，用其父亲名字的首字母组合来设计官方徽标。随后引入瞩目的红、绿色条纹，与之相结合而成为品牌的代名词。

20世纪30年代，由于第二次世界大战导致皮革材料短缺，古驰从那不勒斯引进了一种特殊的卡纳帕纤维和大麻纤维的交织物，将这种织物作为皮革替代品。并以此为契机，出现了品牌的第一个签名印花：在黄褐底色上印以深棕色、小巧而相互交织的钻石图案。

1953年，古驰在纽约设立办事处，进一步扩大公司规模，相继推出手表、珠宝和眼镜等系列产品[①]，并迎来了古驰的黄金时代，直至20世纪80年代。

图1–15　古驰酒神单肩手袋

① 该品牌历代标志性产品为作者手绘。

1947年推出的Bamboo Bag，独特之处在于其抛光的竹柄是日本竹子经由独特工艺制成，好莱坞明星伊丽莎白·泰勒是其忠实爱好者。

In 1947, artisans utilized Japanese bamboo to craft unique handles for their bags, and Hollywood star Elizabeth Taylor was a loyal fan.

1966年，邀请意大利插画家Vittorio Accornero为摩纳哥王妃格蕾丝·凯莉特别设计的Flora印花丝巾。

In 1966, the Italian illustrator Vittorio Accornero was invited to design the Flora printed silk scarf specially made for Grace Kelly, the Princess of Monaco.

20世纪60年代，为美国第一夫人杰奎琳·肯尼迪设计以其名字命名的手袋——Jackie o Bag，以坚固的O形手柄、厚实的皮革和金色金属装饰为标志。

The bag made famous by former first lady Jackie Kennedy Onassis in the 1960s, is with a sturdy O shaped handle, thick leather and decorated with gold hardware.

1976年，女演员朱迪·福斯特在滑板时穿着标志性的古驰马衔扣乐福鞋。

In 1976, actress Jodie Foster wore these iconic Gucci horsebit loafers while skateboarding.

图1-16 古驰历代标志性产品

Gucci

Brand Introduction

Gucci is a luxury brand that represents the pinnacle of Italian craftsmanship. It specializes in high-end leather goods and clothing. Without a doubt, it is one of the industry's most buzzing brands right now for its influence and innovation, redefining luxury for the 21st century and promoting the growth of Kering Group (formerly known as PPR, Pinault-Printemps-Redoute was a French luxury group founded in 1962 by Francois Pinault and acquired Gucci in 1999).

Brand Strategy

Owing to its active participation in major social media platforms, including Facebook, Twitter, Instagram, YouTube, Google, Pinterest and Snapchat, Gucci has successfully captured future customers and positively differentiates from other luxury brands, which in turn results in higher market share and sales. For example, the "Collaborative Art Project" campaign, which aims to promote a series of new products, includes generating headlines for unveiling its new collection of watches through creating a series of branded memes ("meme" usually refers to content that spreads on the Internet in a humorous tone) in collaboration with artists and popular Instagram meme accounts. Gucci attempts to effectively translate conversations into actual sales in the digital world.

Gucci has focused on the online shopping experience as well. One of the important initiatives of Alessandro Michele is to redesign and relaunch its website, sharing the inspiration and thought processes behind them and telling the stories of the individual patterns and items. This has allowed consumers to gain a stronger emotional relationship with the brand.

Gucci has created strong partnerships with Hollywood celebrities. For example, with the influence of contemporary style icons like Rihanna, Blake Lively and Harry Styles, try to resonate with millennials. Along with this, Gucci has worked closely with opinion leaders who try to influence the purchasing behaviors of opinion seekers.

Key Designers

Tom Ford (1994–2004)

Tom Ford, the Texas-born designer, was appointed as Creative Director of Gucci in 1994, when the brand was going through its hardest phase—sales dropping, products lacking of identification, and brand story hard to tell. Gradually tasked with all aspects of the company—including ready-to-wear, visual merchandising, packaging, interior design, advertising, etc., Tom Ford focused more on luxury retail, bringing Gucci into a new era.

Tom Ford infused the brand with an overt sex appeal that at the time couldn't be found and infiltrated it into the runway show and advertising. The famous sensual white dresses with provocative cut-outs in 1995 and hyper-sexy outfits for women in 1996 which contrast to the minimalist trend of the 1990s were totally embraced by consumers. Provocative campaigns released during this period also quickly contributed to the label's rapidly growing success.

Tom Ford's tenure at Gucci marked the beginning of the era of star designers, powerful creative directors, whose responsibilities span over designing and marketing.

Alessandro Michele (2015–)

In 2015, the current Creative Director Alessandro Michele, who had been working with the company for over 12 years, took over the brand. The brand's success lies in its creation of a lifestyle that people want to emulate, with its unique aesthetic and aspirational story, which promotes strong growth in the brand business.

Since debuting the first collection in Milan Fashion Week in 2015, Michele has coordinated the rich history of this Italian brand melds with the present. Inspired by the vast archives, Michele brought back the iconic Gucci logo, daubing it with flowers or pairing it with cartoonish motifs in accessories that appeal to a younger demographic. Michele's new Gucci champions a maximalist approach: ruffles, frills, prints, layers, a cacophony of color—all of which consumers have welcomed with open arms.

Brand History

The young Guccio Gucci (1881—1953) was inspired by the luxurious luggage he saw sophisticated guests brought with. Upon returning to his birthplace of Florence in 1921, he opened his own eponymous leather goods store to sell fine leather goods with classic styling.

In the beginning, Gucci's main business was making saddles and other accessories for horseback riders. As the company opened stores in Milan and Rome, it began to feature the leather accessories as handbags, shoes, as well as silks and knitwear.

The double-G design, symbolized by high-end quality, was created in 1933. Aldo Gucci, the eldest son of Guccio Gucci, joined the family business and combined the initials of his father into a double-G design as the official logo. And the prominent red and green bands introduced later became synonymous with the brand.

In the 1930s, as leather was hard to come by due to the Second World War, Gucci developed a specially woven canapa, or hemp, from Naples as the alternative to leather, and printed with the first signature print — a series of small, interconnecting diamonds in dark brown on a tan background.

Gucci further expanded the company's horizons in 1953 by establishing offices in New York City, and launched a series of watches, jewelry and glasses, contributing to the golden age of Gucci until the 1980s.

乔治·阿玛尼 Giorgio Armani

品牌简介

乔治·阿玛尼集团是意大利成衣设计领域极具权威的品牌，于1975年由乔治·阿玛尼与其合作伙伴塞尔吉·奥加莱奥蒂在米兰共同创立。集团旗下的多个品牌从设计、制造、分销到零售，涉及众多时尚领域，包括成衣、皮具、鞋靴、手表、珠宝、眼镜、化妆品、家居设计和酒店。

图 1-17　乔治·阿玛尼集团主要品牌一览表

作为少数几家依旧保持独立的意大利知名品牌之一，阿玛尼并未跟随其他品牌一同投入奢侈品行业整合的浪潮中去。“我创造了一个由完全不同的品牌构成的世界，包括安普里奥·阿玛尼（Emporio Armani）、阿玛尼精选（Collezioni）和阿玛尼高定（Privé）等，它们都适时地起到了作用。这个做法是毋庸置疑的，因为各品牌具有不同的故事、

图 1-18 阿玛尼将传统英式剪裁与意大利定制工艺相结合，实现了正式服装与宽松随意的运动服的融合。阿玛尼的女装也更为简洁和现代化——无衬里的柔软外套和舒适的裤装。

风格、质量和价格。”面对外界对其不断延伸的产品线的质疑，阿玛尼先生回应道：“对于我来说，我无须移除任何一个品牌，因为它们有各自的消费者基础，能够行之有效。”

然而，面对自2009年以来首次出现的年度销售下滑，阿玛尼开始推进合并产品线和削减店铺的计划，包括将高级定制系列Privé和家居品牌Armani Casa收归乔治·阿玛尼高端品牌旗下，Collezioni和Jeans将并入轻奢定位的Emporio Armani。

另外，面对近年来奢侈品行业向年轻消费群体靠拢的趋势，以及亚洲市场越来越重要的倾向，以中国为例，集团旗下的Armani Jeans系列和Emporio Armani EA7系列也已于2017年进驻天猫和京东，开设了官方旗舰店。

品牌战略

“我是第一个这么做的设计师：在柔化男性形象的同时强化女性形象。我将女性服装的面料运用在男装中，并且将男性服饰中为女性所渴望的‘权力套装’应用于女装。

1975年10月，阿玛尼推出了以自己名字命名的第一个系列——1976春夏男士成衣，同时也推出了女装线。品牌第一年的销售额就达到了100万美元，获得了巨大的成功。

而成功的原因之一在于阿玛尼适时地创造出新的设计方法——无衬里和未经整理的外套——恰好反映了1968年之后社会的变化，满足了当时占社会大多数的中产阶级无法承担高级定制，但同时也希望为自己塑造一个独特形象的需求。

外套始终是阿玛尼时装中的核心，通过采用不同的面料、比例和颜色创造出新的设计。而出自1997年的“greige”（灰色和米色之间）也仍然是阿玛尼调色板中最典型的元素，通常搭配以白色、黑色、柔和的大地色调和灰蓝色调。

关键人物

“大家意识到我创造的时尚一以贯之，但并非一成不变。我认为这就是我成功的秘诀。发挥创造力有许多不同的方式，比如你可以像一名艺术家一样去创作，将生意或是业务置之度外。而我选择的创造方式是沿着产业的路径——一种美国式的商业模式，我将此奉为我事业的哲学。”

1982年，乔治·阿玛尼先生出现在《时代周刊》的封面，作为继克里斯汀·迪奥之后第二位登上该杂志封面的时装设计师，阿玛尼在向全世界展示他作为一名优秀时装设计师所具有的眼界的同时，又展现了他前瞻性的商业意识。

品牌历史

阿玛尼不仅积极地进行品牌扩展，还成功地运用了借助明星进行营销推广的手段。以合作1980年的电影《美国舞男》为开端，阿玛尼标志性的服装相继出现在《蝙蝠侠》（1989）和《低俗小说》（1994）中。此外，阿玛尼还为电视连续剧《迈阿密风云》（1984-1989）和流行音乐家提供了服饰品的赞助。不久，许多顶级好莱坞明星也开始在红地毯上穿戴阿玛尼系列，包括米歇尔·菲佛、朱迪·福斯特和约翰·特拉沃尔塔等。

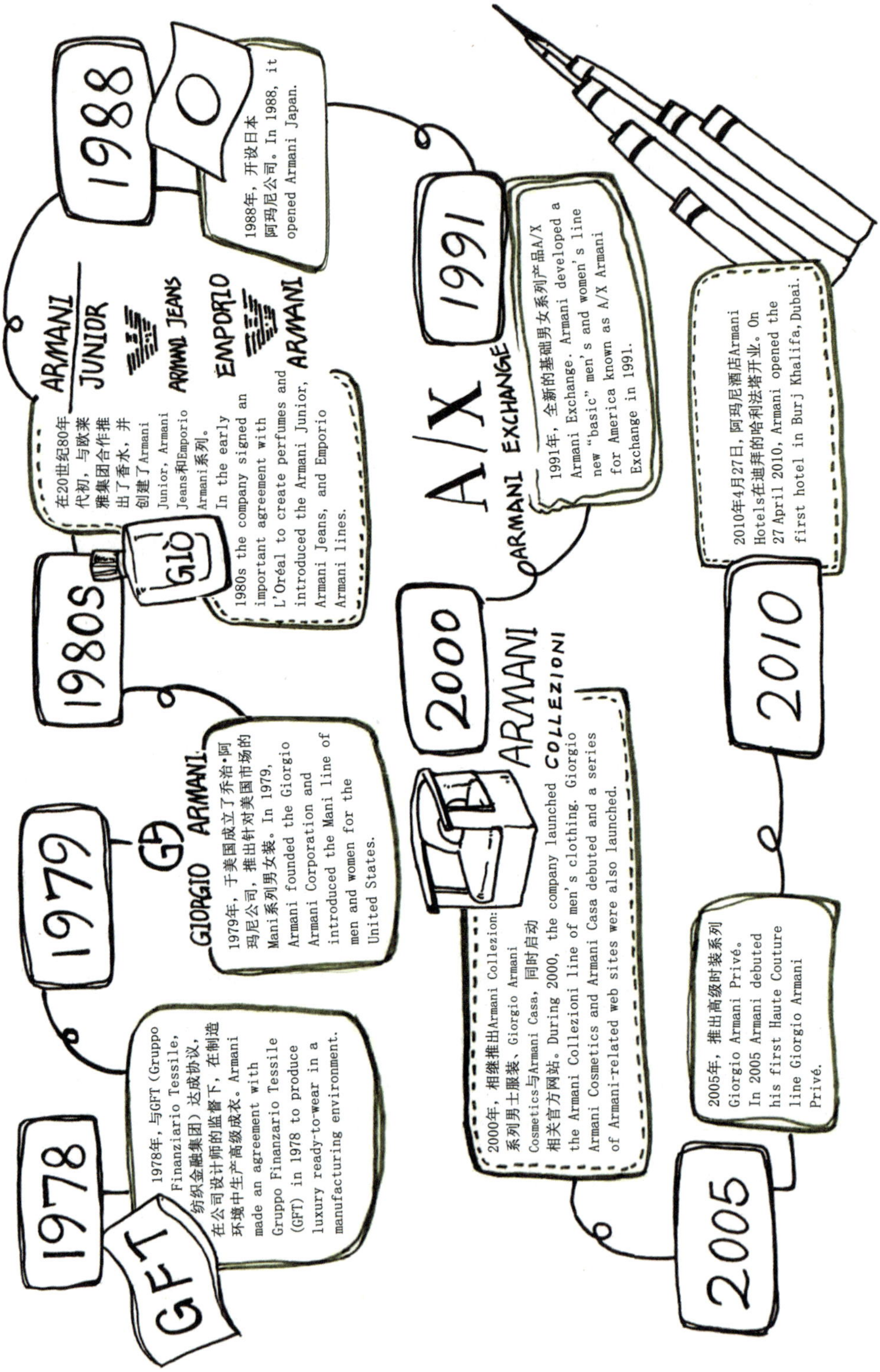

图1–19 Giorgio Armani 品牌发展历程图①

① 该品牌发展历程图由作者手绘制成。

Giorgio Armani

Brand Introduction

Giorgio Armani is an authoritative brand in Italian ready-to-wear design, founded by Giorgio Armani in Milan with his partner Galeotti in 1975, whose designs, manufactures, distributes and retails involve with numerous fashion fields including ready-to-wear, leather goods, footwear, watches, jewelry, eyewear, cosmetics, home design and hotels.

The group is unique in remaining aloof from waves of consolidation in the luxury goods industry. "I have built a world made of totally different brands including Emporio Armani, Collezioni, Privé and soon, which have worked in time, and I don't think it was confusing because there's different stories, styles, qualities and prices point behind each brand." Mr. Armani responded, "As for me, right now I don't see the need to remove any brands because they work, they have their customer base."

However, Giorgio Armani is pushing ahead with plans to streamline its brands and store network after the fashion brand recorded its first annual sales decline since 2009. Armani would bring its Privé haute couture line and the furniture and homewares brand Armani Casa under the umbrella of the high-end Giorgio Armani brand, while the Collezioni and Jeans labels will be folded into the more accessibly priced Emporio Armani.

In addition, in the face of the trend of the luxury goods industry moving closer to the young consumer groups in recent years, and the Asian market that continues to show importance, taking China as an example, the group's Armani Jeans series and EA7 Emporio Armani have also entered T-mall and Jingdong in 2017 and opened its official flagship stores.

Brand Strategy

"I was the first to soften the image of men, and harden the image of women. I dressed men in women's fabrics, and stole from men what women wanted and needed—the power suit."

In October, 1975, Armani presented his first collection of men's ready-to-wear for spring and summer 1976 under his own name. He also produced a women's line at the same time. The brand's first year sales reached $1 million. The secret of Armani's great success seems to derive from his having introduced, at the right moment, a new approach—the first unstructured jackets for men, unlined and unironed—to clothing design that reflected the changes in post-

1968 society, which was composed essentially of the middle-class people who could no longer afford to wear couture clothing but at the same time wanted to construct a distinctive image for themselves.

Over time, the jacket has continued to remain the centerpiece of the Armani wardrobe, changing year by year through using new materials, new proportions, and new colors. And for Armani, the "greige" (between gray and beige) of 1997 remained the most typical element in a palette often centered on shades of white and black, soft earth tones, dusty blues.

Key Person

"They found my way of doing fashion very consistent, but also very innovative. I think this is the secret of my success. You can be creative in different ways. You can be creative without worrying business or industrial issues, like an artist, who doesn't care about or has make sure that the stores are filled with goods and then emptied by customers. Then there is a kind of creative person who works alongside the industry. That is an American model of business and I embraced it myself as a philosophy and a way of working."

Official recognition of his fame came in 1982 when he appeared on the cover of *Time* magazine, only the second fashion designer, after Christian Dior, to do so. Armani showed the world his vision as a good fashion designer with a forward-looking business sense.

Brand History

Giorgio Armani not only actively promotes brand expansion, but also exploits the marketing power of media stars. He designed Richard Gere's wardrobe for the film *American Gigolo* (1980). A string of other movie credits would accumulate throughout the next two decades, including *Batman* (1989) and *Pulp Fiction* (1994). He also provided much of the wardrobe for *Miami Vice* (1984—1989) and pop musicians. Soon, many top Hollywood stars started wearing Armani on the red carpet, including Michelle Pfeiffer, Jodie Foster and John Travolta, among others.

第三节

本章讨论与阅读推荐

Discussion and Reading Recommendation

本章讨论

1. 在全球经济衰退风险威胁众多（如英国“无协议脱欧”）的环境下，你认为奢侈品是否还能保持强劲的增长势头？

2. 部分奢侈品牌（如古驰）通过年轻化品牌在短期内取得了一定的成功，而面对存在风险的年轻消费群体，奢侈品牌应该如何应对？

3. 试分析向来注重品牌体验的奢侈品牌，在中国市场更加喜欢以微信小程序为发售和营销渠道的原因。

Discussion

1. In the context of the global economic recession risk threats (such as the Brexit), do you think luxury goods can maintain a strong growth momentum?

2. Some luxury brands (such as Gucci) have achieved certain success in the short term through making the brand younger, and how should luxury brands deal with unstable young consumers?

3. Try to analyze why luxury brands that have always focused on brand experience have preferred the use of WeChat as a distribution and marketing channel in the Chinese market.

阅读推荐 Reading Recommendation

《可可·香奈儿的传奇一生》

作　者：［英］贾斯迪妮·皮卡蒂

出版社：广西科学技术出版社

译　者：郭昌京、张宏、邵志杰、李庆

出版年：2011

ISBN：9787807636038

《克里斯汀·迪奥自传》

作　者：［法］克里斯汀·迪奥

出版社：湖南人民出版社

译　者：熊娅

出版年：2013

ISBN：9787543889101

《阿玛尼传奇——挚爱一人，优雅一生》

作　者：［意］勒娜特·莫尔霍（Renata Molho）

出版社：中国经济出版社

译　者：李海鹏等

出版年：2012

ISBN：9787501795604

参考资料 References

奢侈品市场分析

http：//www.sohu.com/a/116432839_516256

http：//36kr.com/p/5136197.html

http：//36kr.com/p/5136358.html

https：//weibo.com/ttarticle/p/show？ id=2309404245304542138273#related

https：//weibo.com/ttarticle/p/show？ id=2309404244266120560168#related

https：//weibo.com/ttarticle/p/show？ id=2309404240249562753084#related

http：//fashion.chinadaily.com.cn/2018-05/24/content_36261649.htm

https：//weibo.com/ttarticle/p/show？ id=2309404237415639337276#related
https：//weibo.com/ttarticle/p/show？ id=2309404246787660608126

博柏利

https：//en.wikipedia.org/wiki/Burberry
https：//www.grailed.com/drycleanonly/history-of-the-burberry-check
https：//theculturetrip.com/europe/united-kingdom/england/london/articles/the-history-of-burberry-and-its-famous-fashion-comeback/
https：//www.tradesy.com/blog/a-short-history-of-burberry/
https：//cn.burberry.com/our-history/
https：//www.gq-magazine.co.uk/article/how-burberry-became-britains-most-important-brand
http：//www.historyhouse.co.uk/articles/burberrys.html
https：//en.wikipedia.org/wiki/Thomas_Burberry
https：//magazine.themall.it/en/thomas-burberry-biography
https：//www.nytimes.com/2018/03/01/fashion/burberry-riccardo-tisci.html
https：//www.businessoffashion.com/articles/news-analysis/riccardo-tisci-is-the-new-creative-director-of-burberry
https：//www.harpersbazaar.com/fashion/designers/a22623947/burberry-new-logo-monogram/
https：//en.wikipedia.org/wiki/Christopher_Bailey_（fashion_designer）
https：//www.hollywoodreporter.com/news/burberry-appoints-new-chief-creative-officer-replacing-christopher-bailey-1089763
https：//www.virginmediatelevision.ie/xpose/article/beauty/262476/Burberry-has-announced-its-new-creative-director-Meet-Riccardo-Tisci
https：//www.gq-magazine.co.uk/article/christopher-bailey-burberry-interview
https：//www.linkedin.com/pulse/why-burberry-so-successful-digital-marketing-yanzhu-chen
https：//www.business2community.com/social-media/social-media-strategy-rebranding-heritage-at-burberry-02138561
https：//socialwall.me/en/burberry-social-media-use-luxury-brands/
https：//www.marketing91.com/marketing-mix-of-burberry-burberry-marketing-mix/
https：//www.harpersbazaar.com/uk/fashion/fashion-news/a13134055/christopher-bailey-burberry-profile-legacy/

香奈儿

https：//www.biography.com/people/coco-chanel-9244165
https：//en.wikipedia.org/wiki/Chanel
https：//www.metmuseum.org/toah/hd/chnl/hd_chnl.htm
https：//www.harpersbazaar.com/uk/fashion/style-files/news/g30003/a-history-of-chanel/？ slide=1
https：//inside.chanel.com/en/timeline/1955_255-bag
https：//www.businessoffashion.com/articles/education/gabrielle-coco-chanel-1883-1971
https：//www.businessoffashion.com/organisations/chanel
https：//www.businessoffashion.com/community/people/karl-lagerfeld

https：//www.referralcandy.com/blog/chanel-marketing-strategy/
https：//econsultancy.com/why-chanel-is-the-most-influential-luxury-brand-on-social/
https：//insights.newscred.com/chanel-social-media-content-marketing/
https：//cn.businessoffashion.com/2019/02/karl-lagerfelds-greatest-legacy-is-a-business-model-chanel.html
https：//insights.newscred.com/chanel-social-media-content-marketing/
https：//econsultancy.com/why-chanel-is-the-most-influential-luxury-brand-on-social/
https：//www.referralcandy.com/blog/chanel-marketing-strategy/
https：//www.businessoffashion.com/community/people/karl-lagerfeld

克里斯汀·迪奥

https：//theculturetrip.com/europe/france/articles/the-history-of-the-house-of-dior/
https：//www.designer-vintage.com/en/masterclass/gallery/the-ultimate-timeline-of-the-house-of-dior
https：//www.savoirflair.com/fashion/93326/brief-history-of-dior
https：//en.wikipedia.org/wiki/Christian_Dior_SE
https：//www.ukessays.com/essays/marketing/marketing-analysis-of-christian-dior-marketing-essay.php
https：//fashionunited.uk/news/fashion/why-christian-dior-and-lvmh-are-co-dominating-the-luxury-industry/2015100217868
https：//ecommercechinaagency.com/dior-first-luxury-brand-sell-wechat/
https：//en.wikipedia.org/wiki/Christian_Dior
http：//www.hautecouturenews.com/2015/story/christian-dior/
https：//fashion-history.lovetoknow.com/fashion-clothing-industry/fashion-designers/christian-dior
https：//zh.wikipedia.org/wiki/%E4%BC%8A%E5%A4%AB%C2%B7%E5%9C%A3%E6%B4%9B%E6%9C%97
https：//museeyslparis.com/en/stories/les-annees-dior-1-1#photos-of-the-trapeze-collection-24
https：//www.dior.com/diormag/nl_nl/article/yves-saint-laurent-dior
https：//en.wikipedia.org/wiki/John_Galliano
https：//www.anothermag.com/fashion-beauty/10931/the-dior-obsessive-chronicling-a-golden-decade-of-john-galliano
https：//www.harpersbazaar.com/fashion/trends/a81/galliano-glorious-reign-0307/
https：//en.wikipedia.org/wiki/Raf_Simons
https：//www.vogue.co.uk/gallery/raf-simons-leaves-dior
https：//www.lvmh.com/news-documents/news/dior-and-i-raf-simons-debuts/
https：//fashionista.com/2015/10/raf-simons-legacy-dior
https：//www.businessoffashion.com/community/people/maria-grazia-chiuri
https：//www.scmp.com/magazines/style/news-trends/article/2167470/diors-maria-grazia-chiuri-what-you-need-know-about-how
https：//www.wmagazine.com/story/maria-grazia-chiuri-dior-feminism
https：//www.viva.co.nz/article/fashion/maria-grazia-chiuri-dior-artistic-director/

古驰

https：//www.harrods.com/en-gb/designers/gucci
https：//www.businessoffashion.com/organisations/gucci

https://en.wikipedia.org/wiki/Gucci

https://hypebae.com/2018/5/gucci-history-alessandro-michele-tom-ford

https://blog.logomyway.com/history-of-gucci-and-their-logo-design/

https://bagista.co.uk/blogs/news/gucci-brand-story

https://fashion-history.lovetoknow.com/fashion-clothing-industry/fashion-designers/gucci

https://www.kering.com/en/houses/couture-and-leather-goods/gucci/history/

https://wwd.com/fashion-news/designer-luxury/history-lesson-3512770/

https://www.crfashionbook.com/fashion/a26934683/evolution-gucci-designer/

https://www.crfashionbook.com/fashion/g27114227/gucci-muses-throughout-history/

https://isys6621.com/2017/03/20/winning-the-internet-in-gucci/

https://digiday.com/marketing/digital-strategy-driving-guccis-growth/

https://medium.com/rta902/gucci-old-world-luxury-meets-digital-marketing-e427df076bc7

https://www.forbes.com/

https://www.telegraph.co.uk/luxury/womens-style/guccis-alessandro-michele-and-the-rebirth-of-the-logo/

https://www.businessoffashion.com/community/people/alessandro-michele

https://www.businessoffashion.com/community/people/frida-giannini

https://www.sleek-mag.com/article/why-tom-fords-tenure-at-gucci-was-so-memorable/

https://www.vogue.co.uk/gallery/suzy-on-tom-ford-rooms-at-gucci

乔治·阿玛尼

https://en.wikipedia.org/wiki/Armani

https://www.marketing91.com/marketing-strategy-armani/

https://www.fundinguniverse.com/company-histories/giorgio-armani-s-p-a-history/

https://fashion-history.lovetoknow.com/fashion-clothing-industry/fashion-designers/giorgio-armani

https://www.businessoffashion.com/community/people/giorgio-armani

https://www.biography.com/people/giorgio-armani-9188652

https://www.businessoffashion.com/articles/news-analysis/armani-streamlines-brands-and-store-network-as-sales-drop

https://www.britannica.com/biography/Giorgio-Armani

第二章

快时尚品牌

Fast Fashion Brands

第一节

快时尚市场分析

Analysis of Fast Fashion Market

快时尚，是全球化、民主化、年轻化和网络化这四大社会潮流共同影响下的产物。快时尚源自20世纪的欧洲，欧洲人将其称为“Fast Fashion”，而美国人则把它叫作“Speed to Market”。快时尚提供当下流行的款式和元素，以快速上新、价格低廉和款式丰富为特点，能够最大限度地满足消费者的需求。

凭借高端设计与低廉价格相结合的快时尚商业模式，飒拉、海恩斯莫里斯等品牌成为打破传统时尚行业规则的黑马。这种先进性也使得快时尚在短期内迅速获得成功。而近来，无处不在的快时尚市场趋于饱和状态，消费者的品牌新鲜性已经消失，因此出现了销售停滞、关闭门店的局面，Forever 21、GAP与Topshop等品牌陷入低潮也成事实。此外，可持续时尚概念引发了消费者对服饰这一高耗能、劳动力密集产业未来发展问题的思考，消费者也意识到优势在于便宜、快速以及低价的快时尚产业隐藏了大量的漏洞，包括环境污染、劳工权益、女性权益等诸多问题。

由于中国消费环境发生的剧变，快时尚在中国面临的处境更为复杂，国外快时尚品牌集体势微。

首先，在消费升级之下，消费者的需求呈现多样化发展，同时中国服装产业的销售渠道愈加多元化，包括淘宝、京东等线上购物平台，使得消费者有更多的选择。这对快时尚产生了重大打击，ASOS、Topshop以及New Look等先后退出了中国市场。除此之外，不断崛起的国产服饰品牌，带来了更多的同质化竞争，加剧了其在中国市场生存的危机，包括近年来加速扩展的URBAN REVIVO、热风、太平鸟，以及依靠渠道下沉占据中低端市场的森马、美特斯邦威等。

其次，受消费升级和理性消费观念影响，快时尚正逐渐失去一、二线城市的消费者。同时得益于智能手机的普及和电商的迅猛发展，三、四线城市的消费习惯跟一、二线城市越来越接近。这就要求国外快时尚品牌努力适应中国市场的要求。

Analysis of Fast Fashion Market

Fast fashion is the product of the four social trends of globalization, democratization, youthfulness and networking. Originated in Europe in the 20th century, Europeans call it "Fast Fashion", while the Americans call it "Speed to Market". Fast fashion offers the current popular styles and elements, featuring fast, new, low-cost and rich styles to maximize consumer satisfaction.

With the fast fashion business model combining high-end design and low price, Zara, H&M and other brands have broken the rules of the traditional fashion industry. This advancement also makes fast fashion a success in the short term. Recently, the ubiquitous fast fashion market has become saturated. It shows that consumers' freshness towards these brands has disappeared. Sales have stagnated, and stores are to be closed. Brands as Forever 21, GAP, Topshop, and other brands have fallen into a low tide.

On the other hand, with the concept of sustainability, consumers are aware that the fast fashion supply chain is a high-energy-consuming and labor-intensive industry. More and more people realize that fast fashion's advantage lies in the cheap, fast and low-cost business mode which also contains a large number of loopholes, including environmental pollution, labor rights, women's rights and many other issues.

Due to the drastic changes in consumer environment, the situation fast fashion faces in China is more complicated, and the foreign brands are collectively going weak.

Firstly, under the circumstance of consumption upgrade, consumers' demand has developed. Meanwhile, the marketing channels of China's fashion industry have become more diversified, including online shopping platforms such as Taobao and Jingdong, which have made consumers have more choices. It has brought a major blow to fast fashion industry that brands like ASOS, Topshop and New Look have all withdrawn from the Chinese market. In addition, the rising domestic apparel brands have brought more homogenization competition and intensified their crisis in the Chinese market, including the accelerated expansion of brands like URBAN REVIVO, Hot Wind, Peace Bird, and also the ones relying on the channel sinking to occupy the middle- and low-end market, like Semir, and Metersbonwe.

Another important reason is that fast fashion is gradually losing consumers in the first-and second-tier cities due to consumption upgrades and rational consumption concepts. At the same time, owing to the popularity of smart phones and the rapid development of e-commerce, the consumption habits of the third- and fourth-tier cities are getting closer and closer to those of the first-and second-tier cities. This requires foreign fast fashion brands to adapt to the requirements of the complicated Chinese market.

第二节

快时尚品牌分析

Analysis of Fast Fashion Brand

海恩斯莫里斯 H&M

品牌简介

海恩斯莫里斯（Hennes & Mauritz AB，缩写为H&M）是来自瑞典的服装零售企业。其在全球范围内开展业务，包括亚洲、欧洲和美洲等均设有分店，提供的产品范围涵盖所有年龄群体，并为女性、男性、青少年和儿童提供服装和配饰。除此之外，海恩斯莫里斯还开发了家居用品和美妆用品，以实现品牌产品多样性。

海恩斯莫里斯从服装设计到成为专卖店中商品的时间极短——在斯德哥尔摩的总部，设计师根据潮流趋势开发出新产品后，世界各地的供应商在短短一个月内便能将产品推向商店。这使得消费者能够迅速接触到最前卫的时尚产品，也有助于降低品牌运营成本。海恩斯莫里斯款式多、数量少的销售理念是对长尾效应的成功运用。

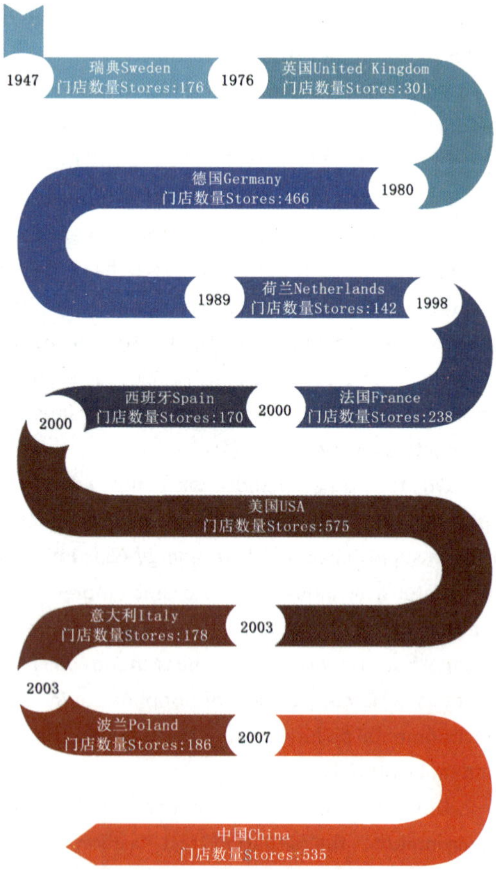

图2-1 海恩斯莫里斯集团的十大市场（截至2019-02-28品牌官网）

海恩斯莫里斯集团不断通过集团旗下各品牌进行市场拓展，并且每个品牌都有自己独特定位。除H&M品牌外，还包括COS（Collection of Style）、&other stories、Monki、Weekday、Cheap Monday、ARKET、Afound和H&M Home。

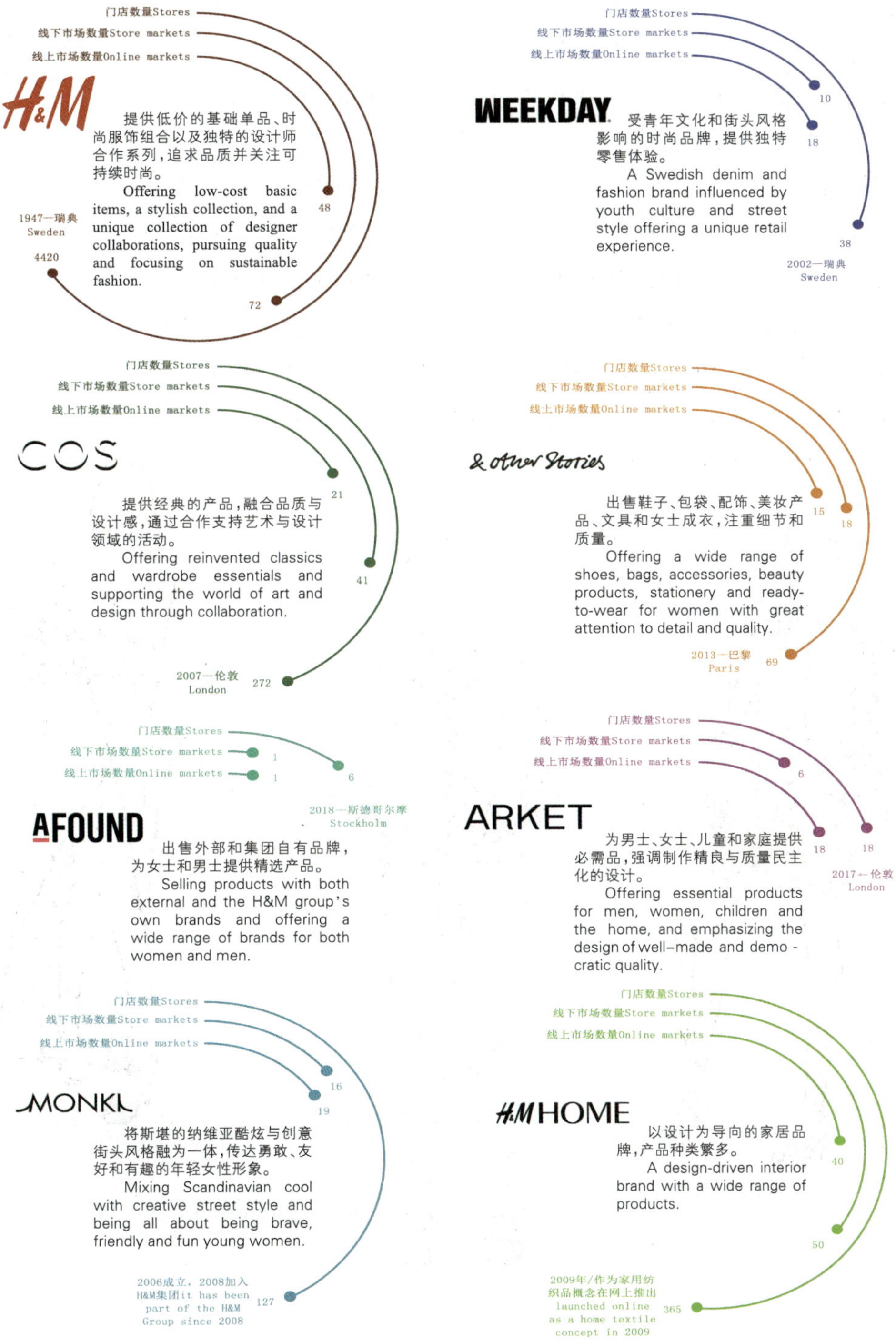

图2-2 旗下品牌一览表（截至2019-02-28品牌官网）

品牌战略

作为全球第二大服装零售商（仅次于西班牙的Inditex集团），海恩斯莫里斯集团将依靠全面循环和可再生能源引领可持续时尚产业的变革作为目标，旨在减少浪费并坚持品牌的环保理念。比如，在2013年推出服装收集计划，并于2018年收集了客户提供的20649吨旧纺织品，用于再利用或回收利用。

扫一扫

海恩斯莫里斯在宣传方面投入也很多，除了广告投放外，它还与著名设计师或是名人联手设计服装以吸引消费者。2004年，海恩斯莫里斯与卡尔·拉格斐以惊人的方式开启了奢侈品牌和平价快时尚的跨界联名，推出的系列产品由知名设计师设计①，价格却十分亲民。随后合作的对象包括Stella McCartney，Viktor & Rolf，Roberto Cavalli，Comme des Garçons，Matthew Williamson，Jimmy Choo，Sonia Rykiel，Lanvin，Versace，Marni等。

扫一扫

图2-3　海恩斯莫里斯设计师合作系列

① 该品牌设计师合作系列为作者手绘。

品牌历史

1947

一次美国之旅激发了埃林·佩尔森以低廉价格提供时尚女装的创意，并于1947在韦斯特罗斯开设了第一家女装店。

A trip to the United States inspired Erling Persson to offer women's fashion at low prices, and he opened the first women's clothing store in Vasteras in 1947.

1968

创始人埃林·佩尔森购买了枪械及打猎用品商店Mauritz Widforss，因此开始拓展男装和童装业务。这之后的Hennes更名为Hennes & Mauritz。

Erling Persson, the founder of Hennes, acquired the Stockholmbased hunting apparel and firearms retailer Mauritz Widforss. This was the start of expanding the business of men's and children's clothing. And the name of Hennes was changed to Hennes & Mauritz.

1974

1974年，海恩斯莫里斯在斯德哥尔摩证券交易所上市。同年，品牌更名为"H&M"。

In 1974, Hennes&Mauritz was listed on the Stockholm Stock Exchange. The same year, the brand was renamed as "H&M".

1980

在电子商务诞生之前，通过1980年收购瑞典邮购公司Rowells，海恩斯莫里斯的服装销售进入客户家中。

Long before the term e-commerce was even born, sale of H&M fashion moved into the customer's homes through the acquisition of Swedish mail order company Rowells in 1980.

1998

随着在法国巴黎开设第一家商店，海恩斯莫里斯在欧洲继续扩张，同时，从瑞典市场开始提供在线购物服务。

With the opening of the first store in Paris, France, H&M continued to expand in Europe, while offering online shopping services from the Swedish market.

2000

第一家海恩斯莫里斯旗舰店在纽约第五大道开业，标志着其在欧洲以外的扩张的开始。

The H&M flagship store opened on Fifth Avenue in New York, marking the start of the expansion outside Europe.

2007

首批亚洲门店在香港和上海开业，并推出全新品牌COS。

The first Asian stores opened in Hong Kong and Shanghai and launched a new brand COS.

2008

海恩斯莫里斯在日本东京开设了第一家店。收购时装公司FaBric Scandinavian AB，包括Weekday、Monki和Cheap Monday。

H&M opened its first store in Tokyo, Japan. Weekday, Monki, and Cheap Monday were welcomed to the H&M group through the purchase of FaBric Scandinavian AB.

图2-4 品牌发展历史

Hennes & Mauritz (H&M)

Brand Introduction

Hennes & Mauritz AB is a Swedish multinational clothing-retail company which operates globally, with branches in countries including Asia, Europe and America, offering products for all age groups and apparel and accessories for women, men, teenagers and children. In addition, H&M has developed household items and beauty products to achieve a wide range of branded products.

For H&M, it takes short time to design and produce new styles. At its headquarters in Stockholm, H&M employs designers who watch for fashion trends and then bring them to life in new products. Suppliers around the world help push the products to stores in just a month. This allows consumers to quickly access the most cutting-edge fashion products and helps reduce brand operating costs. The sales concept of Hennes & Mauritz AB with many styles and small quantities is the successful application of the long tail effect.

The H&M group continues to grow. The expansion takes place through its different brands, each of which has its own unique identity. In addition to the H&M, it also includes COS (Collection of Style), &other stories, Monki, Weekday, Cheap Monday, ARKET, Afound and H&M Home.

Brand Strategy

As the second-largest global clothing retailer (just behind Spain-based Inditex), H&M Group aims to reduce the waste and adhere to the brand's environmental philosophy by transforming the sustainable lifestyle industry through a comprehensive cycle and renewable energy. For example, in 2013, the clothing collection program was launched, and in 2018, 20649 tons of old textiles supplied by customers were collected for reusing or recycling.

H&M has invested a lot in propaganda. In addition to advertising, it also works with famous designers or celebrities to design clothing to attract consumers. In 2004, H&M and Karl Lagerfeld opened a cross-border cooperation between luxury brands and fast fashions in an amazing way. The series of products were designed by well-known designers at a very affordable price. Subsequent collaborators include Stella McCartney, Viktor&Rolf, Roberto Cavalli, Comme des Garçons, Matthew Williamson, Jimmy Choo, Sonia Rykiel, Lanvin, Versace, Marni and so on.

优衣库 UNIQLO

品牌简介

优衣库由柳井正创立，主要业务为休闲运动服装的设计、制造和零售。自1984年在广岛中区的袋町开设首间店铺后，以自有品牌专业零售商经营模式（SPA）活跃于全球，在世界各地大型购物商场开设门店。优衣库作为当下全球快时尚龙头之一，以“服饰人生”为理念，生产和销售适合所有人穿着的衣服，同时兼顾审美与实用。截至2018年8月底，优衣库在日本国内及海外的店铺总数达2000间，其海外销售额占优衣库整体销售额的51%。

图2-5 优衣库品牌标志

优衣库隶属于日本迅销集团，该集团前身为1963年成立于日本山口县宇部市的男性服饰公司——小郡商事株式会社。除核心业务优衣库外，集团旗下还拥有多个品牌，包括GU、Theory、Comptoir des Cotonniers、Princesse tam.tam及J Brand等。

图2-6 优衣库集团旗下品牌概览

品牌战略

不同于其竞争对手品牌，在产品设计与开发上，优衣库将极简主义与功能性作为品牌差异化的重点。以“为每个人制作的服装”的理念为出发点，优衣库专注于提供高性价比的基础款服装，做工精细、细节设计、尺码齐全，并通过强化研发来提升服装穿着性能。创造的HeatTech（有助于保持热量的轻薄织物）、AIRism（一种带有快干内层面料的柔软面料）、3D U-Knit（无缝立体针织技术）和UV Cut（用于防止90%紫外线到达穿着者的材料）技术，均成为其具有核心竞争力的主推产品。

在全球开启数字化时代之前，优衣库将营销传单和电视广告作为其主要推广手段。如今，优衣库借助其独特的店内环境、名人品牌大使、数字营销、与设计师的合作等品牌活动来传达其品牌地位和理想。

◎门店环境：通过宽阔的过道、明亮的灯光和整齐陈列的产品来提供舒适的购物体验，并通过店内设置数字显示屏来展示其面料选用和设计理念。

◎品牌大使：与许多全球品牌类似，优衣库还使用名人代言扩展品牌形象并与大众产生联系，比如赞助世界级运动员，这有助于优衣库打开欧美新市场。

◎数字营销：随着智能手机的普及和在线销售重要性的提升，优衣库通过本土化社交媒体推广，培养消费者的品牌忠诚度，并利用移动应用程序获取客户信息以扩大在线销售。

◎与设计师的合作[①]：优衣库定期与不同的设计师进行联名合作，创造独特风格，开拓其知名度较低的欧美市场。

同时，优衣库积极承担企业的社会责任，将可持续性作为实现其品牌价值的重点之一。比如发起名为“全产品回收计划”的倡议，鼓励客户回收衣服进行再利用，将其作为纺织工业材料，并且承诺消除所有危险化学品的使用，以最大限度地减少公司在化学品排放和用水方面的环境影响。

图2-7 优衣库联名系列

① 该品牌联名系列插图为作者手绘。

品牌历史

1984–1998

以低价产品打开本土市场。

1984 在广岛市中区袋町开设了第一家综合服饰店"Unique Clothing Warehouse"，简称为"UNI - CLO"(1988年注册"UNI-QLO"为商标)。

1991 母公司小郡商事株式会社更名为迅销集团。

1997 优衣库以美国零售集团GAP为参考，开始进行改革以转变品牌形象。

1998–2003

根据业绩调整定位与战略。

1998 面对依赖爆款(摇粒绒衫)增长动力不足导致营收增速下滑的状况，推出ABC (All Better Change)计划。

2001 集团营业额达到高峰，在中国成立子公司迅销(江苏)服饰有限公司，并在英国伦敦开设首家优衣库海外店铺。

2004–2009

初探国际市场，扩充品牌矩阵。

2004 迅销集团投资Theory的开发商。

2005 海外市场持续扩张，在美国纽约，中国香港尖沙咀和韩国首尔开设店铺，并成立Comptoir des Cotonniers Japan Co.，Ltd。

2006 收购Princesse Tam.Tam，并成立GU，开发低价时尚休闲服装品牌。

2010–NOW

加码全球布局，加速海外扩张。

2011 优衣库第五大道商店在纽约开设全球旗舰店。

2012 收购JBrand的大部分股份(J Brand是一家位于洛杉矶的时尚品牌)。

2016 全球优衣库商店开始零售由艺术总监Christophe Lemaire及其团队在优衣库巴黎研发中心开发的全新优衣库U系列。

图2-8 集团发展历史

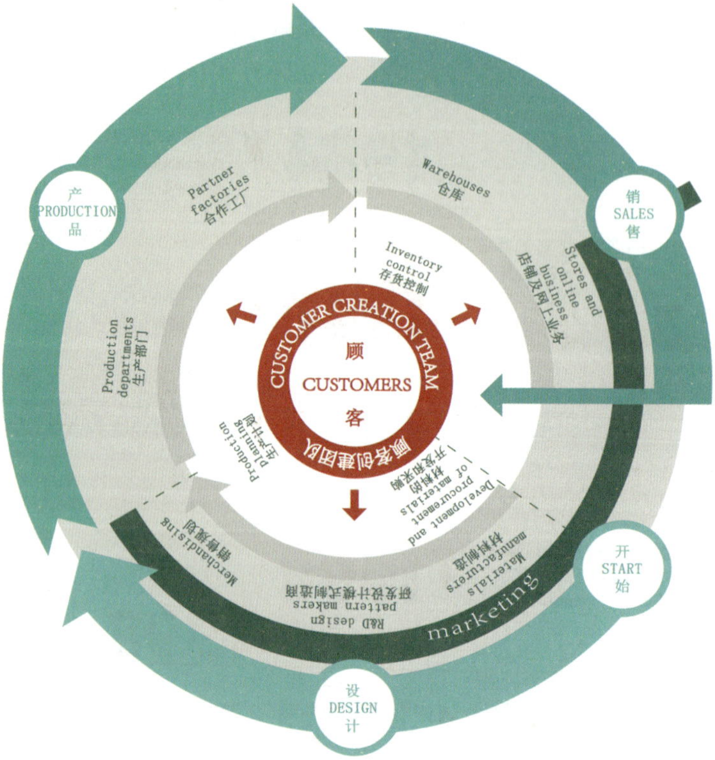

图2-9 优衣库的产品开发方法和高效供应链

UNIQLO

Brand Introduction

UNIQLO was founded by Tadashi Yanai, which specializes in the design, manufacture and retail of casual sportswear. Since opening its first store in Fukuro-machi, Naka-ku, Hiroshima in 1984, it has been active in the world with its business model SPA (Speciality Retailer of Private Label Apparel) and has opened stores in major shopping malls around the world. As one of the leading global fashion retailors, UNIQLO is based on the concept of "Lifewear", which produces and sells clothes suitable for everyone, while considering aesthetics and practicality. At the end of August, 2018, UNIQLO had a total of 2,000 domestic and overseas stores, and its overseas sales accounted for 51% of UNIQLO 's overall sales.

UNIQLO is part of Fast Retailing Co., Ltd., formerly known as Men's Shop Ogori Shoji, a male apparel company founded in 1963 based in Yamaguchi. In addition to the core business UNIQLO, the group also has a number of brands, including GU, Theory, Comptoir des Cotonniers, Princesse tam.tam, J Brand and so on.

Brand Strategy

Unlike its competitors' brands, UNIQLO has made minimalism and functionality a key part of brand differentiation in product design and development. Starting from the concept of "Made for all", UNIQLO focuses on providing cost-effective basic clothing with fine workmanship, detailed design and complete sizes, and enhances the performance of clothing through intensive research. The HeatTech (lightweight fabric that helps maintain heat), AIRism (a soft fabric with quick-drying inner fabric), 3D U-Knit (seamless stereo knitting) and UV Cut (material designed to prevent 90% of ultraviolet rays from reaching the wearer) have all become the main products of its core competitiveness.

Until the digital age started to gain rapid global momentum, UNIQLO had traditionally relied on marketing flyers and TV commercials as its primary means of advertising. Today, it uses a plethora of methods to communicate its brand position and ideals, including its unique in-store environment, celebrity brand ambassadors, digital marketing, brand campaigns such as collaborations with designers and so on .

◎ In-store environment: Through its wide aisles, bright lights, neatly stacked shelves to create a comfortable and welcoming shopping experience. It also has digital screens in-store explaining the practical benefits of its fabrics and apparels.

◎ UNIQLO Global Ambassadors: Similar to many global brands, UNIQLO also uses celebrity endorsements to extend the brand's image and connect with the masses. For example, sponsoring world-class athletes could help UNIQLO open new markets in Europe and America.

◎ Digital marketing: With the popularity of smartphones and the increasing importance of online sales, UNIQLO promotes consumer brand loyalty through localized social media and uses mobile applications to capture customer information to expand online sales.

◎ Collaborations with designers: UNIQLO regularly collaborates with different designers to create a unique style to gain quicker access into American and European markets where it has a weaker brand awareness.

At the same time, UNIQLO actively assumes corporate social responsibility and regards sustainability as one of the key points in achieving its brand value. For example, an initiative called "All-Product Recycling initiative" was launched to encourage customers to recycle the clothes and use them as textile industry materials. And it promised to eliminate the use of all hazardous chemicals to minimize the company's environmental footprint specifically in chemicals, emissions and water usage.

飒拉 ZARA

品牌简介

作为西班牙服装零售商Inditex集团的旗舰品牌，飒拉创始于1975年，以合理的价格为客户提供优质的时尚产品，除了贡献大部分利润的女装外，还出售男士、儿童服装以及大码和孕妇装。目前，飒拉已在全球96个国家和地区开设2259家店铺，销售额占到集团总销售额的75%左右。

图2-10 飒拉品牌标志变更

而作为全球知名的服装零售商，其母公司Inditex集团为了满足不同细分市场的需求，开始了多品牌运作，先后推出Massimo Dutti、Pull & Bear、Bershka、Stradivarius、Oysho、Zara Home和Uterqüe等主要品牌。每个品牌都围绕“提供消费得起的流行时装”的理念进行独立运作，实行同样的管理模式和统一的供应链控制，以实现对市场响应速度的最大化。

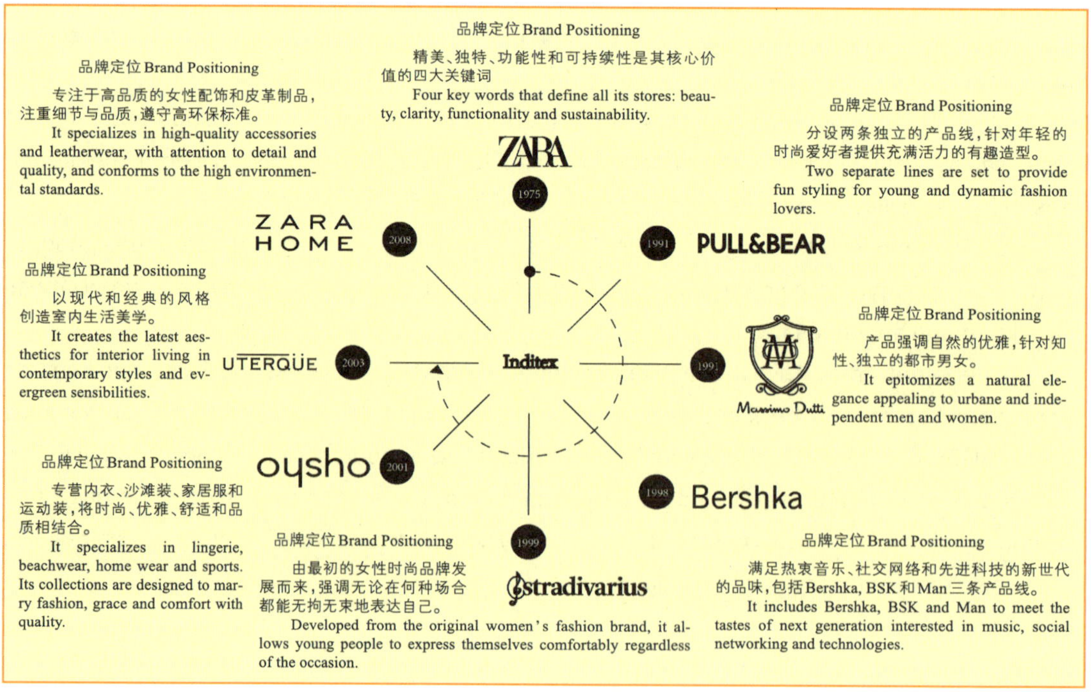

图2-11 集团旗下品牌概览

品牌战略

将快速、敏捷、多品类、小规模、大终端作为竞争战略，飒拉成为Inditex集团最具价值的品牌。而手握八个知名服装品牌的Inditex公司，则毫无悬念地跻身于西班牙最大商业奇迹之一。飒拉成功的秘诀可以概括为商店、内部设计师和工厂之间的联系。

◎商店：不同于一般时装零售商通常将其收入的3.5%用于广告，飒拉只将其中的0.3%用于广告，转而将一定比例的收入用于新店铺的开设。创始人阿曼西奥·奥尔特加·高纳认为，广告是一种毫无意义的开销，唯一需要的广告是商店橱窗和消费者的口碑。因此，商店的橱窗成为品牌重要的宣传途径之一，其中展示的往往是飒拉所有需要

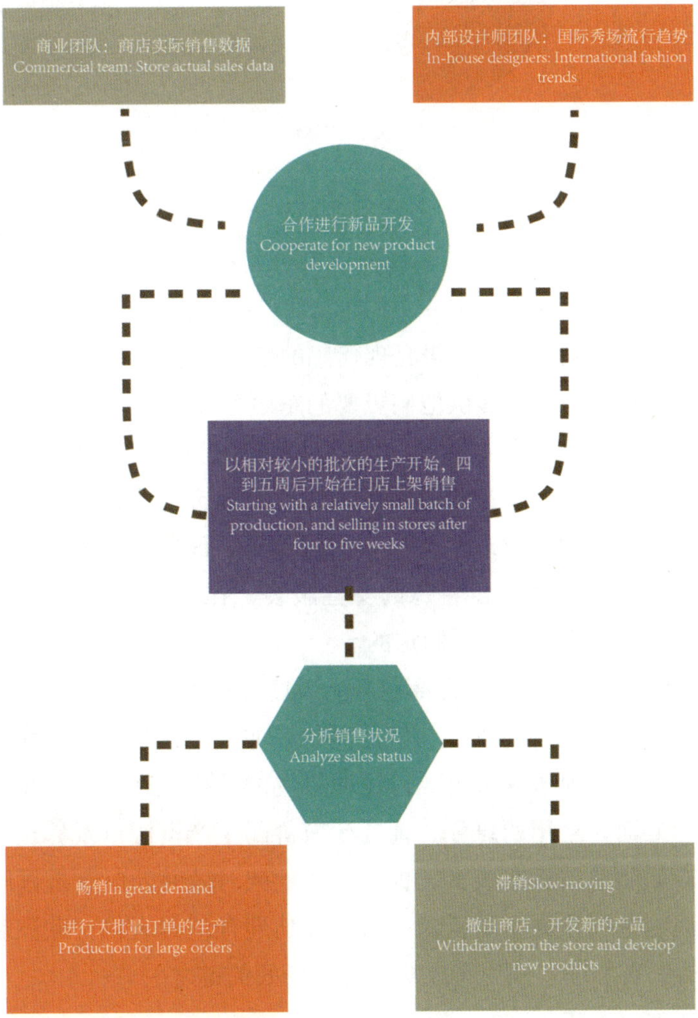

图2-12 飒拉新品开发流程示意图

图2-13 飒拉供货流程示意图

推广的产品。除此之外，90%的飒拉零售商店归公司所有，其余则是归特许经营的合资企业，这意味着客户在进入世界各地的飒拉商店时体验的是统一的购物环境。这些商店位于主要商业区，光线充足，营造出极具现代感的氛围。

◎设计师：飒拉将“为客户提供他们想要的东西”，同时“能够以比其他任何人更快的速度获得它们”视为品牌的基本准则。保持对客户关注成为飒拉成功的核心，可以说消费者是飒拉的首席设计师。飒拉极具竞争力的客户研究能力还在于，其在全球各地的商店提供的产品反映了客户在物理、气候和文化差异方面的独特需求，比如它在日本提供较小的尺寸，在阿拉伯国家提供特殊的女性服装，在南美洲提供不同的季节性服装。价格策略也是根据目标消费市场进行制定的。

◎工厂：“二战”之后，产品制造商们开始无序地在南美洲和亚洲等廉价劳动力地区开设加工厂，以最大限度地节约成本。但是奥尔特加坚持让集团的绝大部分生产和采购都在西班牙国内或欧洲其他国家进行，以证明市场的动机性和必要的少量缺货比廉价劳动力更为重要。一方面，运用西班牙、葡萄牙廉价的生产资源以及邻近欧洲大陆的地缘优势，大幅降低产品制造与运输成本，提升货品上架时效并及时掌握国际流行趋势；另一方面，将“欧洲制造”作为主要营销策略，成功迎合消费者将“欧洲制造”等同于高级流行服饰品牌的消费心理，成为其成功打开市场的关键之一。

品牌历史

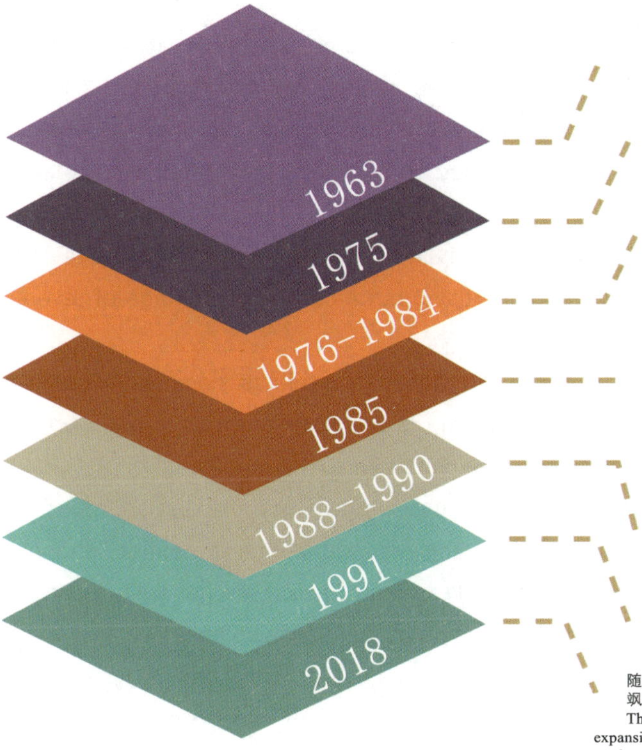

Inditex集团由服装商阿曼西奥·奥尔特加·高纳创立，最初主要为服装批发商生产女性睡衣和贴身内衣。

The Inditex Group was founded by clothing manufacturer Amancio Ortega Gaona and initially produced women's pajamas and lingerie for clothing wholesalers.

第一家零售门店飒拉开设于西班牙拉科鲁尼亚市，初衷是为了销售批发商取消订单后的存货。

First store of Zara opened in the Spanish coastal city of La Coruña to sell the inventory after the wholesalers canceled the order.

在西班牙各大城市开设飒拉分店，使得飒拉的时尚概念得到广泛的认可。

The opening of ZARA stores in major cities in Spain has made ZARA's fashion concept widely recognized.

确立Inditex为集团母公司，建立起一个能够极快地应对市场变化趋势的分销系统。

Inditex was officially founded and established a distribution system capable of reacting to trends of market change.

相继在葡萄牙波尔图、美国纽约、法国巴黎开设海外门店。

The overseas stores opened in Porto, Portugal; New York, US and Paris, France.

Pull&Bear和Massimo Dutti加入集团，开始将时装市场进一步细分，并开始多元化的扩张。

Pull&Bear and Massimo Dutti joined Inditex. For the first time, Inditex expanded its stable.

随着综合店铺和在线模式的发展，品牌加快了在线业务的扩展。飒拉在其没有线下商店的106个市场推出了全球在线商店。

The evolution of its integrated store and online model prompted the expansion of online business. Zara launched its global online store in 106 markets which have no offline store.

图2-14 Inditex集团发展历史

Zara

Brand Introduction

As the flagship brand of the Spanish fashion retailer Inditex Group, Zara is founded in 1975 to provide customers with high-quality fashion products at affordable prices. In addition to women's clothing, from which most of their profit comes, they also sell clothes for men, children and plus-size and maternity lines to clothe its larger customers. At present, there are 2259 Zara stores in 96 countries(regions), accounting for about 75% of the Group's total sales.

The parent company Inditex Group (INdustrias de DIseño TEXtil, S.A., referred to as INDITEX), as a world-renowned clothing retailer, continued to expand and began multi-brand operation by successively launching Massimo Dutti, Pull&Bear, Bershka, Stradivarius, Oysho, Zara Home and Uterqüe to meet the needs of different market segments. Each brand operates independently around "providing affordable fashion" with the same management model and unified supply chain control to maximize market responsiveness.

Brand Strategy

Taking fast, agility, multi-category, small-scale, and large terminals as competitive strategies, it has become the most valuable brand of the Inditex Group. Inditex, which holds eight well-known clothing brands, is one of the biggest business miracles in Spain without any suspense. The secret of Gala's success can be summed up as a link between stores, in-house designers and factories.

◎Stores: Differing from a fashion retailer that normally spends around 3.5% of its revenue on advertising, Zara only spends 0.3% of it on advertising but a certain percentage of revenue for new stores.

The shop window display is all Zara needs to promote the products since the founder of the company, Amancio Ortega believes that advertising is pointless and the only advertising needed is the shop window or a word of mouth by the consumers.

Other than this, 90% of Zara stores are owned by the company and the rest are owned by joint ventures of franchises. This means that customers experience a unified shopping environment when they enter the Zara stores around the world, which are generally located in the main business district, are filled with light and create a modern atmosphere.

◎ In–house designers: The Zara empire is built on two basic rules: "to give customers what they want", and "get it to them faster than anyone else". It can be said that Zara's principal designer is the customer since Zara's unrelenting focus on the customer is at the core of the brand's success.

Zara's competitive customer research capabilities also lie in its product offerings across its stores globally reflect the unique customer needs in terms of physical, climate and cultural differences. It offers smaller sizes in Japan, special women's clothes in Arab countries, and clothes of different seasonality in South America. And the price strategy is also based on the target consumer market.

◎The factory: After World War II, product manufacturers began to open processing plants in cheap labor areas such as South America and Asia to maximize cost savings. But Ortega insists that most of the group's production and procurement are carried out in Spain or the other European couvtries to prove that the market's motivation and the necessary small shortages are more important than cheap labors.

On the one hand, using the cheap production resources of Spain and Portugal and the geographical advantages of neighboring Continental Europe, the product manufacturing and transportation costs are greatly reduced, the timeliness of goods is improved, and the international fashion trends are grasped in time; on the other hand, "Made in Europe" as the main marketing strategy has successfully catered to consumers' consumption psychology of "Made in Europe" being equivalent to high-end fashion brands, which has become one of the keys of opening its market successfully.

第三节

本章讨论与阅读推荐

Discussion and Reading Recommendation

本章讨论

1. 结合本章内容谈谈快时尚品牌（集团）之所以取得成功，除了能够快速回应消费者需求外，还有哪些原因？

2. 请举例说明快时尚品牌该如何适应时尚产业新的数字化变革。

3. 本章涉及的快时尚品牌均采取了举措，以强调其对可持续发展的承诺，你认为快时尚的概念与可持续理念是否可以并存？

Discussion

1. In combination with the contents of this chapter, what are the reasons for the success of the fast fashion brand (group) in addition to being able to respond quickly to consumer demands?

2. Please give an example of how fast fashion brands can adapt to the new digital transformation of the fashion industry.

3. The fast fashion brands involved in this chapter have taken measures to emphasize their commitment to sustainable development. Do you think that the concept of fast fashion and sustainability can coexist at the same time?

阅读推荐 Reading Recommendation

《如此不同，如此成功——优衣库 VS ZARA》

作　者：［日］斋藤孝浩

出版社：中国大百科全书出版社

译　者：袁丽晖

出版年：2017

ISBN：9787500099987

参考资料 References

快时尚市场分析

https://wiki.mbalib.com/wiki/快时尚

https://cn.fashionnetwork.com/news/shen-du---kuai-shi-shang-wei-he-geng-nan-zai,1079200.html#.XUuo0y-tZQI

https://36kr.com/p/5171688

https://www.tmtpost.com/3126243.html

http://www.xinhuanet.com/fashion/2019-05/22/c_1124527284.htm

https://money.163.com/19/0507/10/EEILOBKR00258105.html

https://www.mings-fashion.com/hm-二手古著-快时尚-250710/

海恩斯莫里斯

https://about.hm.com

https://en.wikipedia.org/wiki/H%26M

https://www.insider.com/surprising-fun-facts-about-hm-clothing-store-2018-6

https://successstory.com/companies/fabulous-fashion-for-all-and-fashion-with-a-conscience-profile-on-hm

https://about.hm.com/en/about-us/history/the-40_s---50_s.html

https://web.archive.org/web/20130319073126/http://about.hm.com/AboutSection/en/About/Facts-About-HM/People-and-History/Our-History.html

https://news.cision.com/h---m-hennes---mauritz-ab/r/versace-to-design-iconic-collection-for-h-m-this-autumn,c9137227

http://www.bbc.co.uk/newsbeat/article/38135969/hm-has-made-a-short-wes-anderson-film-for-its-christmas-ad

https://www.theguardian.com/sustainable-business/zara-h-m-fashion-sustainable-forests-logging-fabric

优衣库

http://www.chinasspp.com/News/Detail/2018-11-23/429807-1.htm
https://www.fastretailing.com/tc/about/business/
https://wiki.mbalib.com/wiki/%E8%BF%85%E9%94%80%E5%85%AC%E5%8F%B8
https://www.fastretailing.com/eng/
https://zh.wikipedia.org/wiki/%E5%84%AA%E8%A1%A3%E5%BA%AB
https://en.wikipedia.org/wiki/Uniqlo
https://martinroll. com / resources / articles / strategy / uniqlo-the-strategy-behind-the-global-japanese-fast-fashion-retail-brand/
https://new.qq.com/omn/20180502/20180502G1AOZX.html
https://m.ef360.com/manager/166.html
https://www.cnblogs.com/canyangfeixue/p/3474690.html
http://www.chinasspp.com/News/Detail/2018-11-23/429807.htm
http://ishare.iask.sina.com.cn/f/RhxgZWRjvb.html

飒拉

https://www.ukessays.com/essays/marketing/history-of-the-famous-fashon-store-zara-marketing-essay.php
https://martinroll. com / resources / articles / strategy / the-secret-of-zaras-success-a-culture-of-customer-co-creation/
https://en.m.wikipedia.org/wiki/Zara_(retailer)
https://www.ukessays.com/essays/marketing/history-of-the-famous-fashon-store-zara-marketing-essay.php
https://www.telegraph.co.uk/finance/newsbysector/retailandconsumer/11172562/How-Inditex-became-the-worlds-biggest-fashion-retailer.html
https://wiki.mbalib.com/wiki/Inditex集团
https://www.inditex.com/en/
https://www.marketing91.com/swot-analysis-zara/
https://www.marketing91.com/marketing-mix-zara/
https://postfunnel.com/spotlight-zara-lessons-brand-spends-next-nothing-ads/
https://www.referralcandy.com/blog/zara-marketing-strategy/
https://www.huffpost.com/entry/if-you-think-zara-does-no_b_12187058
https://www.forbes.com/sites/pamdanziger/2018/04/23/zaras-difference-pull-people-in-not-push-product-out/
https://www.telegraph.co.uk/finance/newsbysector/retailandconsumer/11172562/How-Inditex-became-the-worlds-biggest-fashion-retailer.html

第三章

运动品牌

Sportswear Brands

第一节

运动装市场分析

Analysis of Sportswear Market

狭义上运动服饰是专用于体育运动竞赛，根据运动项目的特定要求进行设计制作；随着运动休闲服装正逐渐突破场景的限制，以及消费者对于运动服饰认知的更新，形成了广义上的“运动风”，成为人们日常时尚的重要组成部分。按运动服饰的产品构成类型来分，可分为专业训练装备、户外服饰用品以及运动衍生类服装。从google搜索指数来看，“athleisure”（运动休闲）的全球搜索热度从2014年开始迅速增长，该类产品也已占据我国运动服饰市场。

目前国内具有影响力的运动鞋服品牌主要有20余家，形成了国际品牌与国内品牌两分天下的局面。海外运动服装行业发展历史悠久，诞生了Adidas，Nike等知名品牌，这些国际知名运动品牌占据我国一线城市运动鞋服市场的领导地位。而李宁、安踏、361度和特步等近年崛起的本土品牌，其优势则在二、三、四线城市更为突出。

由于对运动服饰的消费偏好的加剧，全球运动休闲服装行业将继续保持上涨的势头。运动休闲细分市场现今已是服装产业增长核心驱动力之一。而以中国为主的新兴市场运动服饰渗透率也不断得到提升。得益于消费者健康意识的提升和运动配套设施的完善，我国运动服行业具有了坚实的发展基础，同时运动服饰需求也获得了快速增长。

随着运动消费的日益时尚化、品牌化，以及信息技术的发展和诸多有影响力的赛事的推动，运动服饰成为服装行业中增长最为瞩目的品类之一，并且时尚化和智能化将成为其发展的趋势。此外，市场对差异化、高端化体育产品需求的增加，要求运动服企业通过多维度、全品类产品满足不同消费者对自身个性发展的需求。

Analysis of Sportswear Market

In the narrow sense, sportswear is dedicated to sports competitions, which is designed and produced according to the specific requirements of sports programs. As sports and casual wear gradually break through the limitations of the wearing occasion, as well as consumers' renewed awareness of sportswear, it has formed a "sports style" in a broad sense, which has become an important part of people's daily fashion. According to different types, sportswear products can be divided into professional training equipment, outdoor clothing and sports-derived clothing. From the google search index, the global search popularity of "athleisure" has been growing rapidly since 2014, and such products have also occupied the sportswear market in China.

At present, there are more than 20 influential sports brands in China, which has formed a world of both international and domestic brands. The overseas sportswear industry has a long history of development and has produced well-known brands such as Adidas and Nike. These internationally renowned sports brands occupy the leading position in the market of China's first-tier cities. Local brands such as Li Ning, Anta, 361° and X-tep have emerged in recent years, and they are even more prominent in second, third and fourth tier cities.

Contributed to the intensity of the consumption preferences of sportswear, the global sports and leisure wear industry will continue to maintain its upward momentum. The sports and leisure wear segment is now one of the core drivers of the growth of the apparel industry. The penetration rate of sportswear in emerging markets dominated by China has also been continuously improved. Thanks to the improvement of consumers' health awareness and the improvement of sports facilities, China's sportswear industry has a solid foundation for development, and the demand for sportswear has also grown rapidly.

With the increasing awareness of sports fashion and brands, as well as the development of information technology and also the promotion of many influential sports events, sportswear has become one of the most eye-catching categories in the apparel industry. And fashion and intelligence will become the trend of its development. In addition, the market demand for differentiated and high-end sports products requires sportswear companies to meet the needs of different consumers for their personality development through producing multi-dimensional, all-category products.

第二节

运动品牌分析

Analysis of Sportswear Brand

阿迪达斯 Adidas

品牌简介

阿迪达斯是德国的运动服饰及体育用品制造商，品牌名取自创始人——阿道夫·达斯勒名字的缩写，其前身为成立于1924年的达斯勒兄弟鞋厂（Gebrüder Dassler Schuhfabrik）。作为遍布全球市场的知名跨国公司，阿迪达斯位于德国Herzogenaurach的总部负责设计和制造鞋子、服装和配饰等，并在世界各地设有分公司。

阿迪达斯已在运动服装市场占据主导地位，是仅次于耐克的世界第二大运动服饰制造商。该集团旗下各品牌涵盖了不同类型的设备和服饰。

adidas

图3-1 阿迪达斯集团旗下各品牌

品牌战略

1. 产品

阿迪达斯的目标是通过设计与技术的结合，为客户提供优质的运动装备，有利于品牌建立稳定的品牌形象，并在其多元化品牌过程中提升品牌价值以扩大其在不同消费者群体中的市场份额。

图3-2　代表性产品

2. 速度

阿迪达斯将速度用于业务模式的“重塑”，从规划到产品开发、采购、供应链和销售渠道，提高其产品每一季度的上市速度，比如在安斯巴赫的Speedfactory通过3D打印技术和机器人数字化生产过程。同时也实施以限制供应的举措，避免流行的阿迪达斯鞋款，如“Stan Smith”和“Superstar”等过度曝光。

3. 数字化

阿迪达斯从2015年开始致力于将数字化作为其营销战略的关键部分，并将其营销预算的90%用于数字营销和社交媒体，以此不断提高品牌的数字化能力，与消费者进行互动，创造优质、互联和个性化的体验。

4. 细分市场

在其主要战略城市（伦敦、洛杉矶、纽约、巴黎、上海和东京）实施不同的定位策略和产品差异化。在欧洲，他们特别专注于销售足球产品，在美国则是篮球和棒球等产品。针对亚洲市场尤其是印度和巴基斯坦，阿迪达斯则开发出适合中产阶级消费者的低成本产品。

“三条纹”作为标志性的徽标，没有特定的外观，以不同的形式出现在阿迪达斯所有系列产品中（最初该商标由小型芬兰运动服品牌Karhu在20世纪40年代进行了注册）。

图3-3 三条纹标志

三叶草诞生于1972年，原始的三条纹在三片叶子交叉的底部做横向切割，以示品牌比以往更加多样化的同时仍保持经典的外观。现在，三叶草是Originals的标志。

图3-4 三叶草标志

对性能、技术和进展的重新关注激发了阿迪达斯于1997年推出三条纹的三角形版本。这一标志酷似山的形状，代表着“面临的挑战和要实现的目标”，现在通常被作为设备标识，在阿迪达斯的篮球性能鞋类的设计运用中尤为突出。

图3-5 三斜杠标志

阿迪达斯的三条纹最新版本是Adidas Style的标志——一个与三个爪状条纹相交的圆圈。

图3-6 圆球型标志

品牌历史

1924

阿道夫·达斯勒与他的哥哥鲁道夫·达斯勒在黑措根奥拉赫创立了达斯勒兄弟鞋厂，并开始制造基本的钉鞋。

Adolf Dassler and his brother Rudolf Dassler founded the Gebrüder Dassler Schuhfabrik in Herzogenaurach and began to manufacture basic running spikes.

1936

杰西·欧文斯在柏林奥运会上穿着达斯勒的手工钉鞋为美国赢得四枚金牌，使之开始在全球享有盛誉。

Jesse Owens, wearing Dassler's handmade spikes, won four gold medals at the Berlin Olympics for the United States, making it a global reputation.

1947

达斯勒兄弟分道扬镳，成为彼此的商业竞争对手。鲁道夫创办了一家名为RuDa的新公司(后来更名为PUMA)，阿道夫则注册了"Adi Dassler adidas Sportschuhfabrik"。

The Dassler brothers parted ways and became each other's commercial competitors. Rudolf founded a new company called RuDa (later renamed PUMA), and Adolf registered "Adi Dassler adidas Sportschuhfabrik".

1967

最初为足球传奇人物Franz Beckenbauer设计的运动服，是阿迪达斯推出的第一款服装。

The first apparel launched by Adidas was originally designed for the legend footballer Franz Beckenbauer.

1970

阿迪达斯开始为FIFA世界杯提供官方比赛用球TELSTAR。

Adidas began to provide the official football TELSTAR for the FIFA World Cup.

1997

阿迪达斯收购所罗门集团(包括其旗下品牌TaylorMade，Mavic和Bonfire)。

Adidas acquired Solomon Group (including its brands TaylorMade, Mavic and Bonfire).

2000s

阿迪达斯成为业内首家推出全新生活方式细分市场的公司，专注于运动风格的街头服饰，与Yohji Yamamoto(2002)和Stella McCartney(2004)建立新合作伙伴关系，并诞生了Y-3(2003)和Porsche Design Sport(2007)。

Adidas became the first company in the industry to launch a new lifestyle segment, focusing on sports-style streetwear. It established new partnerships with Yohji Yamamoto (2002) and Stella McCartney (2004), and developed the brands Y-3 (2003) and Porsche Design Sport (2007).

2005

阿迪达斯出售所罗门集团给亚玛芬体育(芬兰)，次年收购锐步Reebok(包括Rockport、Reebok-CCM Hockey等)。

Adidas sells Solomon Group to AmerSports (Finland) and acquired Reebok in the following year (including Rockport, Reebok-CCM Hockey, etc.).

2010

DirkSchonberger成为阿迪达斯的创意总监，这促成了之后与拉夫·西蒙、法瑞尔·威廉姆斯、瑞克·欧文斯和坎耶·维斯特的合作关系。

DirkSchonberger became the creative director of Adidas, which led to the subsequent partnerships with Raf Simons, Pharrell Williams, Rick Owens and Kanye West.

2011

阿迪达斯收购了户外专业品牌Five Ten。

Adidas acquired the outdoor professional brand Five Ten.

图3-7 品牌发展历程

Adidas

Brand Introduction

Adidas is a German manufacturer of sportswear and sporting goods. The brand name is taken from the founder—Adolf Dassler's name abbreviation. It was formerly known as the Gebrüder Dassler Schuhfabrik in 1924. As a well-known multinational company in the global market, Adidas is headquartered in Herzogenaurach, Germany, responsible for the design and manufacture of shoes, clothing and accessories. It also has branches around the world.

Adidas has dominated the sportswear market and is the second largest sportswear manufacturer in the world after Nike. The group's brands cover different types of equipment and apparel.

Brand Strategy

The product:

Adidas' goal is to provide customers with high-quality sports equipment through the combination of design and technology, which helps the brand to establish a stable brand image. At the same time, in the process of diversifying its brand, it constantly enhances its brand value to expand its market share among different consumer groups.

The speed:

Adidas uses speed for the "remodeling" of business models, from planning to product development, procurement, supply chain and sales channels, to increase the speed of its products in every quarter, such as Speedfactory in Ansbach digitizing production process through 3D printing technology and robotics. At the same time, measures to limit supply were implemented to avoid over-exposure of popular Adidas shoes such as "Stan Smith" and "Superstar".

Digitalization:

Since 2015, Adidas has been committed to treating digital as a key part of its marketing strategy and used 90% of its marketing budget for digital marketing and social media to continuously improve the digital capabilities of its brands, interact with consumers and create quality, connected and personalized experiences.

Market segmentation：

Implement different positioning strategies and product differentiation in its major strategic cities (London, Los Angeles, New York, Paris, Shanghai and Tokyo). In Europe, they focus on selling products, especially football, and in the US, they focus on basketball and baseball. For Asian markets, especially India and Pakistan, Adidas has developed low-cost products for middle-class consumers.

李宁 LI-NING

扫一扫

品牌简介

李宁是中国领先的体育品牌之一，由体操运动员李宁[①]在1990年创立，主要提供专业及休闲运动鞋、服装、器材和配件等产品。李宁拥有品牌营销、研发、设计、制造、经销及零售能力，主要采用外包生产和特许分销商模式，已在中国建立起庞大的供应链管理体系以及零售分销网络。来自中国的收入是李宁集团收入的主要来源，其渠道主要分布在大陆二、三线城市。截至2018年12月31日，李宁品牌在中国境内的线下店铺总数为6344家，并持续在东南亚、印度、中亚、美国和欧洲等地区开拓业务。

图3-8 李宁旗下品牌

李宁集团聚焦自有品牌李宁的同时，采取多品牌业务发展。

① 李宁是中国家喻户晓的“体操王子”，1984年，在洛杉矶奥运会上，他夺得了男子自由体操、鞍马和吊环的3枚金牌。有赖于李宁本人在体育界中的声誉和地位，李宁品牌在成立后的短时间内就占领了市场。

李宁长期致力于体育事业的发展，从1992年巴塞罗那奥运会开始，先后为中国体操、跳水、射击、乒乓球、羽毛球等运动队提供装备。在国际方面，李宁公司与NBA、ATP等国际赛事，以及西班牙奥委会、西班牙篮协、瑞典奥委会、阿根廷篮协等组织合作；先后签约达蒙·琼斯、奥尼尔、伊辛巴耶娃、安德烈亚斯·托希尔德森、德维恩·韦德等国际顶级运动员。李宁也积极承担社会责任，资助希望小学、援建灾区、关爱艾滋孤儿、并且长期支持“一起运动”公益培训项目。

品牌战略

李宁将创新作为品牌发展的根本，比如其于1998年建立中国第一家服装与鞋产品设计开发中心以及于2004年成立香港设计研发中心。2014年回归后的李宁重新将公司的经营方向调回运动领域，将品牌发展集中于运动生活、跑步、篮球和羽毛球等运动类别，并向“互联网+运动生活体验提供商”转型，辅以多维度的营销策略，致力于提供与数字化结合的李宁体验式价值。

李宁意在成为有国际竞争力的体育用品品牌。与电子商务巨头天猫合作亮相纽约时装周，将“潮流”“国际化”“李宁”“国货”等标签与李宁联系起来，使得对中国文化的深刻理解成为李宁的优势，改变了过往消费者对李宁的认识同时强调了李宁国产运动品牌形象。这一举措在18至35岁的中国消费者中取得了巨大反响。

图3-9 李宁参与2018纽约时装周秀场图

扫一扫

品牌历史

1989–2009 开端与发展 Beginning and development

1989

注册"李宁牌"商标。

Registered the "LI-NING" trademark.

1990

李宁公司正式在广东三水成立。

LI-NING Company was officially established in Sanshui, Guangdong Province.

1992

为第二十五届巴塞罗那奥运会上的中国代表团提供服饰。

Provided clothes for the Chinese delegation on the 25th Barcelona Olympics.

2002

确立全新品牌定位：李宁，一切皆有可能。

Established a new brand positioning: LI-NING, anything is possible.

2004

相继推出李宁专业足球鞋Tie和专业篮球鞋Free jumper，并于香港上市。

LI-NING professional football shoes Tie and professional basketball shoes Free jumper were launched and listed in Hong Kong.

2006

推出"李宁弓"减震科技。

Launched "LI-NING Gong", the shock absorption technology.

2010–2014 转型与触底 Transformation and bottoming

2010

推出全新LOGO，并将口号"一切皆有可能"改为"让改变发生"；将消费人群定位为"90后"，大幅提高产品价格。

Launched a new LOGO, and changed the slogan "anything is possible" to "make the change happen"; positioned the consumer group as "post-90s" while greatly increased product prices.

2011

停止Z-DO（新动）品牌业务以及红双喜发展计划。

Quited the Z-DO (New Action) brand business and the Development Plan of DHS.

2014

创始人李宁回归，担任CEO。

Founder Li Ning returned to serve as its CEO.

2015–NOW 复苏 Recovery

LI-NING 让改变发生

图3-10 品牌发展历史

LI–NING

Brand Introduction

LI–NING is one of the leading sports brands in China. Founded in 1990 by gymnast Li Ning, LI–NING mainly provides professional and casual sports shoes, clothing, equipment and accessories. LI–NING has brand marketing, R&D, design, manufacturing, distribution and retail capabilities. It mainly adopts outsourcing production and franchise distributor model. It has established a huge supply chain management system and retail distribution network in China. The income from China is the main source of its group income. Its channels are mainly distributed in the second- and third- tier cities of the mainland. Till December 31, 2018, the total number of offline stores of Li Ning brand in China was 6, 344, and it continued to develop business in Southeast Asia, India, Central Asia, the United States and Europe. LI–NING Group focuses on its own brand LI–NING while taking multi–brand business development.

LI–NING has long been committed to the development of sports. Since the 1992 Barcelona Olympic Games, it has provided equipment for Chinese gymnastics, diving, shooting, table tennis, badminton and other sports teams. Internationally, LI–NING cooperates with NBA, ATP and other international events, as well as the Spanish Olympic Committee, the Spanish Basketball Association, the Swedish Olympic Committee, the Argentine Basketball Association and other organizations. It has also signed some international top athletes, such as Damon Jones, O'Neal, Isinbayeva, Andreas Thorkildsen and Dwyane Wade. LI–NING also undertakes social responsibilities actively. It subsidizes Hope Primary School, assists in building disaster areas, cares for AIDS orphans, and supports the "Sports Together" charity training program for a long time.

Brand Strategy

LI–NING regards innovation as the foundation of brand development. For example, it established the first clothing and footwear product design and development center in China in 1998 and the Hong Kong Design and Development Center in 2004. After the founder Li Ning's return in 2014, LI–NING Group retransferred the company's business direction back to the sports field, focusing on running, basketball and badminton. And it transformed to the idea of "Internet + Sports Life Experience Provider", supplemented by multidimensional marketing strategies to provide LI–NING experience value combined with digitization.

LI–NING intends to be an internationally competitive sports brand. Cooperating with e–commerce giant T–mall in New York Fashion Week, it linked the labels of "trend", "internationalization", "LI–NING" and "Chinese goods" with LI–NING, making the deep understanding of Chinese culture an advantage of LI–NING to change consumers' understanding of Li–Ning in the past and emphasize the image of LI–NING as a domestic sports brand. This move has had a huge response among Chinese consumers aged 18 to 35.

耐克 NIKE

品牌简介

耐克是当今世界上最大的运动鞋服供应商以及主要的运动器材制造商，也是体育企业中最有价值的品牌之一。作为一家从事设计、开发、制造，并在全球范围内销售鞋类、服装、设备、配件及其相关服务的跨国公司，在美国本土，耐克的产品通过约20000个零售店铺进行销售；在全球范围内，其产品销往约200个国家。

1971　　1978

1985　　Solo swoosh

图3-11　耐克品牌标志[1]

耐克的前身蓝丝带体育（Blue Ribbon Sports），成立于1964年1月25日，创始人为比尔·鲍尔曼（Bill Bowerman）（比尔·鲍尔曼是菲尔·奈特作为中长跑运动员时所在的俄勒冈大学田径队的教练）和菲尔·奈特（Phil Knight），最初是日本制鞋商Onitsuka Tiger在美国的经销商。1971年，BRS开始通过独立承包商在海外制造自己的产品系列，并推出标志性商标“Swoosh”和品牌名“Nike”。从20世纪80年代后期开始，耐克通过众多收购稳步扩展其业务并实现产品线多元化（其中一些已经被出售）。

---

① 品牌标志由来与演变：“NIKE”这一品牌名称来自希腊神话中的胜利女神Νίκη，由耐克的第一位全职员工杰夫·约翰逊提出。而如今已是价值数十亿美元品牌基础的“Swoosh”旋风标志，由波特兰州立大学的平面设计专业学生卡罗琳·戴维森（Carolyn Davidson）以胜利女神的翅膀为灵感进行创作，当时她收取的设计收费仅为35美元。

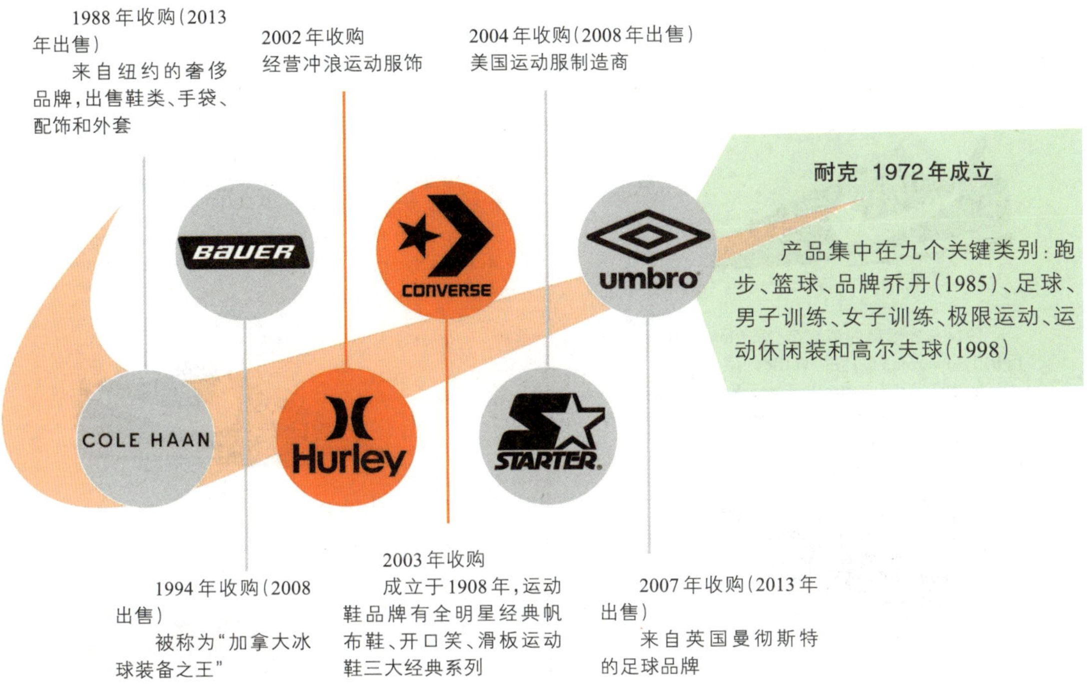

图3-12 耐克旗下品牌

品牌战略

营销对耐克来说至关重要，2018年其用于广告和促销的费用高达35亿美元，通过在线商店、线下商店、公关、电视、口碑和赞助等渠道进行主要产品的推广，保留忠实客户的同时吸引潜在消费者。

品牌情感化是耐克营销成功的关键。耐克被消费者视为出售高品质产品的品牌，这使其能够充分利用其品牌力量，与消费者建立起某种情感上的互动，并塑造积极正面的品牌形象。极具影响力与创意的广告是耐克数字营销的重要手段，相比直接向受众展示所要推广的产品，耐克的广告更倾向于借助情感唤起消费者特定的感受。正如耐克标志性口号“Just do it”所传达的，其每个广告也都在激励其消费者“只要我们勇于尝试，我们可以做任何事情”。

耐克另一个关键营销策略是赞助知名体育明星和大型体育赛事，以“获得品牌知名度和亲和力”，赞助的对象包括老虎伍兹（高尔夫）、迈克尔·乔丹（篮球）、克里斯蒂亚诺·罗纳尔多（足球）、罗杰·费德勒（网球）等运动员，以及NBA、奥运会等赛事。同时，耐克能够及时捕捉消费者的偏好，与Off-White、Yeezy和Raf Simons等高端时尚品牌的合作，成为其进入时尚领域的有效营销方式之一。

品牌历史

1972—第一款用于缓冲的泡沫鞋“Nike Cortez”在墨西哥奥运会期间发布。

In 1972, the Nike Cortez is released during the Mexico Olympics. It's the first foam shoes featuring cushioning.

1974—最畅销的训练鞋“Waffle Racer”底部采用Bill Bowerman设计的Waffle外底。

In 1974, the bestselling sneaker Waffle Racer was released, using the sole inspired by Bill Bowerman's original creation called Waffle.

1978—公司正式更名为Nike。

In 1978, the company officially changed its name to Nike.

1979—推出的“Tailwind”首次采用先进专利技术Air-Sole缓震系统。

In 1979, Nike released the Tailwind, the first running shoes to include air pockets in its outsole.

1982—第一款采用Nike Air缓震技术的耐克篮球鞋Air Force 1推出。

In 1982, the Air Force 1 was released and it was the first basketball shoes with air pockets in the outsole.

1984—为篮球运动员迈克尔·乔丹(Michael Jordan)设计的新款篮球鞋“Air Jordan”推出，并首次使用著名的“Jumpman”标志。

In 1984, the Air Jordan was produced exclusively for Michael Jordan with the famous Jumpman' logo used for the first time.

1987—第一款Nike Air Max首次采用耐克气囊，并将英伦摇滚乐队披头士(The Beetles)的歌曲“Revolution”用于电视广告。

In 1987, the first Nike Air Max shoe with a visible air pocket was released. It was on the advertisement with the song “Revolution” from the British rock&roll band, The Beetles.

1988—在广告中首次使用“Just Do It”的口号。

In 1988, the very first campaign featuring the now iconic slogan “Just Do It” launches.

图3-13 品牌发展历程(1)

1990—在俄勒冈州波特兰市中心开设第一家零售店。

In 1990, Nike opened its first retail store in Downtown Portland, Oregon.

1991—以潜水服为灵感的 Air Huarache 迅速成为主流休闲服装。

In 1991, inspired by diving suits, Air Huarache quickly became mainstream casual wear.

1993—实施 Reuse-A-Shoe 计划，回收旧运动鞋用于制造篮球场、跑道和游乐场。

In 1993, it implemented the Reuse-A-Shoe program to recycle used sneakers for basketball courts, runways and playgrounds construction.

1999—NikeTown 在伦敦牛津街开业，是世界上最大的耐克商店。

In 1999, NikeTown, the largest Nike store in the world opened in London's Oxford Street.

2000—推出采用手工编织鞋面和 Zoom 空气单元的 Nike Woven，以及全新鞋类缓震系统 Nike Shox。

In 2000, it launched the Nike Woven, featuring a handwoven woven upper and Zoom air unit, together with the new footwear cushioning system Nike Shox.

2005—推出的专业跑鞋 Nike Free 采用高度灵活的鞋底设计。

In 2005, Nike introduced "Free" shoe technology which used highly flexible soles.

2006—和 Apple 合作推出 Nike+，使得使用者能够获得跑步的路程、速度和时间。

In 2006, it teamed up with Apple to launch "Nike+" technology, allowing runners to track their distance, speed and time.

图3–14 品牌发展历程（2）

NIKE

Brand Introduction

Nike is the world's largest supplier of sportswear and apparel, as well as a major sports equipment manufacturer and one of the most valuable brands in sports. As a multinational company that designs, develops, manufactures, and sells footwear, apparel, equipment, accessories and related services worldwide, Nike sells its products in approximately 20000 retail stores in USA, and 200 countries overseas.

Nike's predecessor, Blue Ribbon Sports, was born on January 25, 1964, founded by Bill Bowerman and Phil Knight (Bill Bowerman is the coach of the University of Oregon track and field team where Phil Knight plays as the middle-distance runner), which was originally the dealer of Japanese shoemaker Onitsuka Tiger in USA. In 1971, BRS began to manufacture its own product line overseas through independent contractors, and launched the iconic trademark "Swoosh" and the brand name "Nike".

Since the late 1980s, Nike has steadily expanded its business and diversified its product lines through a number of acquisitions (some of which have already been sold).

Brand Strategy

Marketing is critical to Nike, with $3.5 billion in advertising and promotion in 2018. To retain old customers while attracting new consumers, it promotes major products through online store, offline store, public relations, TV, word of mouth and sponsorship.

Emotion branding is the key to Nike's marketing success. Nike is seen by consumers as a brand that sells high-quality products, which enables it to leverage its brand power, build some emotional interaction with consumers, and shape a positive brand image. Influential and creative advertising is an important means of Nike digital marketing. Compared with directly showing the products to be promoted to the audience, Nike's advertisements tend to use emotions to arouse consumers' specific feelings. As Nike's iconic slogan "Just do it" conveys, each of its ads is also motivating its consumers "as long as we try it, we can do anything".

Another key marketing strategy for Nike is to sponsor well-known sports stars and major sports events to "get brand awareness and affinity". Nike sponsored athletes such as Tiger Woods (golf), Michael Jordan (basketball), Cristiano Ronaldo (soccer), Roger Federer (tennis), as well as NBA, Olympics and other events. At the same time, Nike is able to capture consumer preferences in a timely manner, and cooperation with high-end fashion brands such as Off-White, Yeezy and Raf Simons has become one of the effective marketing methods for entering the fashion field.

第三节

本章讨论与阅读推荐

Discussion and Reading Recommendation

本章讨论

1. 耐克与阿迪达斯作为全球两大运动服饰零售商巨头，请你谈谈其发展侧重点的异同。

2. 李宁是由知名体操运动员创立的国内运动服饰品牌，你认为该品牌哪些优势有助于其成功转型？

3. 试分析国外知名运动品牌可为本土运动品牌借鉴的发展策略。

Discussion

1. Nike and Adidas are the two major sportswear retailers in the world. Please talk about the similarities and differences of their development priorities.

2. LI-NING is a domestic sportswear brand founded by a well-known gymnast. Which advantage of the brand do you think has contributed to its successful transformation?

3. Try to analyze the development strategies that local sports brands can learn from foreign well-known sports brands.

阅读推荐 Reading recommendation

《鞋狗——耐克创始人菲尔·奈特亲笔自传》

作　者：［美］菲尔·奈特

出版社：北京联合出版公司

译　者：毛大庆

出版年：2016

ISBN：9787550284463

《没有不可能——商业史上伟大的复兴故事：再造阿迪达斯》

作　者：［美］布伦纳

译　者：严丽川

出版社：中信出版社

出版年：2007

ISBN：9787508608648

参考资料 References

运动装市场分析

https：//bg.qianzhan.com/trends/detail/506/190313-c531fe8d.html
https：//www.qianzhan.com/analyst/detail/220/190122-5fbcb159.html
http：//www.ebrun.com/20190111/316576.shtml

阿迪达斯

http：//adidasfutures.blogspot.com/2013/04/brand-portfolio.html
https：//www.britannica.com/topic/Adidas-AG
https：//en.wikipedia.org/wiki/Adidas
https：//web.archive.org/web/20150208215436/http：//www.adidas-group.com/en/group/history/
https：//www.thoughtco.com/quick-history-of-adidas-1444319
https：//www.highsnobiety.com/2017/04/20/adidas-history-10-facts-you-didnt-know/
https：//www.logaster.com/blog/adidas-logo/
https：//www.highsnobiety.com/2017/07/12/adidas-three-stripes-history/

https：//www.adidas-group.com/en/group/strategy-overview/
https：//digitalagencynetwork.com/digital-marketing-strategy-of-adidas/
https：//www.marketing91.com/marketing-mix-adidas/
https：//www.marketingweek.com/2016/07/19/adidas-details-revolutionary-three-pillar-strategy-as-it-aims-to-reclaim-lost-ground/
https：//www. forbes. com / sites / alapshah / 2018 / 09 / 05 / the-adidas-brand-climbing-up-or-decelerating/#45e369cf77f4
https：//www.thinkwithgoogle.com/marketing-resources/experience-design/adidas-marketing-collaboration/
https：//ivypanda.com/essays/advanced-marketing-strategy-of-adidas-group/
https：//www.thedrum.com/news/2015/03/28/how-adidas-creating-new-recapture-its-winning-streak

李宁

https：//zh.wikipedia.org/wiki/李宁有限公司
https：//www.mings-fashion.com/李宁-时装周-访问-186377/
https：//www.lining.com
https：//www.lining.com/brand/history.html
https：//en.wikipedia.org/wiki/Li-Ning
https：//en.people.cn/200608/15/eng20060815_293127.html
https：//www.espn.com/nba/news/story？ id=2550832
https：//www.globalassignmenthelp.com/samples/marketing/marketing-strategy-of-li-ning
https：//www.businessoffashion.com/articles/global-currents/china-sportswear-giant-li-ning-spars-with-nike-and-adidas
https：//baijiahao.baidu.com/s？ id=1614990442656477619&wfr=spider&for=pc
https：//baijiahao.baidu.com/s？ id=1623998072079943328&wfr=spider&for=pc
https：//www.huxiu.com/article/263554.html？ rec=manual
https：//wiki.mbalib.com/wiki/李宁公司

耐克

https：//www.britannica.com/topic/Nike-Inc
https：//en.wikipedia.org/wiki/Nike， _Inc。
https：//fashiongear.fibre2fashion.com/brand-story/nikeinc/history.asp
https: //www. businessinsider. com / history-of-nike-facts-about-its-50th-anniversary-2014-11？ interna-tional=true&r=US&IR=T
https：//www.fundinguniverse.com/company-histories/nike-inc-history/
https：//didyouknowfashion.com/the-history-of-nike/
https：//www. independent. co. uk / news / media / logos-that-became-legends-icons-from-the-world-of-advertising-768077.html
https：//en.wikipedia.org/wiki/Swoosh
https：//www.oregonlive.com/business/2008/07/nikes_just_do_it_slogan_celebr.html
https：//www.todayifoundout.com/index.php/2014/07/history-nike/
https：//successstory.com/companies/nike-inc

https：//media.corporate-ir.net/media_files/IROL/10/100529/nike-gs09/docs/nike-growth-story.pdf
https：//www.oprah.com/oprahshow/the-evolution-of-the-nike-shoe/all
https：//www.fatbuddhastore.com/nike-sneaker-history-i195
https：//coschedule.com/blog/nike-marketing-strategy/
https：//profitworks. ca / blog / marketing-strategy / 545-nike-strategy-how-nike-became-successful-and-the-leader-in-the-sports-product-market.html

第四章

牛仔品牌

Jeanswear Brands

第一节

牛仔装市场分析

Analysis of Jeanswear Market

世界上第一件牛仔服诞生于19世纪中叶的美国，最初是淘金工人的工作服装。19世纪50年代，牛仔服装成为叛逆青年人的时尚标志，并于70年代开始大量生产，逐渐在全球范围内流行。

众多服装品牌推出具有特定市场定位的新牛仔成衣系列，面向不同类别消费者。牛仔品牌大致可分为：奢侈品时尚品牌，如意大利品牌Diesel，突出美式流行文化和性感元素的Calvin Klein；中高端品牌，如将牛仔服饰变为年轻人的生活方式的Levi's、Lee、Guess等；大众品牌有主打牛仔产品的美国快时尚品牌Gap；等等。

20世纪70年代，牛仔服饰进入中国，尽管当下中国已成为牛仔布生产及销售的重要大国，但相对来说，以中国为代表的亚洲牛仔服装市场还未成熟，仍具有很大的发展潜力。就目前国内牛仔服装市场而言，一线品牌由国际品牌占据，其品牌文化占据绝对的主流；国产品牌利用自身渠道优势占据中低端市场，代表性品牌包括Jason Wood、美特斯邦威、森马等。

牛仔服饰已被迅速认知和消费并成为日常服饰，如今亦在经历降温后逐渐回潮。由于休闲服愈来愈受欢迎，牛仔服装的发展呈现追求时尚及功能两者并重的趋势，包括推出全新的设计风格，开发功能性牛仔布等。而消费者品牌意识的不断上升，将进一步推动中高端牛仔服装市场发展。除此之外，面对牛仔产业普遍存在的污染和排放的问题，现在已经有牛仔企业采用数字化加工技术取代传统生产中的手擦、喷砂等工艺，缩短牛仔服装的制作流程，让牛仔服装产业实现可持续发展。

Analysis of Jeanswear Market

The world's first denim was invented in the United States in the mid-19th century, initially as working costume for gold rush workers. In the 1850s, denim clothing became a fashion symbol for rebellious young people. It began mass production in the 1970s and gradually became popular worldwide.

Numerous apparel brands have launched new denim ready-to-wear collections with specific market positioning for different categories of consumers. Denim brands can be broadly divided into: luxury fashion brands, such as Diesel, the Italian brand, and Calvin Klein, Which highlights American pop culture and sexy elements; mid- and high-end brands, such as Levi's, Lee, Guess, etc., which transform denim into a young lifestyle; the Volkswagen brand, such as American fast fashion brand Gap; and so on.

In the 1970s, denim apparel entered China. Although China has become an important country in the production and sales of denim, relatively speaking, the Asian denim clothing market represented by China is still immature and has great development potential. As far as the domestic denim clothing market is concerned, the first-line brands are occupied by international brands, and their brand cultures are dominant. Domestic brands take advantages of their own channel to occupy the mid- and low-end market. Representative brands include Jason Wood, Metersbonwe, Semir and so on.

Denim clothing is quickly recognized and consumed and becomes a daily dress, and it is gradually regaining its momentum after experiencing hard times. As casual wear is becoming more and more popular, the development of denim apparel has a trend to pursue both fashion and functionality, including the introduction of new design styles and the development of functional denim. And as consumers' brand awareness continues to rise, it will further promote the development of mid- and high-end denim clothing market. In addition, in the face of the pollution and emissions problems which are common in the denim industry, there are already denim enterprises using digital processing techno-logy to replace the hand brushing, sand blasting and other processes in traditional production to achieve sustainable development.

第二节

牛仔品牌分析

Analysis of Jeanswear Brands

卡尔文·克莱因 Calvin Klein

品牌简介

CALVIN KLEIN

图4-1 品牌标志

卡尔文·克莱因是世界上最具代表性的设计师品牌之一，由设计师卡尔文·克莱因和其搭档巴里·施瓦茨共同创立于1968年，总部位于纽约曼哈顿，并于2003年被Phillips Van Heusen Corp（PVH）[①]收购。1978年，其推出的Calvin Klein Jeans被视为业界第一个设计师牛仔时装系列，提供兼具性感、时尚和舒适的男女士休闲牛仔服饰产品。这对于此前一直被视作功能性工作服的牛仔服饰是一次革命性的转变，“以卡尔文·克莱因品牌的力量重塑牛仔裤形象，而不是使牛仔裤成为卡尔文·克莱因标志”。

该品牌在零售和商业领域以及高级时装中拥有可观的市场份额，通过直营、特许经营及网络，将主线设计师系列的服饰及其他副线的商品进行全球性销售。除标志性产

① PVH Corp.，鹏卫齐商业有限公司，拥有并经营全球的Calvin Klein等各大品牌，是全球最大的服装企业之一。它也是全世界最大的衬衫制造商，通过旗下品牌销售多元产品，包括Van Heusen，Calvin Klein，Tommy Hilfiger，IZOD，ARROW，Warner's及Olga。其代理品牌包括Speedo，Geoffrey Beene，Kenneth Cole New York，Kenneth Cole Reaction，MICHAEL Michael Kors，Sean John，Chaps，Donald J. Trump Signature Collection，JOE Joseph Abboud，DKNY，Ike Behar及John Varvatos。

品牛仔裤（1978）、内衣（1982）和香水（1979）外，还涉及成衣、家居用品、珠宝、手表等领域①。

品牌战略

图4-2 品牌历代标志性广告片

② 该品牌代表性设计与产品为作者手绘。

卡尔文·克莱因作为全球性生活方式品牌，采用灵活的细分策略，提供多元化的产品，以满足不同目标客户群的需求，让忠实客户感兴趣的同时吸引新客户。该品牌用于推广的众多营销策略包括电视广告、直接营销、社交媒体营销、促销优惠等。其发展历史上一些最具代表性的广告邀请知名人士出镜，呈现的影像近乎简洁，却非常清晰地传达了其设计美学。

于2017年重新启动的“我的卡尔文”活动（最初于2014年首次亮相，在品牌官网上，有一个“我的卡尔文”画廊，鼓励顾客在社交媒体上传自己的照片并有机会展示在网站上）是第一次完全依靠数字营销，充分利用其社交媒体影响力开展的全球多媒体广告活动。在新的主题“我们的家庭”“我的卡尔文”之下，卡戴珊姐妹、耶贝尔兄妹等明星家庭成员穿着卡尔文内衣和卡尔文牛仔的单品出镜。

为了突破卡尔文·克莱因逐渐固化为牛仔裤和内衣品牌形象，集团在2016年任命拉夫·西蒙成为品牌首席创意官，在全球范围内负责监督设计和创意战略，包括成衣系列、休闲装、牛仔裤、内衣和家居用品①等。除了将Calvin Klein Collection更名为Calvin Klein 205W39NYC之外，他还与建筑师斯特林·卢比合作，改造了纽约麦迪逊大道旗舰店。如今，品牌已宣布将关闭其高端设计师系列，专注于其现有的类别，包括牛仔时装系列和内衣。

图4-3　拉夫·西蒙任职期间设计

① 拉夫·西蒙任职期间设计为作者手绘。

品牌历史

1997

沃纳科集团取得卡尔文·克莱因内衣裤及牛仔裤系列销售授权

Warnaco wins sales license for Calvin Klein lingerie and Jeans

2001

卡尔文·克莱因牛仔进入中国开设首间专卖店

Calvin Klein Jeans entered China to open its first store

2003

PVH买入高级时装和运动系列专营及销售权

US apparel manufacturer PVH acquired the franchise and sales rights of high fashion and sports series

2012

被美国服装生产商PVH以29亿美元收购

Acquired by PVH for $2.9 billion

$2900000000

2013

拥有该品牌多个产品线的Warnaco集团被PVH收购，PVH正式将卡尔文·克莱因的牛仔时装、高级成衣和内衣整合在一起

The Warnaco Group, which owns multiple product lines of the brand, was acquired by PVH. PVH officially unified jeans, R-T-W and lingerie.

图4–4　品牌发展重大记事

在Calvin Klein Jeans于1978年推出之前，卡尔文·克莱因已凭借极简的时尚风格取得了成功：简洁而性感的迷你裙，利落线条和纯净色调的外套。

早在1976年，牛仔裤就首次出现于该品牌的时装发布会，之后克莱因对牛仔裤的设计进行调整以强调裆部和臀部，使紧身牛仔裤与性感的概念联系得更为紧密。之后于1978年正式推出卡尔文·克莱因牛仔时装系列，彻底改变了牛仔服饰市场，并将卡尔文·克莱因从设计师品牌转向大众市场，据称该系列牛仔裤推出一周后的销售量就高达20万条。在20世纪70年代中期，克莱因将其名字置于后袋，掀起了名牌牛仔裤的热潮。

扫一扫

扫一扫

时装牛仔系列作为卡尔文·克莱因的副线不仅改变了作为商品的牛仔裤本身，同时，以迥异于传统的广告宣传创造了全新的市场趋势，开启了设计师牛仔系列的浪潮。其最为颠覆的广告片由理查德·阿维登（Richard Avedon）拍摄并指导，15岁的女演员布鲁克·希尔兹（Brooke Shields）出演，广告台词已成为经典“你知道我和我的Calvins之间发生了什么吗？没什么”。该广告颇具争议，在当时遭到诸多投诉，但对于提升销售量效果显著。

图4-5 CK旗下品牌线

Calvin Klein

Brand Introduction

Calvin Klein is one of the world's most iconic designer brands. Founded in 1968 by designer Calvin Klein and his partner Barry Schwartz, headquartered in Manhattan, New York, it was acquired by Phillips Van Heusen Corp (PVH) in 2003. In 1978, Calvin Klein Jeans was regarded as the industry's first designer denim collection, offering men's and women's casual denim products that are sexy, stylish and comfortable. "Lend the Calvin Klein image to jeans and not a jeans image to Calvin Klein." This was revolutionary for denim which previously had always had a functional workwear angle.

It has a significant market share in the retail and commercial sectors as well as in high fashion, and through the direct sales, franchise and network, the main line of designer clothing and other secondary products are sold globally. In addition to the iconic jeans (1978), lingerie (1982) and perfume (1979), it also covers the fields of ready-to-wear, household items, jewelry, watches and so on.

Brand Strategy

As a global lifestyle brand, Calvin Klein uses a flexible segmentation strategy to provide a diverse range of products to meet the needs of different target customers, attracting new customers with loyal customers. The brand's many marketing strategies for promotion include TV commercials, direct marketing, social media marketing, promotional offers, and so on. Some of the most representative advertisements in its history have invited celebrities, and the images presented are almost concise when convey its design aesthetics in clear way.

The MYCALVINS event (originally debuted in 2014, on the brand's official website, there is a MYCALVINS gallery that encourages customers to upload their photos on social media which provide the opportunity to display on the website), which was relaunched in 2017, is the first global advertising campaign to fully leverage digital marketing to use its social media influence. Under the new theme "Our Family" MYCALVINS, celebrity families like Kim Kardashian and Kendall Jenner, Kaia and Presley Gerber dressed in Calvin Klein Lingerie and Calvin Klein Jeans.

To break through Calvin Klein's gradual solidification into a brand of jeans and lingerie, the group appointed Raf Simons as the brand's chief creative officer in 2016, overseeing design and creative strategies worldwide, including high-end collection, ready-to-wear, jeans, lingerie and household items. In addition to changing the Calvin Klein Collection to Calvin Klein 205W39NYC, he also worked with architect Sterling Ruby to transform the flagship store on Madison Avenue in New York. Today, the brand has announced that it will close its high-end designer collection, focusing on its existing categories, including jeans and lingerie.

Brand History

Prior to the launch of Calvin Klein Jeans in 1978, Calvin Klein had succeeded with a minimalist fashion style: simple and sexy mini skirts, neat lines and pure-toned jackets.

As early as 1976, jeans appeared on the brand's fashion show for the first time. After that, Klein adjusted the design of the jeans to emphasize the crotch and hips, which made the skinny jeans more closely related to the sexy concept. Then in 1978, the Calvin Klein denim fashion collection was officially launched, which completely changed the denim market and shifted Calvin Klein from the designer brand to the mass market. It is said that the sales of the jeans had reached 200,000 in one week. During the mid-1970s, Klein put his name in the back pocket and set off a wave of designer jeans.

As the vice line of Calvin Klein, Calvin Klein Jeans not only changed the jeans itself as a commodity, but also created a new market trend with the advertisements far from the tradition, which opened the wave of designer denim products. The most subversive commercial was directed by Richard Avedon, and casted with a 15-year-old actress, Brooke Shields, which became a classic advertisement. "You want to know what happens between me and my Calvins? Nothing." The advertisement was controversial and received many complaints at the time, but it was effective in increasing sales.

李 Lee

品牌简介

李是来自美国堪萨斯州的牛仔裤品牌，是休闲服饰和工作制服的国际零售商、制造商，由亨利·大卫·李创立于1912年，并在1969年被威富公司①收购。该品牌提供优质的产品，始终保持创新与变革，并且洞察客户的需求，从工人制服供应商逐渐转变为时尚休闲品牌，成为世界上最成功的服装公司之一。其提供的产品组合包括：牛仔裤、休闲裤、短裤、衬衫、夹克、裙子、连衣裙和配饰等。

图4-6 品牌标志

该品牌的零售店遍布全球200多个国家和地区，产品通过分销商、代理商、许可证持有者和单一品牌或多品牌合作零售店进行销售。在美国本土，中档和传统百货商店以及官方网站是其主要销售渠道。同时，其在欧洲和亚洲的国家特定网站开展电子商务，并提供量身定制服务。

图4-7 Buddy LEE

品牌战略

早在1920年，李就曾推出一款12.5英寸高的促销玩具Buddy LEE②，以推广其工作服。之后，李开始向时尚品牌转变，邀请玛丽莲·梦露和平·克劳斯贝作为代言人，在全球范围内进行品牌推广。李也是第一个通过电视广告进行宣传的品牌，并且每年在广告上投入大量资金，另外也借助媒体和杂志进行促销，提升品牌知名度。

---

① 威富公司(VF Corporation)成立于1899年，是一家美国的跨国服饰公司，品牌分为四类：户外、运动、工作制服和牛仔裤，包括Vans、JanSport、Timberland及The North Face等品牌。2018年合并两大牛仔裤部门Lee和Wrangler成为独立公司Kontoor Brands。

② 该插画为作者手绘。

图4–8　Lee x Smiley联名合作系列

图4–9　Lee x Cushnie et Ochs合作系列

1996年，李推出了“世界牛仔日”以提高对乳腺癌研究的认识。参与活动的公司要求员工捐赠5美元，以换取穿着李的牛仔裤的机会。从1996年到2015年，该活动筹集金额已超过9800万美元。同时，李开发循环生产的Rethink系列产品，能有效实现节能、节水和碳排放。这些活动作为其营销策略，有利于塑造其积极承担社会责任的企业形象。

扫一扫

如今，李正在开展品牌重塑的一系列举措，包括重新设计广告、网站和店内体验，以及借助公共关系和数字渠道的力量，旨在帮助品牌引入新一代消费者。其中一项名为“Move Your LEE”的广告，通过轻松的风格来“引领年轻丹宁爱好者活在当下，享受乐趣，突破自我”。借助YouTube，Instagram，Twitter和Facebook等社交平台进行最新动态展示①，并与客户建立联系，是这个拥有130年历史品牌的数字营销策略之一。

扫一扫

① 该品牌合作系列插画均为作者手绘。

品牌历史①

亨利·大卫·李在萨利纳成立H.D.Lee Mercantile公司，最初是一家批发杂货和干货的经销商。

Henry David Lee founded H. D. Lee Mercantile in Salina, which was initially a distributor of wholesale groceries and dry goods.

1889

亨利认识到耐穿工作服的巨大市场潜力及其批量生产的可能性，在堪萨斯州开设了第一家服装厂，向服装制造商转变。

Recognizing the huge market potential of durable workwear and the possibility of mass production, Henry opened the first garment factory in Salina, KS to transform into a clothing manufacturer.

1912

第一款具有保护性的连身工装服“Union-Alls”面世。

The first protective one-piece work clothes “Union-Alls” was launched.

1913

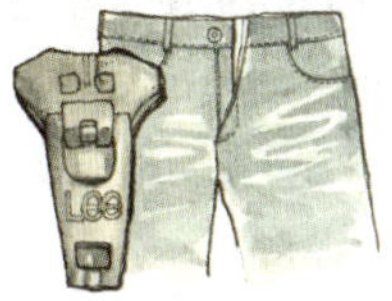

推出13盎司重磅丹宁布制作的经典101牛仔系列。

The classic 101 collection made of denim weighing 13-ounce was launched.

1924

第一条带拉链的牛仔裤——101Z系列正式面世。

The first Jeans with zipper—the 101Z series was officially available.

1926

标志性的马毛皮牌出现在牛仔裤后腰位置。

The iconic Horse-on-Hide appears in the back waist position of the jeans.

1936

另一标志性的“Lazy S”装饰缝线开始出现在后袋和“Twitch”皮革标签上使用。

Another iconic “Lazy S” decorative stitching began to appear on the back pocket and the “Twitch” leather label.

1944

推出修身的女装牛仔裤Lady Lee Riders系列。The slim women’s jeans Lady Lee Riders collection launched.

1949

詹姆斯·迪恩和马龙·白兰度穿着李的牛仔裤亮相银幕，牛仔裤成为时尚单品。

James Dean and Marlon Brando wear Lee jeans on the screen making jeans become a fashion item.

1954

Lee正式登陆中国，同时在亚太地区急速发展。Lee officially landed in China and is growing rapidly in the Asia.

1995

图4-10 品牌发展历程

①该品牌发展历程中的插画均为作者手绘。

Lee

Brand Introduction

Lee, a jeans brand from Kansas, USA, is an international retailer and manufacturer of casual wear and work uniforms, founded in 1912 by Henry David Lee and acquired by VF Corporation in 1969. It offers quality products, always innovates and transforms, and has an insight into the needs of its customers, becoming one of the most successful apparel companies in the world by gradually transforming from a uniform supplier to a fashion brand. Its products includes jeans, slacks, shorts, shirts, jackets, skirts, dresses and accessories.

Its products are sold through distributors, agents, licensees and single-brand or multi-brand cooperative retail stores that located in more than 200 countries and regions around the world. In the United States, department stores and official websites are its main sales channels. At the same time, e-commerce is carried out on country-specific websites in Europe and Asia, and tailor-made services are provided.

Brand Strategy

As early as 1920, Lee launched a 12.5-inch promotional toy Buddy LEE to promote its products. After that, Lee began to change to fashion brands, and invited Marilyn Monroe and Bing Crosby as spokespersons to promote the brand on a global scale. Lee is also the first brand to promote through TV commercials, and invests a lot of money in advertising every year. In addition, it also promotes brand awareness through media and magazines.

In 1996, Lee launched “World Denim Day” to raise awareness of breast cancer research. The participating companies require employees to donate $5 in exchange for the opportunity to wear Lee's jeans. From 1996 to 2015, the event raised more than $98 million. At the same time, the development of recycled Rethink series products can effectively achieve energy economizing, water saving and carbon emissions reducing. As a marketing strategy, these activities are conducive to shaping their corporate image of active social responsibility.

Lee is working on rebranding initiatives nowadays, including redesigning advertisements, websites and in-store experiences, and leveraging the power of public relations and digital channels to attract new generation of consumers. One of the advertisements, called "Move Your LEE", “leads young Denim fans to live in the moment, enjoy the fun, and break through themself" in a relaxed style. With the latest developments on social platforms such as

YouTube, Instagram, Twitter and Facebook, it establishes contact with customers, which is one of the digital marketing strategies of this 130–year–old brand.

李维斯 Levi's

品牌简介

19世纪50年代，正值美国淘金热时期，品牌创始人李维·斯特劳斯①受到矿工们对耐用裤子需求的启发，开始使用粗糙帆布来制作工人服装，之后则将材质替换为牛仔布，并在口袋接缝中添加铜铆钉。经过150余年制造经验的积累，李维斯已成为世界知名牛仔裤品牌，也是世界上最大的牛仔裤生产商之一。

图4-11 李维斯产品组合

① 李维·斯特劳斯（Levi Strauss，1829年2月26日—1902年9月26日），美籍德国犹太人，出生于巴伐利亚。

李维斯在成立之初仅是美国西部一家经营干货的批发商，发展至今，其零售业务已分布于加拿大、美国、欧洲、拉丁美洲、澳大利亚、日本、中国等国家和地区，而制造业务则主要由提供廉价劳动力和原材料的发展中国家承担，如印度、斯里兰卡、越南和印度尼西亚等。

品牌旗下的牛仔裤系列众多，包括拥有“世界上最畅销的服装”称号的传奇501牛仔裤。其他产品包括休闲裤、夹克、毛衣、T恤、衬衫、裙子和配饰等。

图4-12 李维斯经典产品

品牌战略

扫一扫

面对服装市场牛仔裤类别销售额的下降，李维斯逐渐拓展其业务范围至更为多元化的服装产品组合，并向生活方式品牌转变，并在首席执行官奇普·伯格（曾在宝洁公司担任品牌经理）的领导下，于2017年成功实现连续五年的利润增长，并将其“重塑”为新一代品牌。

伯格扩大了服装范围，将女装作为重点，不断拓展俄罗斯、中国和印度等相对尚未开发的市场，同时顺应电子商务的发展趋势，为年轻消费者提供现代化技术和定制产品的服务，以赢得更多服装市场份额。比如推出李维斯虚拟造型师——一款智能聊天机器人，向客户提供样式和尺寸建议以提高转换率。

为了提高其产品的知名度，李维斯采取了积极的广告投放策略，通过电视、报纸、广告牌和时尚杂志等途径展示其非常规商业广告的概念，使其定期推出新产品以获得持续的关注。同时，该品牌深谙名人效应。比如为庆祝Type III Trucker Jacket成立50周年，邀请50名社交影响力者为其定制独特版本的传统Trucker Jacket，并且在活动结束后，请数十名备受瞩目的名人在杂志和日常生活中进行穿着，如卡莉·克洛斯、贾斯汀·汀布莱克和吉吉·哈迪德等，提高产品曝光度。

除此之外，推出“Water Less”活动，实现在生产过程中的重复用水，创造出比传统工艺更为节水的新面料，以此将可持续性因素纳入他们所经营的每一项活动中，成为品牌的官方核心价值。

图4–13　Levi's Type III Trucker Jacket款式图

品牌历史

1853

李维·斯特劳斯在加利福尼亚州旧金山成立了LEVI STRAUSS&CO。

Levi Strauss founded LEVI STRAUSS&CO in San Francisco, California.

1873

获得了在男性工作裤上使用铜铆钉的制作专利权，第一条蓝色牛仔裤由此诞生。

The patent for the use of copper rivets on men's work trousers was obtained, and the first blue jeans were born.

1886

象征铆钉服饰耐穿性的双马皮印标志诞生。

1886 saw the birth of the double horse leather logo symbolizing the durability of rivet clothing.

1934

推出首款女式蓝色牛仔裤Lady Levi's。

The first women's blue jeans Lady Levi's.

1936

首次使用红色标签，缝制在501牛仔裤的右后侧口袋。

The red label was first used and was sew in the right rear pocket of the 501 jeans.

1960s

"蓝色牛仔裤热潮"成为品牌发展的催化剂；期间收购加拿大服装制造商Great Western Garment Company，并引入现代"石洗"技术。

The "Blue Jeans boom" became a catalyst for brand development; it acquired Canadian clothing manufacturer Great Western Garment Company and introduced modern "stone wash" technology.

1965

随着牛仔裤、夹克和其他Levi's产品的普及，在欧洲和亚洲设立了办事处和工厂。

With the popularity of jeans, jackets and other Levi's products, offices and factories have been established in Europe and Asia.

1980s

Levi Strauss开始将生产转移到海外。

Levi Strauss began to shift production overseas.

1986

在美国推出Dockers®khakis，提供工作场所可穿着的休闲服装。It launched Dockers®khakis in the United States to provide casual wear in the workplace.

2006

在沃尔玛独家销售Signature系列的牛仔裤和其他服饰。

The Signature collection of jeans and other apparel were exclusively sold at Walmart.

2018

推出了Project FLX，旨在响应和实现可持续的供应链。

It launched Project FLX to respond to and achieve a sustainable supply chain.

图4-14　品牌发展历程

Levi's

Brand Introduction

In the 1950s, during the Gold Rush era, the founder Levi Strauss was inspired by the miners' demand for durable trousers, using rough canvas to make workers' clothing, and then replacing the material with denim and adding copper rivets to the pocket seams. After more than 150 years of manufacturing experience, Levi's has become a world-renowned jeans brand and one of the world's largest jeans manufacturers.

At the beginning of the establishment, Levi's was only a wholesaler of dry goods in the western United States. Today, its retail business has been distributed in Canada, the United States, Europe, Latin America, Australia, Japan, China and other countries and regions, while the manufacturing business is mainly committed by developing countries that provide cheap labors and raw materials, such as India, Sri Lanka, Vietnam and Indonesia.

Under the brand, there are many kinds of jeans, including legendary 501 jeans with the title of "the world's best-selling clothing". Other products include pants, jackets, sweaters, T-shirts, shirts, skirts, accessories and so on.

Brand Strategy

Faced with the decline in sales of the jeans in the apparel market, Levi's gradually expanded its business scope to a more diversified apparel product portfolio, transforming into a lifestyle brand, and under the leadership of CEO Chip Bergh (who was a brand manager at P&G), in 2017, it achieved a five-year profit growth and "remodeled" into a new generation brand.

Bergh has expanded the scope of clothing, focusing on women's wear, expanding the relatively untapped markets of Russia, China and India, while complying with the development trend of e-commerce, providing young consumers with modern technology and customized products to win more clothing market share. For example, it launched Levi's Virtual Stylist, an AI bot that provides customers with style and size suggestions to increase conversion rates.

In order to increase the visibility of its products, Levi's has adopted a proactive advertising strategy to showcase its concept of unconventional commercial advertising through television, newspapers, billboards and fashion magazines, so that it can keep its regularly new products for continuous attention. At the same time, the brand is familiar with the celebrity effect. For example, to celebrate the 50th anniversary of the Type III Trucker Jacket, 50 social influencers were invited to customize their unique version of the traditional Trucker Jacket, and after the event, dozens of celebrities were dressed in magazines and daily wear, such as Karlie Kloss, Justin Timberlake and Gigi Hadid, to increase the product exposure.

In addition, the "Water Less" campaign was launched to achieve reuse of water during the production process and to create new fabrics that are more water efficient than traditional processes. Sustainability factors are incorporated into a series of activities that make it the official core value of the brand.

第三节

本章讨论与阅读推荐

Discussion and Reading Recommendation

本章讨论

1. 比较Lee和Levi's这两个历史悠久牛仔品牌，分析其发展策略的异同与其发展趋势，你认为哪个品牌更具前景？

2. Calvin Klein深谙通过打造争议性的广告引发品牌热度，你认为这是否有助于其建立新的品牌形象，并扭转下滑的销售业绩？

3. 尝试说明随着千禧一代购买力的上升，牛仔品牌应该如何进行有针对性的扩张与数字化改革。

Discussion

1. Compare Lee with Levi's , the two long-established denim brands , analyze the similarities and differences of their development strategies and trends. Which brand do you think is more promising?

2. Calvin Klein knows well how to create brand awareness by creating controversial advertising. Do you think this will help it build a new brand image and reverse the decline in sales?

3. Try to explain how the denim brand should carry out targeted expansion and digital reforms as the rise in purchasing power of millennials.

阅读推荐 Reading recommendation

Calvin Klein
作　者：Calvin Klein
出版社：Rizzoli
出版年：2017
ISBN：9780847860142

参考资料 References

牛仔装市场分析

https：//news.cfw.cn/v247540-1.htm
http：//www.ef360.com/subject/news/cowboy-wear/
https：//cj.sina.com.cn/articles/view/5115326071/130e5ae7702000l53b？ from=finance
http：//www.xinhuanet.com/fashion/2019-04/11/c_1124352625.htm
http：//www.linkshop.com.cn/web/archives/2013/275174.shtml
https：//new.qq.com/omn/20180408/20180408A0VT5Q.html
http：//www.sohu.com/a/331101620_100189737

卡尔文・克莱因

http：//www.clerkenwellvintagefashionfair.co.uk/a-brief-history-of-calvin-klein/
https：//www.vogue.com/article/calvin-klein-jeans-90s-ads-kate-moss-mark-wahlberg-controversy
https：//en.wikipedia.org/wiki/Calvin_Klein_（company）
https：//zh. wikipedia. org / wiki/% E5%8D% A1%E7%88%BE% E6%96%87%C2%B7%E5%85%8B% E9%9B% B7%E6%81%A9
https：//www.calvinklein.cn/static/brand-introduction#bottom
https：//www.calvinklein.cn/static/ckstory#bottom
https：//theidleman.com/blogs/style/history-calvin-klein-2
https：//www.highsnobiety.com/2016/08/04/calvin-klein-brand-history/
https：//indie-mag.com/2017/11/calvin-klein-history/
https：//www.thefactshop.com/blog/fashion-facts/calvin-klein-facts
https：//www.theguardian.com/business/2019/mar/07/calvin-klein-to-axe-luxury-collections-business
https：//hypebeast.com/2018/7/calvin-klein-jeans-est-1978-delivery-1
https：//www.businesswire.com/news/home/20171120005606/en
https //www.marketingdive.com/news/calvin-klein-embraces-digital-in-global-ad-campaign-starring-solange/511402/

https：//juicestore.com/blogs/editorial/calvin-klein-jeans-est-1978-ss-19-latest-arrivals
https：//www.vogue.com/article/calvin-klein-jeans-est-1978-new-collection
https：//lesfacons.com/2018/09/10/calvin-klein-jeans-fall-2018-ad-campaign/
https：//www.teenvogue.com/gallery/calvin-klein-ads-iconic-justin-bieber-kendall-jenner-kate-moss
https：//qz.com/quartzy/1482441/calvin-klein-is-facing-that-its-a-jeans-and-underwear-company-now/
https：//www.marketing91.com/marketing-strategy-of-calvin-klein/
https：//www.marketing91.com/marketing-mix-calvin-klein/
https：//www.marketing91.com/swot-analysis-of-calvin-klein/
https：//www.mbaskool.com/marketing-mix/products/17411-calvin-klein.html
https：//www. businesswire. com / news / home / 20190110005675 / en / Calvin-Klein-CEO-Outlines-Strategic-Brand-Organization
https：//www.mediapost.com/publications/article/332274/in-new-digital-first-strategy-calvin-klein-tries.html
https：//www.pvh.com/brands/calvin-klein
https：//www.businessoffashion.com/community/people/calvin-klein

李

https：//www.marketing91.com/top-10-levis-competitors/
https：//en.wikipedia.org/wiki/Lee_（jeans）
https：//lee.com.cn/brand-history.html
https：//www.lee.com/about/history.html#
https：//www.mbaskool.com/marketing-mix/products/17480-lee.html
https：//www.denimhunters.com/the-big-three-levis-lee-wrangler/
https：//www.marketing91.com/swot-analysis-of-lee-jeans/
https：//www.marketingdive.com/news/lee-jeans-rebrands-with-lighthearted-ad-campaign/425926/
https：//digiday.com/marketing/lees-vp-marketing-not-just-mom-jeans/

李维斯

《哈佛商业评论》，2018年7月至8月，第33—39页
https：//www.levi.com.cn/landing/brand-story？fix=1
https：//zh.wikipedia.org/wiki/Levi%27s
http：//www.levis.co.za/About.aspx
https：//www.britannica.com/topic/Levi-Strauss-and-Co
https：//www.levistrauss.com/levis-history/
https：//theidleman.com/blogs/style/the-history-of-levis
https：//en.wikipedia.org/wiki/Levi_Strauss_%26_Co.
https：//www.marketing91.com/marketing-strategy-levis/
https：//www.marketing91.com/marketing-mix-of-levis/
https：//adage.com/article/cmo-strategy/true-blue-levi-s-remains-relevant-165-years/315488
https：//beeketing.com/blog/levis-growth-story/
https：//www.entrepreneur.com/article/243412
https：//hbr.org/2018/07/the-ceo-of-levi-strauss-on-leading-an-iconic-brand-back-to-growth

第
五
章

童装品牌

Children's Wear Brands

第一节

童装市场分析

Analysis of Children's Wear Market

相关报告显示，40.4%的零售商已开发或计划开发童装自有品牌。这是由于童装业务具有巨大的增长潜力，使之成为国内服饰品牌新的增长点。

当前，我国服饰集团正在经历消费者自身及其需求的变化。85后、90后年轻父母成为童装市场消费的主力军，他们多数为独生子女，受过良好教育，主张高品质、品牌特性与审美消费。这为时尚儿童服装业创造了更多发展契机。另外，二胎政策的施行，以及父母晚生晚育、财务状况稳定、出生率增加和祖辈对孙辈的溺爱等中国社会复杂因素，都成为童装市场持续发展的推动因素。

同时，童装业务自身所具备的稳定属性使之能够不受经济波动影响，中高端儿童服饰市场前景广阔。正因为此，已经相当成熟的海外童装市场至今仍然发展强劲。明星设计师维多利亚·贝克汉姆（Victoria Beckham）也曾在采访中表示，她认为童装是值得投入的第二大品类，其女儿小七（Seven）的着装一直以来都是舆论热议的焦点。

在这些客观原因的共同作用下，森马旗下巴拉巴拉、安奈儿，起步旗下ABCKids等专业童装品牌均发展稳健，其他诸多成人服饰品牌、运动品牌等也纷纷进军童装市场。

就运动品牌而言，其出色的功能性设计更易获得消费者的信赖。凭借此“先天”优势，该类童装在当前的童装市场中占有重要份额。其中包括国外运动品牌阿迪达斯（Adidas）、耐克（Nike）和国内运动品牌安踏（Anta）的童装线。随着成人装延伸童装，童装成人化的趋势愈发明显——时尚化、多元化、个性化，其原因之一在于绝大多数时候，父母才是最终的购买决策者。本土服装品牌MO&Co、太平鸟、美特斯邦威、江南布衣、七匹狼等均已相继进行童装产品的开发。

总体看来，一方面，随着二胎开放政策和消费升级，中国童装市场规模增长趋于稳定，且成长空间巨大；另一方面，童装行业品牌集中度低，市场占有率相较于国外成熟市场仍有待提升。同时，随着对外贸易活动的增加以及信息网络技术的发展，众多国外的童装品牌开始进入国内童装市场，国内童装市场已经开始呈现出多样化的特征。这要求国内童装品牌开展精细化经营，并且更加注重产品研发、品牌文化和品牌服务。

Analysis of Children's Wear Market

According to relevant reports, 40.4% of retailers have developed or planned to develop their own brands of children's wear. This is due to the huge growth potential of the children's wear business, making it a new growth point for domestic apparel brands.

Today, China's apparel enterprises are experiencing changes in consumers and their needs. Young parents became the main force in the children's wear market. Most of them once were the only children and well-educated, who also advocated high quality, brand characteristics and aesthetic consumption. This creates more opportunities for the development of the fashion industry of children's wear. In addition, the implementation of the second child policy, the complex factors of Chinese society such as parents' late birth and late childbearing, stable financial situation, increasing birth rate, and patriarchal love from grandparents, are the driving factors for the sustainable development of the children's wear market.

At the same time, the stable attributes of the children's wear business itself can be immune to economic fluctuations, and the market for mid- and high-end children's apparel is promising. Because of this, the international children's wear market which has already become mature is still growing strongly. Celebrity designer Victoria Beckham also said in an interview that she thinks that children's wear is the second largest brand worth investing in. The dress of her daughter, Seven, has always been the focus of public opinion.

Under the combined effect of these objective reasons, the professional children's wear brands such as Balabala, Annil, and ABC Kids have developed steadily. Many other adult apparel brands and sports brands have also entered the children's wear market.

As far as sports brands are concerned, their outstanding functional design is more easily trusted by consumers. With this "innate" advantage, this type of children's wear has a significant share of the current children's wear market, which includes the foreign sports brands Adidas, Nike and the domestic sports brand Anta. With the extension of adult wear to children's wear, the adultification of children's wear has become more and more obvious—fashion, diversification and personalization. One of the reasons is that most of the time, parents are the ultimate purchase decision makers. The local clothing brand MO&Co., as well as its parent company EPO Group, Peace Bird, Metersbonwe, JNBY, Seven Wolves, etc. have had all developed children's clothing products.

In general, on one hand, with the second-child policy and consumption upgrade, the growth of China's children's wear market tends to be stable and there is huge space for growth; On the other hand, the brand concentration of children's wear industry is low, and its market share still needs to be improved compared with mature foreign markets. At the same time, with the increase of foreign trade activities and the development of information network technology, many foreign children's wear brands have begun to enter the domestic market, creating diversified characteristics in the domestic children's wear market. These require domestic children's wear brands to carry out refined operations, and lay more emphasis on product development, culture and services.

第二节

童装品牌分析

Analysis of Children's Wear Brands

巴拉巴拉 Balabala

品牌简介

巴拉巴拉是由森马集团于2002年推出的中端童装品牌，面向0—14岁中产阶级及小康家庭的童装消费群体。以“童年不同样”作为品牌主张，具有丰富的产品线。

图5-1 品牌标志

图5-2 品牌产品分类

巴拉巴拉具有其较早进入童装市场的先发优势，同时针对的是具有较大规模的中端市场。此外，得益于母公司在成人服饰领域积累的运营及管理经验，巴拉巴拉得以成功切入童装市场。自成立以来，其国内童装市场的占有率一路走高，并于2018年达到5%水平。

图5-3 森马旗下其他儿童服装品牌

品牌战略

巴拉巴拉的销售渠道覆盖线下的旗舰店、体验店、商超专营店、特许经营店和线上的淘宝、天猫、京东等平台，国内线下门店已由2003年的110家发展到2017年的近4000家；而经过两年多的海外市场布局，目前在伊朗、俄罗斯、阿联酋等多个国家也已开设11家专卖店。

除了全渠道发展，森马也积极打造儿童全产业链，实现多品牌运营以加快布局童装市场，助推巴拉巴拉触达更多用户圈层。为适应市场需求，森马近年已着手进行业务细分升级，于2013年推出马卡乐、梦多多（低于主品牌约10%的价格），以及巴拉巴拉旗下的婴幼童服饰品牌迷你巴拉巴拉（Mini Balabala）；同时引入意大利奢侈童装品牌

Sarabanda的中国区销售业务。

森马也将目光瞄准更广阔的海外市场，通过全球化供应链布局，提升在其他国际市场的市场进入和经营能力。

2018年3月，森马与北美童装品牌THE CHILDREN'S PLACE[①]签署长期合作协议。THE CHILDREN'S PLACE将授权森马在指定区域内使用其商标、知识产权和专有技术；森马除了从THE CHILDREN'S PLACE采购产品，为满足中国市场需求，还将进行自主设计开发、生产和销售。

2018年5月，森马收购Sofiza SAS，获得其拥有的欧洲童装Kidiliz集团[②]全部资产。这意味着森马服饰一举跃升为全球第二大童装公司，成为全球童装行业重要的参与者。

与此同时，面对国内童装市场，巴拉巴拉始终坚持对新一代消费者展开研究，并围绕儿童生活方式展开品牌塑造，通过品牌社群及会员访谈，深挖消费者需求。在"新零售"背景下，积极运用不断迭代的品牌终端形象，提升品牌在消费者心中的美誉度与辨识度，灵活运用数字化营销、建立主题快闪店、加强与知名IP的合作、打造自有时尚活动，持续扩大品牌曝光率和影响力。

Balabala

Brand Introduction

Balabala is a mid-end children's wear brand launched by the Semir Group in 2002. It aims at children's wear groups of middle-aged and well-off families from 0 to 14 years old. With the brand concept of "not the same childhood", it has a rich product line.

Balabala has its first-mover advantage in entering the children's wear market, and aims at the mid-end market with a large scale. In addition, thanks to the parent company's operation and management experience in the field of adult apparel, Balabala has successfully entered the children's wear market. Since its establishment, its market share in the domestic children's wear market keeps rising, and reached 5% in 2018.

① THE CHILDREN'S PLACE成立于1969年，是北美第一大全年龄段(0–14岁)专业童装零售商，销售高性价比大众童装、鞋类及配饰。

② Kidiliz于1982年在法国巴黎成立，该集团旗下拥有包括Z、Catimini、Absorba等10个风格各异的自有品牌，并代理包括Kenzo Kids等知名时尚品牌的童装线，定位于中高端，产品年龄段覆盖从婴童到青少年。

Brand Strategy

Balabala's sales channels cover from the flagship stores, experience stores, franchise stores to online Taobao, T-mall, Jingdong and other platforms. Domestic offline stores have grown from 110 in 2003 to nearly 4,000 in 2017; and after more than two years of overseas market layout, 11 stores have been opened in Iran, Russia, the United Arab Emirates and other countries.

In addition to full-channel development, Semir is also actively building a children's entire industry chain, achieving multi-brand operations to speed up the layout of the children's wear market, and boosting Balabala to reach more user circles. To meet the market demand, Semir has started to carry out business segmentation and upgrade in recent years. In 2013, it launched MarColor and Mongdodo (price is about 10% lower than the main brand), and Balabala's baby's clothing brand Mini Balabala; it also introduced the sales of the Italian luxury children's wear brand Salabanda in China.

Semir also aims to target a broader overseas market and enhance its market entry and operation capabilities in other countries through a global supply chain.

In March 2018, Semir signed a long-term cooperation agreement with North American children's wear brand THE CHILDREN'S PLACE. THE CHILDREN'S PLACE will authorize Semir to use its trademarks, other intellectual property rights and proprietary technology in the assigned regions; Semir will also purchase products from THE CHILDREN'S PLACE, and to meet the needs of the Chinese market, Semir will independently design, develop, produce and sell.

In May 2018, Semir acquired Sofiza SAS and acquired all its assets of the European children's clothing Kidiliz Group. This means that Semir apparel has jumped to become the world's second largest children's wear company, and is playing an important role in the global children's wear industry.

At the same time, in the face of the domestic children's wear market, Balabala has always insisted on study of the new generation of consumers, branding around children's lifestyles, and digging into consumer demand through brand community and member interviews. In the context of "new retail", it actively uses the image of brand terminals that are constantly iterative to enhance the reputation and recognition of the brand in the eye of consumers, and flexibly use digital marketing, promote the theme flash shop, cooperate with well-known IP, build its own Fashion activities, and continue to expand brand exposure and influence.

小樱桃 Bonpoint

扫一扫

扫一扫

品牌简介

Bonpoint是来自法国巴黎的高端童装品牌，由Marie France Cohen创建于1975年。其设计部门保留巴黎高级定制的传统工作形式，并且一年两次在巴黎高级定制时装周期间举办发布会[①]。

图5-4　品牌标志

Bonpoint的品牌理念是将奢华与童装完美结合，在其精心打造的颇具童话氛围的店铺里，出售的童装品质上乘——尖端的剪裁、严格的选料和精巧的细节兼具优雅浪漫与经典传统的风格特点，其产品平均售价为120欧元至280欧元。

如今，Bonpoint在27个国家拥有120多家店铺，遍及纽约麦迪逊大街、巴黎蒙田大道、巴黎胜利广场、巴黎皇家大道、好莱坞比弗利山庄等各大国际时尚地标。

图5-5　Bonpoint 2017春夏秀场造型

图5-6　Bonpoint店铺橱窗

① 该品牌秀场造型及店铺橱窗为作者手绘。

品牌战略

有别于其他奢侈品牌开发童装系列（如范思哲、迪奥、古驰和巴宝莉等）作为其培育未来消费者的途径，童装于Bonpoint而言是其核心业务。

通常情况下，童装的制作将平均六岁的孩子作为尺码指南，并以数学公式来推算其他年龄组的尺寸，而Bonpoint的尺寸则是以特定年龄儿童的具体数据作为参考资料。比如，Bonpoint使用的两岁儿童的人体模型，有着微微弯曲的膝盖，向前倾斜的肩膀和明显突出的腹部，确保了服装的合体性。

同时，Bonpoint积极向生活方式品牌转变，以赢得更广泛的消费群体。除了开发青少年系YAM系列，还推出全天然美妆产品线。占其销售额25%至30%的香水和护肤品已成为品牌业绩增长的重要动力，在中国上海和北京设有化妆品专柜，并在天猫进行线上销售。

在全球范围内，只有最富有的1%的人才熟悉该品牌，因此Bonpoint核心业务过半的营业额来自娱乐明星（维多利亚·贝克汉姆、凯特·摩丝、麦当娜等）和皇室贵族等社会知名人士，并邀请其子女参加其巴黎高级定制时装周期间的发布会，以实现口碑推广。而其在2009年启动的数字战略则是为了进一步增强客户对品牌的认知和理解，包括更新电子商务平台、加入社交网络等。

图5-7 Bonpoint X John Nollet合作系列

品牌历史

1975

Marie-France和Bernard Cohen在巴黎开设第一家Bonpoint店铺。

Marie-France and Bernard Cohen opened their first Bonpoint store in Paris.

1978

Bonpoint以自营或特许经营的形式在法国以及海外扩张。

Bonpoint expands in France and overseas in the form of self-operated or franchised distribution.

1988

纽约麦迪逊大街上的第一家Bonpoint店铺开张。

The first Bonpoint store on Madison Avenue in New York opened.

1994

Bonpoint跃身成为世界奢侈品牌的一员。

Bonpoint has become a member of the world's luxury brands.

1999

Bonpoint亚洲首家店铺于日本东京开业。

Bonpoint's first store in Asia opened in Tokyo, Japan.

2006

Bonpoint进军中国，首家旗舰店位于上海；同年，位于巴黎Rue de Tournon的1000平米品牌概念店开幕。

Bonpoint entered China and its first flagship store was in Shanghai. The 1,000-square-meter brand concept store in Rue de Tournon, Paris, opened in the same year.

2007

Bonpoint加入了法国奢侈品牌集团EPI（EPI, Societe Europeenne de Participations Industrielles，由Christopher Descours经营的家族式奢侈品控股公司，也拥有其他高端品牌，包括JM Weston、高级鞋履MichelPerry和法国香槟酒庄Piper-Heidsieck等）。

Bonpoint joined the French luxury brand group EPI（EPI, Societe Europeenne de Participations Industrielles, a family-owned luxury holding company run by Christopher Descours, also owns other high-end brands, including JM Weston, Michel Perry, and Piper-Heidsieck.）

图5-8 品牌发展历程

Bonpoint

Brand Introduction

Bonpoint is a high-end brand of children's wear from Paris, France, which was founded in 1975 by Marie France Cohen. Its design department retains the traditional work of Paris Haute

Couture and holds a press conference twice a year during the Haute Couture Fashion Week in Paris.

Bonpoint's brand philosophy is to combine children's wear with luxury. In its carefully crafted fairy-tale shop, the children's wear is of the highest quality—cutting-edge tailoring, strict material selection and intricate details, with elegant romance and traditional style. The average price of its products ranges from €120 to €280.

Today, Bonpoint has more than 120 stores in 27 countries, extending all over New York's Madison Avenue, Paris Avenue Montaigne, Paris Victory Square, Royal Paris Avenue, Hollywood Beverly Hills and other international fashion landmarks.

Brand Strategy

Different from other luxury brands (such as Versace, Dior, Gucci and Burberry), Bonpoint is dedicated to developing children's wear series, which is regarded to as a way cultivate future consumers. Children's wear is the core business of Bonpoint.

Normally, children's wear regards an average of six-year-old child as a size guide, and mathematical formulas are used to estimate the size of other age groups. Bonpoint's size is based on concrete data for children of a specific age. For example, the two-year-old child's mannequin used by Bonpoint has a slightly curved knee, a forwardly inclined shoulder and a prominent abdomen to ensure the fit of the garment.

At the same time, Bonpoint is actively shifting to lifestyle brands to win a wider consumer base. In addition to the development of the youth YAM series, it also launched a line of all-natural beauty products. Perfume and skin care products, which account for 25% to 30% of its sales, have become an important driver of brand growth, with cosmetic counters in Shanghai and Beijing, and online sales at T-mall.

Globally, only the richest 1% of the people is familiar with the brand, so more than half of Bonpoint's core business comes from social celebrities such as entertainment celebrities (Victoria Beckham, Kate Moss, Madonna, etc.) and the royal family. Bonpoint invites their children to participate in the launch of their Paris Haute Couture Fashion Week to promote word of mouth. Hence, the digital strategy launched in 2009 was to further enhance customers' awareness and understanding of the brand, including updating e-commerce platforms and joining social networks.

江南布衣 jnby by JNBY

品牌简介

图5-9 品牌标志

江南布衣集团旗下的高端童装品牌jnby by JNBY以“自由的想象力”为设计理念[1]，针对育有3—10岁孩童的富裕中产阶级家庭而推出。在国内婴童市场消费升级的背景下，jnby被视为该集团男女服饰业务的有益补充。自2011年成立以来，已开设有461家jnby by JNBY门店（截至2018年），是当前国内发展最迅猛的童装品牌之一。

在jnby by JNBY的强劲业绩刺激之下，针对小学至初中低年级的少年，江南布衣集团于2016年推出另一童装品牌蓬马（Pomme de terre），以填补青少年品牌市场的空缺。品牌以名叫“蓬马”的10岁男孩为原型展开设计，为正处在“自我探索期”和“半自治期”的少年提供注重设计质感的轻松着装，目前已开设76家门店（截至2018年）。

图5-10 品牌搭配造型

品牌战略

凭借母公司江南布衣集团企业文化和发展经验构建的品牌生态圈，jnby塑造的形象有别于传统两大童装阵营——以迪士尼人物形象为代表的卡通形象阵营和以Nike耐克、Adidas阿迪达斯童装为代表的运动阵营。其“自由、想象力、惊喜、真实”的核心文化

① 该品牌搭配造型为作者手绘。

和设计理念，更符合当下中国富裕中产阶级家庭教育理念和母公司持续在企业文化及价值方面的探索。这使之以独特的辨识度在童装市场占有一席之地。

jnby与女装品牌JNBY一脉相承，但在设计元素上又明显有别于成人装。jnby在进行服饰的设计时会从儿童的角度出发，构建一种属于孩子的美感，展现孩子们真实的天性，比如通过故事的讲述把孩子带入想象的空间，并且通过强调互动与体验宗旨，鼓励家长与孩子一同成长。

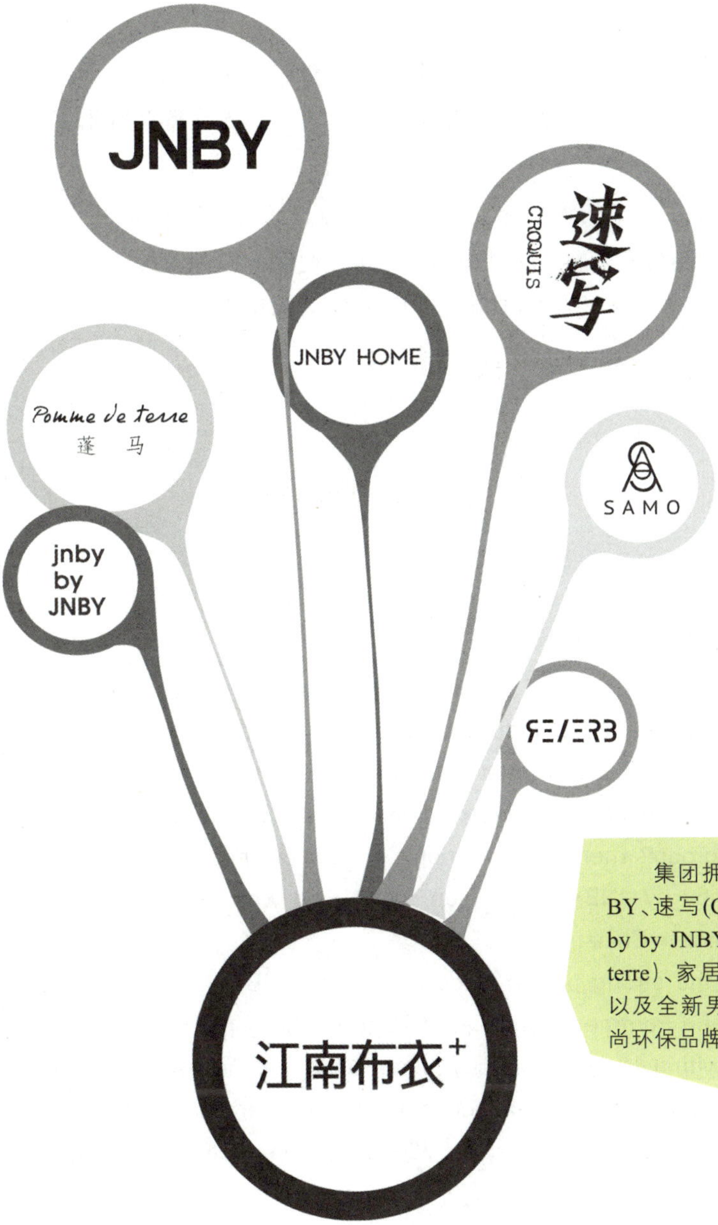

集团拥有设计师品牌JNBY、速写(CROQUIS)、less、jnby by JNBY、蓬马(Pomme de terre)、家居系列JNBY HOME以及全新男装品牌SAMO、时尚环保品牌REVERB。

图5-11 集团旗下品牌

同时，jnby积极进行品牌公益实践活动，比如2017年联合网易LOFTER举办的“我眼中的小世界”摄影征集活动，鼓励家长把相机交给孩子，让孩子通过摄影向大人展示他们眼中的那个“小小世界”。这为与现实儿童教育相关联的具体操作提供了更多可能，同时符合并强化品牌定位。

品牌历史

品牌母公司江南布衣集团创立于1994年，总部位于中国杭州。其主营业务为品牌服装的创意设计、工艺技术研发及生产销售，实施以“设计诠释趣味和品质生活”理念为主导的多品牌组合战略，积极、持续地打造品牌形象。

2013年5月初，JNBY的童装系列以单独柜台的形式首次亮相杭州，JNBY推出独立童装的想法源于女装与童装混搭出售获得的良好业绩。而此前，JNBY进行了为期一年的实验，在全国100多家年销售额500万元以上的店铺里混入童装售卖，其销售业绩在半年内就已达到JNBY一年销售的10%。

jnby by JNBY

Brand Introduction

jnby by JNBY, a high-end children's wear brand owned by JNBY Group, is designed with the concept of “free imagination” for wealthy middle-class families with children aged 3—10. In the context of the domestic baby market consumption upgrade, jnby is regarded as a useful supplement to the group's men's and women's apparel business. Since its inception in 2011, it has opened 461 jnby by JNBY stores (up to 2018), which is one of the fastest growing children's wear brands in China.

Stimulated by the strong performance of jnby by JNBY, JNBY Group launched another children's wear brand Pomme de terre in 2016 to fill the gap in the youth brand market. The brand is designed with a 10-year-old boy named “Pengma” as prototype to provide a relaxed design with a design-oriented texture for teenagers who are in the “self-exploration period” and “semi-autonomous period”. Currently, 76 stores have been opened (up to 2018).

Brand Strategy

With the brand ecosystem based on corporate culture and development experience of JNBY Group, jnby's image is different from the traditional two children's clothing camps—the cartoon image represented by Disney characters and the Sports camp represented by Nike and Adidas children's wear. Its core culture and design philosophy of "freedom, imagination, surprise, and truth" is more in line with the current Chinese middle-class family education philosophy, and the parent company's continued exploration of corporate culture and value. This enables it to play an important role in the children's wear market.

jnby is in line with the women's brand JNBY, but the design elements are obviously different from the adult clothes. When designing the costumes, jnby will construct a child's beauty from the perspective of children and show the children's true nature, such as bring children into the space of imagination through storytelling, and encourage parents to grow with their children by emphasizing interaction and experience.

At the same time, jnby is actively engaged in brand public welfare practice activities. For example, in 2017, the "Little World in My Eyes" photography collection event organized with NTES LOFTER encouraged parents to give the camera to children and let the children show the "small world" in their eyes. This provides more possibilities for specific operations associated with real-life children's education, while meeting and strengthening brand positioning.

Brand History

JNBY Group was founded in 1994 and is headquartered in Hangzhou, China. Its main business is creative design, technology research, production and sales development. It implements a multi-brand combination strategy led by "design interpretes taste and quality life" to actively and continuously build brand image.

At the beginning of May, 2013, JNBY's children's wear series debuted in Hangzhou in the form of a separate counter. The idea of JNBY's launch of independent children's wear was due to the good performance of mixed sales of women's and children's wear. Previously, JNBY conducted a one-year experiment, selling children's clothing in more than 100 stores that annual sales are over 5 million yuan. Its sales performance has reached 10% of JNBY's overall sales within six months.

The group owns the designer brands "JNBY", "CROQUIS", "less", "jnby by JNBY", "Pomme de terre", home series "JNBY HOME" and the new menswear brand SAMO, fashion and environmental protection Brand REVERB.

第三节
本章讨论与阅读推荐
Discussion and Reading Recommendation

本章讨论

1. 在森马推出童装十年后，国内服饰市场又掀起了一股童装潮，包括江南布衣、太平鸟等国内服饰品牌相继推出童装产品，试分析这其中的原因。

2. 多品牌矩阵战略已经成为服饰集团的普遍发展方向，童装为何能成为矩阵的利润中心?

3. 在二孩政策、消费升级的大环境下，中国童装市场规模不断扩大，同时也对童装行业提出了更全面的要求，国产童装品牌应如何抓住机遇实现转型?

Discussion

1. Ten years after the launch of children's wear of Semir, the domestic apparel market has set off a wave of children's wear, including domestic apparel brands such as JNBY and PEACE BIRD, which have launched children's wear products one after another. Try to analyze the reasons.

2. The multi-brand matrix strategy has become the general development direction of the apparel group. Why can children's wear become the profit center of the matrix?

3. Under the environment of the two-child policy and consumption upgrading, the scale of China's children's wear market is expanding, and it also puts forward more comprehensive requirements for the children's wear industry. How should domestic children's wear brands seize the opportunity to achieve transformation?

阅读推荐 Reading Recommendation

Bonpoint：Parisian Chic for Children's Fashion

作　者：Natasha Fraser-Cavassoni

出版社：Harry N. Abrams

出版年：2017

ISBN：1419721461，9781419721465

参考资料 References

童装市场分析

https：//cn. fashionnetwork. com / news / xin-sheng-er-jian-shao---lao-pai-fu-shi-wei-he-hai-yao，1013259. html#. XOZAy1MzbjA

https：//cn.fashionnetwork.com/news/shen-du---tong-zhuang-zen-me-tu-ran-cheng-wei-guo-nei-fu，851747. html#. XOZBRlMzbjA

http：//news.baobei360.com/research/2018-09-04/10008339.html

巴拉巴拉

https：//www.fuzhuangnet.com/reading/201803/08/23.html

http：//www.sohu.com/a/279274920_802361

http：//www.linkshop.com.cn/web/archives/2017/379104.shtml

https：//www.tnc.com.cn/info/c-001006-d-3657016.html

https：//www.docin.com/p-1695712264.html

http：//brands.haibao.com/brand/9853/gushi/

http：//www.semirbiz.com/products/balabala.html

https：//fashionunited. uk / news / business / facts-figures-of-the-biggest-chinese-fashion-companies-semir / 2018060129977

https：//www.fuzhuangnet.com/reading/201803/08/23.html

http：//www.sohu.com/a/279274920_802361

https：//www.tnc.com.cn/info/c-001006-d-3657016.html

http：//news.winshang.com/html/063/4464.html

https：//www.myguancha.com/post/25126

http：//www.ebrun.com/20180805/290188.shtml

小樱桃

http：//www.ef43.com.cn/brands/bonpoint/
https：//baike.baidu.com/item/bonpoint/1897605
https：//www.ft.com/content/372fdf06-1223-11e6-839f-2922947098f0
https：//www.vogue.co.uk/gallery/bonpoint-a-touch-of-french-magic
https：//blogs. wsj. com / indiarealtime / 2014 / 05 / 04 / children-clothing-brand-bonpoint-director-says-she-is-inspired-by-india/
https：//www.nytimes.com/2014/07/09/fashion/french-childrens-label-bonpoint-wants-to-be-lifestyle-brand.html
https：//jingdaily.com/bonpoint-ceo-small-luxury-brand-makes-it-in-china/
https：//www.lesechos.fr/2018/01/bonpoint-cultive-de-nouvelles-clienteles-982672
https：//www. capital. fr / entreprises-marches / bonpoint-le-chanel-pour-enfants-qui-cartonne-a-letranger-1310485

江南布衣

http：//www.chinairn.com/news/20170713/085623788.shtml
http：//www.jnbygroup.com/gotoBrand.do？ p=1
http：//www.jnbygroup.com/gotoBrand.do？ p=1
http：//fashion.ifeng.com/a/20161017/40181219_0.shtml
http：//www.eeff.net/wechatarticle-266348.html
https：//cn.businessoffashion.com/articles/news-analysis/t-mall-china-day-jnby-cn
https：//cn.businessoffashion.com/person/li-lin
http：//www.china-ef.com/brand/newsshow-24338-644012.html
http：//w.huanqiu.com/r/MV8wXzkxMDQ3NTZfOTBfMTQ2NzI1NTE3OA
http：//q.chinasspp.com/1-33216.html
https：//jingdaily.com/20110818jing-daily-qa-jnby-chinas-international-fashion-pioneer/
http：//www.ecns.cn/business/2016/08-26/224037.shtml
https：//finance.yahoo.com/news/china-jnby-introduces-brand-andrea-161729561.html

第六章

内衣品牌

Lingerie Brands

第一节

内衣市场分析

Analysis of Lingerie Market

内衣通常直接接触皮肤穿着，是人们必需的服饰之一。从广义上来说，内衣包括文胸、内裤、塑身衣、保暖衣、运动内衣、泳衣、睡衣、家居服、浴衣等；而狭义上，则通常指文胸、内裤和塑身衣等。其中，女性内衣市场一直被称为“服装界的最后一块蛋糕”。

进入21世纪，国内女性对内衣消费观念和诉求有所转变，认识到内衣不只是功能性服饰，也需要兼具时尚、健康，使得中国女士内衣行业得到了较好的发展。我国内衣生产企业主要集中在珠三角、长三角等产业聚集区域，目前有都市丽人、汇洁股份、华歌尔、安莉芳、爱慕等领先内衣企业。中国女士内衣行业相对于其他发达国家来说还有巨大差距，当前国内女士内衣市场存在的问题是集中度低、结构分散，尽管品牌众多，但高端品牌主要由国外品牌占据，国产品牌则主要集中于中低端市场。因此，国内女性内衣市场发展空间巨大。

现有内衣品牌大致可分为三种模式：以三枪、AB等为代表的日用内衣服饰品牌；依靠塑形、抗菌、保暖等特殊功能定位抢占市场的婷美、北极绒等品牌；女性内衣主导的时装性内衣，包括黛安芬、华歌尔等海外品牌，以及爱慕、都市丽人等国产品牌。随着时尚变成一种大众表达，以及消费者对内衣各方面提出的精细化需求，促使内衣产业酝酿相应的变革。以研发和销售能力为主导的内衣行业需进行新一轮的产业升级。

一方面，消费者更加注重内衣的品牌价值和消费体验，带动了中高端内衣的消费需求。一些高档的服装品牌拓展了内衣产品线。另一方面，内衣品类多样化的概念下，“小众”细分品类在业内份额不断提升，如无钢圈内衣、无模杯内衣等。并且，在互联网环境下成长起来的年轻消费者热衷于表达个性，创造的年轻市场为新兴小众品牌的快速崛起提供了大量机会。

Analysis of Lingerie Market

Lingerie is usually worn directly in contact with the skin and is one of the essential clothings. In a broad sense, lingerie includes bras, panties, corsets, warm clothing, sports lingerie, swimwear, pajamas, leisure wear, bathrobes, etc.; and narrowly speaking, lingerie usually refers to bras, panties and corsets. Among them, the women's lingerie market has always been called "the last piece of cake in the clothing industry".

In the 21st century, domestic women have changed their concept and demand in lingerie consumption, recognizing that lingerie is not only functional clothing, but also needs to be both fashionable and healthy, which has made the Chinese women's lingerie industry get better development. China's lingerie production enterprises are mainly concentrated in the industrial gathering areas of the Zhujiang Delta and the Yangtze Delta, etc. Currently, there are leading lingerie companies such as Cosmo Lady, Huijie Holdings, Wacoal, embryform and Aimer. At present, there is a problem of low concentration and scattered structure in the domestic women's lingerie market, compared with other developed countries. Despite the large number of brands, high-end brands are mainly occupied by foreign brands, while domestic brands are mainly concentrated in the low-end market. Therefore, the domestic women's lingerie market has a huge potential for development.

The existing lingerie brands can be roughly divided into three modes: daily-use lingerie clothing represented by Three Guns, AB, etc.. Relying on special functions such as shaping, antibacteria and warm keeping to locate the market, such as Tingmei, Bejirog, etc.. Fashion lingerie brands including overseas brands such as Triumph, Wacoal, and domestic brands such as Aimer and Cosmo Lady. As fashion becomes a kind of public expression, and consumers'demand for finer aspects of lingerie, the lingerie industry is brewing corresponding changes. The lingerie industry, led by R&D and sales capabilities, needs a new round of industrial upgrading.

On the one hand, consumers pay more attention to the brand value and consumption experience of lingerie, which drives the consumption demand of middle- and high-end lingerie. Even some high-end clothing brands have also expanded the lingerie line. On the other hand, under the concept of diversified lingerie categories, the "niche" sub-categories are constantly increasing in the industry, such as rimless bra and modeless bra. Moreover, young consumers who have grown up in the Internet environment are keen to express their individuality, creating a young market that offers plenty of opportunities for the emerging niche brands.

第二节 内衣品牌分析
Analysis of Lingerie Brands

拉佩拉 La Perla

扫一扫

品牌简介

图6-1 品牌标志

意大利知名高端内衣品牌拉佩拉（荷兰投资集团 Sapinda Holding BV 收购于2018年），是世界顶级内衣、女装和泳装生产商，致力于通过精湛的手工艺诠释品牌深厚的文化内涵和唯美的艺术气息，并以兼具优雅与性感的女性气质而闻名。

在过去近60年的时间里，拉佩拉始终密切关注女性身体的演变，同时捕捉国际流行趋势动态，成为同类品牌中“意大利制造”的奢侈品。其品牌产品种类丰富，主线品牌出售女士内衣、家居服、泳装、香水、成衣、晚礼服和配饰等，同时也包括MALIZIA、MARVEL、GIORGIO PERLA男装、JOELLE睡袍等副线品牌。

拉佩拉通过遍布全球主要城市的150多家旗舰精品店（包括自有和特许经营）销售其系列产品。1994年，第一家La Perla旗舰店在米兰的蒙特拿破仑大街开业。它还在主要的百货商店和专门商店中开展业务。

品牌创始人阿达·马索蒂（Ada Masotti）是一位制作紧身胸衣的传统工匠，因其高超剪裁能力而被称为“金剪刀”。她于1954年在博洛尼亚[①]开设了一家小型内衣精品店，将她专业的紧身胸衣技术应用于各种内衣，通过在女性身体上不断试穿的

① 博洛尼亚(Bologna)是一个意大利小镇，其作为丝绸和高级面料制造商中心的历史可以追溯到17世纪。
Bologna is an Italian town whose history as a centre for silk and high-end fabrics dated back to the 17th century.

方法来创造全新的内衣风格，并重新定义了内衣的穿着方式。

创意总监 Julia Haart 于2016年开始任职，基于对打造贴合女性身体曲线的服装的深刻了解，负责内衣、睡衣、沙滩装、配饰、男装系列以及全新成衣系列。此前她与品牌已经合作推出了两季的配饰系列。

图6-2 旗下主要品牌

品牌战略

拉佩拉（La Perla）将其现有产品线整合为三个核心品牌以重塑其品牌结构。

该品牌的沟通策略旨在吸引更加多元化的女性消费者，比如在2014年春夏内衣系列广告中选择卡拉·迪瓦伊、玛高莎·贝拉和刘雯三位形象迥异的知名模特作为其品牌面孔。

为加强零售网络，该品牌开设30家直营商店，并翻新现有的分店，包括在旧邦德街开设精品店，与亚历山大·麦昆和葆蝶家相邻。这座三层高的精品店由意大利建筑师Roberto Baciocchi（普拉达专用建筑师）的设计，其设计理念同样运用在香港和纽约的精品商店，并提供费用高昂的量身定制服务，从1300英镑的丁字裤到33600英镑的长袖紧身连衣裤不等，采用手工测量和意大利传统裁缝技术，结合个性化的设计，打造专属内衣。

早在1992年，拉佩拉开始进驻中国内地，并曾在北京、上海、广州和大连等城市开设专卖店，但因产品设计并未能成功全面考量亚洲女性的体形，最后不得不逐渐退出中国市场。而随着中国经济的发展和中国中产阶级消费群体的壮大，La Perla集团日益重视亚洲市场，专门根据亚洲女性的体形特征进行产品设计以重返中国市场。

品牌历史①

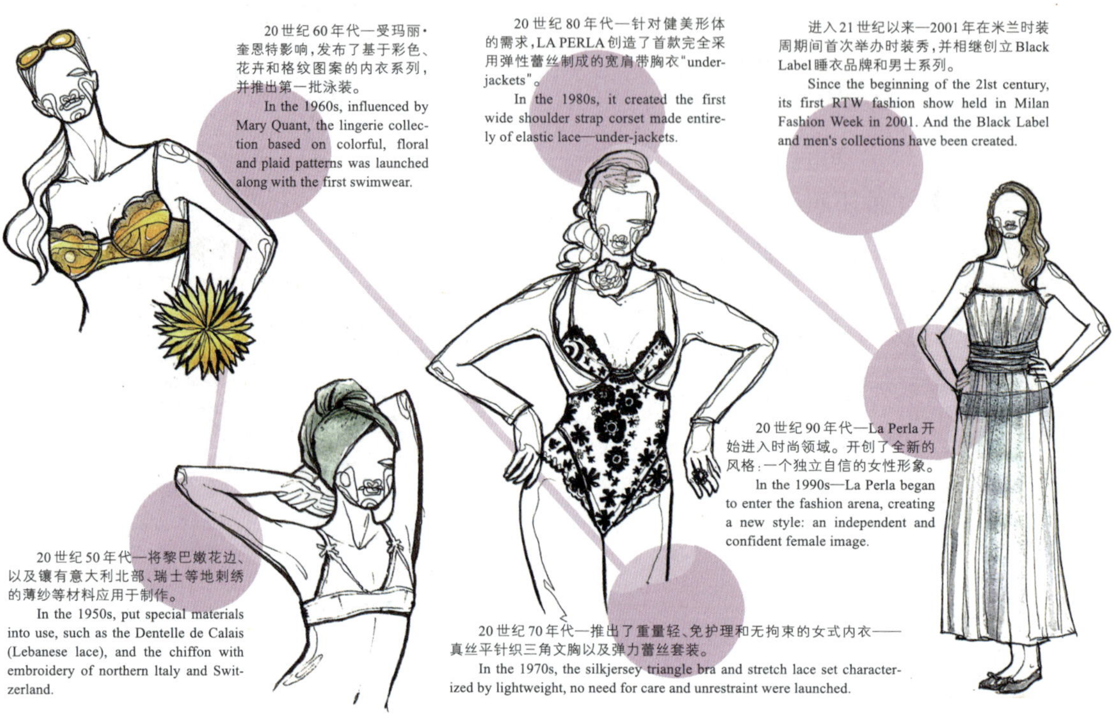

图6-3 品牌发展历程

La Perla

Brand Introduction

Italian well-known high-end lingerie brand La Perla (purchased by Holland investment group Sapinda Holding BV in 2018) is the world's top manufacturer of lingerie, women's wear and swimsuits, dedicated to interpreting the brand's profound cultural and aesthetics through exquisite craftsmanship and being famous for its femininity of elegance and sensuality.

In the past 60 years, La Perla has been paying close attention to the evolution of women's bodies, while capturing the dynamics of international fashion trends to become a luxury of "Made in Italy" among similar brands. Its products are rich in variety, and the main line brand sells women's lingerie, pajamas, swimwear, perfumes, ready-to-wear, evening dresses and accessories. It also includes MALIZIA, MARVEL, GIORGIO PERLA, JOELLE and other

① 该品牌发展历程图为作者手绘。

secondary brands.

La Perla sells its range of products through more than 150 flagship boutiques, including its own and franchise, in major cities around the world. The first La Perla flagship store opened in 1994 in Via Montenapoleone, Milan. It also operates in major department stores and specialty stores.

Brand founder Ada Masotti is a traditional craftsman who makes corsets and is known as the "golden scissors" for his superb tailoring ability. She opened a small lingerie boutique in Bologna in 1954, applying her professional corsage technology to a variety of undergarments, creating a new style of lingerie and refining the way of dressing lingerie by constantly trying on the female bodies.

Julia Haart began her career as Creative Director in 2016 and is responsible for lingerie, pajamas, beachwear, accessories, menswear collections and new ready-to-wear collections based on a deep understanding of the clothing that fits the female body curve. Previously, she has partnered with the brand to launch a two-season collection of accessories.

Brand Strategy

La Perla reinvented its Brand structure by Consolidating its existing product line into three core Brands.

At the same time, the brand aims to attract more diverse female consumers. For example, in the spring/summer 2014 lingerie series, Cara Delevingne, Malgosia Bela and Liu Wen were chosen as its brand faces, which is one of its communication strategies.

To strengthen the retail network, the brand opened 30 direct stores and refurbished existing stores, including opening boutiques on Old Bond Street, adjacent to Alexander McQueen and Bottega Veneta. Designed by Italian architect Roberto Baciocchi, The three-storey boutique is designed by Italian architect Roberto Baciocchi, whose design concept it also used in boutiques of Hong Kong and New York. It offers cost-effective tailor-made services, the costs ranging from £1, 300 thongs to £33, 600 long-sleeved bodysuits, with manual measurement and traditional Italian tailoring techniques, combined with personalized design to create exclusive lingerie.

As early as 1992, La Perla began to enter the Chinese mainland, and opened stores in Beijing, Shanghai, Guangzhou and Dalian. However, due to the product design failure being unable to fully consider the shape of Asian women, they had to gradually withdraw from China market. With the development of China's economy and the growth of China's middle-class consumer groups, La Perla has increasingly attached importance to the Asian market, designing products based on the physical characteristics of Asian women to return to the Chinese market.

黛安芬 Triumph

品牌简介

黛安芬是世界知名的内衣制造和零售商之一，由1886年成立于德国霍伊巴赫的一家小型紧身胸衣工厂演变而来，并在1977年将其总部迁至瑞士楚尔察赫。自20世纪60年代以来，黛安芬一直是女士内衣和睡衣领域的领先品牌，如今已在全世界120多个国家开展业务，建立起一个由3600个控制点组成的网络（截至2017年），包括自营、特许经营和合作运营店铺。就亚洲而言，黛安芬进入该市场已有五十多年历史，其亚太区总部设在香港（1960），并且在日本、中国等地都有领先的销售网络和市场份额。

该公司开发、生产和销售内衣裤、睡衣和泳装等产品，涉及经典型、复古型、功能型、睡衣型、生理型、运动型等多元化产品组合，融合了工艺质量、舒适合身和时尚设计，以优质的产品和服务满足全球消费者的需求。同时，面对不同的客户群体，黛安芬进行不同价位的产品线开发，以涵盖整个女性内衣市场。

图6-4　品牌标志

VALISERE—奢华系列

BeeDees—20世纪80年代推出，针对25岁以下的年轻女性客户群体（2017年出售给德国Jansen Fashion Group）

Triaction—20世纪90年代末推出的运动型文胸系列

Florale—轻熟女系列，由奥斯卡影后茱莉安·摩尔代言

Essence—2011年推出的高端系列，由好莱坞女星莉芙·泰勒代言

Sloggi—20世纪70年代末推出的少女系列，后来添加男士产品(sloggi men)和泳衣(sloggi swim)。

图6-5　黛安芬产品图片

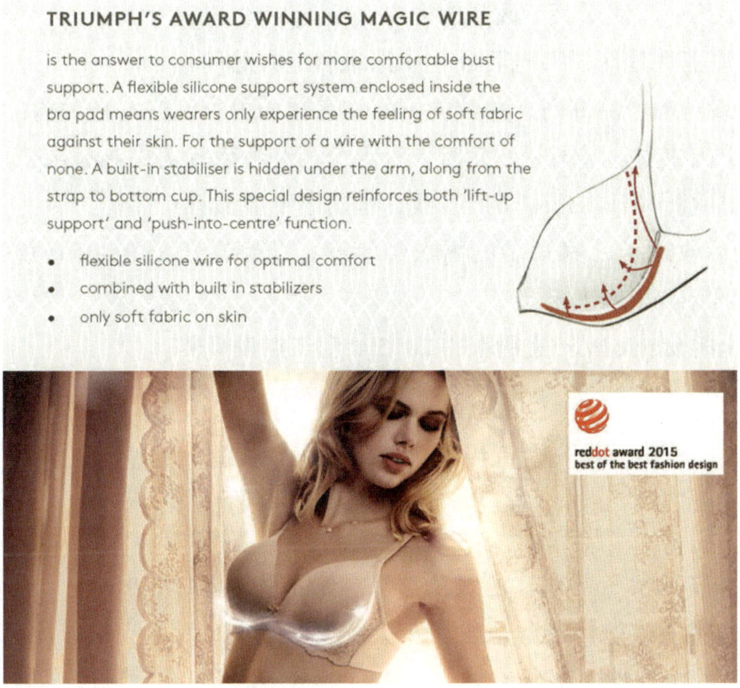

图6-6　黛安芬红点奖产品图片

品牌战略

品牌创立130多年以来，始终洞悉市场变化和消费者需要，与消费者进行有效沟通，以保持敏锐的时尚触觉，都是巩固其全球领先的内衣服装公司之一地位的有效策略，并因此逐步发展为真正的内衣制造商。全新黛安芬标志于2008年推出，成为品牌设计理念的核心，预示着黛安芬更直接地与消费者及其愿望接触。

品牌历史

1886—Johann Gottfried Spiesshofe和Michael Braun在德国霍伊巴赫创办Spiesshofe& Brauno公司，生产紧身胸衣。

1902—受巴黎凯旋门的启发，Triumph成为其品牌名称。

1930—发展成为欧洲境内女士内衣主要制造商，并开始生产塑身内衣。

1933—公司在瑞士楚尔察赫开设了第一家分店。

1953—公司改名为Triumph International（黛安芬国际），随后在比利时、英国、瑞典、意大利、芬兰、挪威、丹麦、奥地利和荷兰开设办事处。

1956—开始与著名的德国女装设计师Heinz Oestergaard进行长期合作。

1959—推出第一款使用莱卡面料的内衣。

1960s—进军亚太地区，并先后成立了泳装和睡衣部门。

1980s—开设运动产品部门，并收购国际知名法国内衣制造商HOM。

1992—在中国成立盐城国际妇女时装有限公司和海南优美内衣有限公司。

2005—针对欧洲和日本延伸了产品线，推出了专业美容产品。

2010s—先后收购了几家知名的内衣经销商，包括瑞士的Beldona Beldona、美国的Journelle和墨西哥的Vicky Form。

2014—推出的Magic Wire文胸获得2015年度红点设计奖。

重大活动

2012—为推广其秋冬系列“曲线诱惑”，该品牌在上海推出全球首个美型工作室。该项目根据全球女性身材数据库，研发出完整的体型自测方案，将女性体型分为Y，S，I，O，A五种类型，并针对不同类型身材给出专属的美体塑身解决方案。

图6–7　2009 Triumph Inspiration Award金奖作品Odette and Odile
（设计师为英国中央圣马丁学生詹姆斯·诺兰）

2015—推出Find the One，内衣领域最大的营销和传播活动之一，支持女性为自己找到最合适的文胸。

2018—推出“一起精彩”，一场属于全球女性的赋能活动，致敬女性之间真挚互助的情谊及同心向前的精神。该活动着重通过社交媒体展开，以视频形式捕捉一系列丰富生活的场景片段，为女性发声。

这些活动都以消费者为中心，与其进行更深层次的情感连接，而非以产品为导向，注重与消费者产生共鸣，全力为女性发声，创造品牌与消费者之间全新的沟通视角。而Triumph Inspiration Award则旨在表彰来自全球各地的有前途的年轻设计师，并在此过程中创造了Triumph与创意年轻消费者之间的对话。

黛安芬推行多品牌策略，并且通过每一年度的市场调查，不断清晰每个品牌线所要针对的消费人群，以期能够有针对性地占领多层次市场。同时，黛安芬在全球各地设立设计师中心，比如设立在香港的亚太总部针对亚洲女性身型打造专属产品，使之成为兼具欧洲和亚洲身型产品的国际产品，因此在中国市场也获得了众多消费者的认可。

Triumph

扫一扫

Brand Introduction

Triumph is one of the world's leading lingerie manufacturers and retailers. It was evolved from a small corset factory founded in 1886 in Heubach, Germany. In 1977, its headquarters was moved to Zurzach, Switzerland. Since the 1960s, Triumph has been a leading brand in lingerie and pajamas, and now has operations in more than 120 countries around the world, establishing a network of 3,600 control points (as of 2017), including self-operated, franchise and cooperative operation stores. As far as Asia is concerned, Triumph has entered the market for more than 50 years. Its Asia-Pacific headquarters is located in Hong Kong (1960) and has leading sales networks and market shares in Japan and China.

The company exploits, manufactures and markets lingerie, pajamas and swimwear in a wide range of products including classic type, retro type, functional type, physiology and sports, and meets the needs of global consumers with quality products and services. At the same time, in the face of different customer groups, Triumph developed product lines at different price points to cover the entire women's lingerie market.

Development Strategy

Over the past 130 years since the brand was founded, insight into market changes and consumer needs, effective communication with consumers, and a keen sense of fashion are all effective strategies to consolidate its position as one of the world's leading lingerie apparel companies, making it a true lingerie manufacturer. The new Triumph logo was launched in 2008 and became the brand's design core, indicating that Triumph is more directly connected with consumers and their wishes.

Brand History

1886—Johann Gottfried Spiesshofe and Michael Braun founded Spiesshofe&Brauno in Heubach, Germany, to produce corsets.

1902—Inspired by the Arc de Triomphe in Paris, Triumph became its brand name.

1930—The brand developed into a major manufacturer of women's lingerie in Europe and began to produce corselet.

1933—The brand opened its first branch in Zurzach, Switzerland.

1953—The brand changed its name to Triumph International and subsequently opened offices in Belgium, the United Kingdom, Sweden, Italy, Finland, Norway, Denmark, Austria and the Netherlands.

1956—The brand started a long-term cooperation with the famous German women's designer Heinz Oestergaard.

1959—The brand launched the first lingerie using Lycra fabric.

1960s—The brand entered the Asia-Pacific region and established the swimwear and pajamas division.

1980s—The brand opened the sports products division and acquired HOM, an internationally renowned French lingerie manufacturer.

1992—The brand established Yancheng International Women's Fashion Co., Ltd. and Hainan Beauty Underwear Co., Ltd. in China.

2005—The brand extended the product line for Europe and Japan, and launched a professional beauty product.

2010s—The brand has acquired several well-known lingerie dealers, including Beldona Beldona of Switzerland, Journelle of the United States and Vicky Form of Mexico.

2014—The brand launched Magic Wire bra which won the 2015 Red Dot Design Award.

Campaigns

2012—To promote its autumn and winter series, it launched the world's first beauty studio in Shanghai. According to the global female body database, the project develops a complete body self—test program, which will give women a variety of body types, such as Y, S, I, O, and A, and give exclusive body shaping solutions for different types of bodies.

2015—Find the One, one of the largest marketing and communication activities in the field of lingerie, supports women to find the most suitable bra for themselves.

2018—Together We Triumph, a empowering activity for women around the world, paying tribute to the true friendship and mutual spirit of women. The campaign focuses on social media, capturing a series of life-rich scenes in video form to speak for women.

These activities are consumer-centric with deeper emotional connections, rather than product-oriented. They focus on resonating with consumers, and fully mobilize for women, creating a new communication perspective between brands and consumers. The Triumph Inspiration Award recognizes promising young designers around the world and creates a dialogue between Triumph and creative young consumers.

Triumph promotes a multi-brand strategy, and through each year's market research, constantly clarifies the consumer groups that each brand line is targeting, to be able to target multiple levels of market. At the same time, Triumph has set up designer centers around the world, such as the Asia-Pacific headquarters in Hong Kong, to create exclusive products for Asian women, making it an international product Possessing both European and Asian body products, so it has also gained a lot consumer recognition in the Chinese market.

维多利亚的秘密 Victoria's Secret

扫一扫

品牌简介

VICTORIA'S SECRET

图6-8 品牌标志

维多利亚的秘密（Victoria's Secret）是世界上最知名的女性内衣零售商之一，为女性消费者提供优质内衣产品。该品牌拥有多元化的产品组合，其主线经营文胸、内衣裤、家居服、女士服饰和泳装等产品，子品牌包括Pink，Victoria Sport，Victoria's Secret Beauty。

作为L Brands集团①的旗舰品牌，性感和女性化是其核心定位，其竞争品牌包括Sara Lee，True & Co，Adore Me，Fruit of the Loom-Vanity Fair，Enamor，Triumph等。

截至2019年2月2日，维多利亚的秘密在美国已开设了1098家店铺，并通过特许经营的形式在全球开展扩张计划，在澳大利亚、中国、日本、巴西、瑞典、丹麦、法国、英国等国的黄金地段均设有零售商店。

图6-9 旗下品牌

① L Brands, Inc.（前身为Limited Brands, Inc.和The Limited, Inc.）是一家美国时装零售商，总部位于俄亥俄州哥伦布市，除Victoria Secret和Bath & Body Works等品牌外，还包括采购业务Mast Global等。

品牌战略

扫一扫

一年一度的维多利亚的秘密时装秀是其精心设计的营销工具。其最初于1995年推出，在黄金时段通过电视进行放送，此后成为其标志性特征。维多利亚的秘密选择拥有“完美的身材”的模特（被称为“维密天使”，如吉赛尔·邦辰、米兰达·可儿和坎蒂丝·斯瓦内普尔等）展示最新的商品系列，还邀请众多知名嘉宾，如贾斯汀·比伯、泰勒·斯威夫特和爱莉安娜·格兰德。这些超过1000万美元的投入使品牌获得了巨大关注度。

维多利亚的秘密在2009年进军社交网络。除官方网站，还开设有Facebook，Pinterest和Twitter等官方帐户，用于时装秀、广告片、产品目录的展示和年度销售、限时优惠、最新系列产品的发布。

图6-10　2016年维密秀场

为了吸引拥有很高的购买力的亚洲新兴中产阶级，2014年维多利亚的秘密在中国开设了第一家专卖店。但早在2009年，选用亚洲模特的举措就已开启了该品牌在亚洲的扩张（中国模特刘雯是第一个为维多利亚的秘密走秀的东亚模特）。针对保守的亚洲市场，该品牌采取了更为谨慎的方式，将其拓展的重点更多地放在香水、美容产品等其他商品上。

扫一扫

品牌历史

1977年，维多利亚的秘密由美国商人罗伊·雷蒙德于旧金山创立。雷蒙德在传统百货公司为妻子选购女性内衣的尴尬经历，促成了他以维多利亚时代的优雅和

图6-11　品牌标志性包装

浪漫为理念开设女性内衣商店。20世纪60年代末和70年代的女权运动呼吁女性从胸罩的束缚中解放出来，维多利亚的秘密以其新的设计对此做出了回应，改变了过去以实用和耐用为重点的女性内衣。同时，得益于产品目录，其邮购业务逐渐覆盖美国各地区的客户。

1982年，维多利亚的秘密已发展到五家商店，在业务蓬勃发展仅仅几年后，以100万美元的价格出售给The Limited，Inc. 的创始人莱斯利·韦克斯纳（Leslie Wexner）。韦克斯纳将原本针对男性的销售模式转变为专注于女性顾客，在设计上使产品不仅适用于特殊场合，也更符合女性日常穿着的需要。

Victoria's Secret

Brand Introduction

Victoria's Secret is one of the world's best-known Lingerie Brands, offering quality lingerie products to women consumers. The brand has a diversified product portfolio. Its main product line includes bras, lingerie, leisure wear, women's apparel and swimwear, and sub-brand includes: Pink, Victoria Sport, and Victoria's Secret Beauty.

As the flagship brand of L Brands Group, sexy and feminine is its core position, and some brands contest against it, include Sara Lee, True & Co, Adore Me, Fruit of the Loom-Vanity Fair, Enamor, Triumph, etc.

As of February 2, 2019, Victoria's Secret has opened 1,098 stores in the United States, and has carried out its global expansion through franchising. It has retail stores in prime locations in Australia, China, Japan, Brazil, Sweden, Denmark, France, and the United Kingdom.

Brand Strategy

The annual Victoria's Secret Fashion Show is a well-designed marketing tool. Originally launched in 1995, it was broadcast on television during prime time and has become its iconic feature. It chose the models with "perfect figure" to showcase the latest collections (known as " VS Angles", such as Gisele Bündchen, Miranda Kerr, Candice Swanepoel, etc.), as well as many well-known guests such as Justin Bieber, Taylor Swift and Eliana Grande. These investments of more than $10 million have given the brand a lot of attention.

Victoria's secrets entered the social network in 2009. In addition to the official website, official accounts such as Facebook, Pinterest and Twitter are also available for fashion shows, campaigns and catalogues along with annual sales, limited time discounts, and the release of the latest collections.

Noticing the high purchasing ability of Asia's emerging middle class, Victoria's Secret opened its first store in China in 2014. But as early as 2009, the use of Asian models has launched the brand's expansion in Asia (Chinese model Liu Wen is the first East Asian model for its runway show). In response to the conservative Asian market, it has taken a more cautious approach, focusing more on the expansion of perfumes, beauty products and other commodities.

Brand History

In 1977, Victoria's secret was founded in San Francisco by American businessman Roy Raymond. Raymond's embarrassing experience of buying women's lingerie for his wife in a traditional department store led him to open a women's lingerie store with the elegance and romance of Victorian era. The feminist movements of the late 1960s and 1970s called for women to be liberated from the bras, and Victoria's secrets responded with new designs that changed the practical and durable way women's lingerie used to be. At the same time, thanks to the product catalog, its mail order business gradually covers customers in various regions of the United States.

In 1982, Victoria's secrets have grown to five stores. And in just a few years after the booming business, it was sold to Leslie Wexner, founder of The Limited, Inc., for $1 million. Wexner turned the original sales model for men into a focus on female customers, and the design is not only suitable for special occasions but also for the demand of women's daily wear.

第三节

本章讨论与阅读推荐

Discussion and Reading Recommendation

本章讨论

1. 随着时代与市场趋势的变化，维多利亚的秘密2019年度的大秀面临重大的调整，请你谈谈发生该变化的原因。

2. 进入21世纪后遭遇市场份额连续下滑的意大利顶级内衣品牌La Perla应如何调整战略以吸引千禧一代消费者？

3. 内衣行业所受到的关注度与日俱增，请你谈谈国产内衣品牌该如何利用这个时机拓展市场。

Discussion

1. With the changes in the times and market trends, Victoria's secret 2019 show is undergoing major adjustments. Please talk about the reasons for this change.

2. How does La Perla, the top Italian lingerie brand that has suffered a continuous decline in market share after entering the 21st century, adjust its strategy to attract millennials?

3. The lingerie industry has received increasing attention. Please talk about how Could domestic lingerie brands use this opportunity to expand the market.

阅读推荐 Reading Recommendation

《后台秘密——维多利亚的秘密时尚秀十年后台掠影》

作　者：［澳］罗素·詹姆斯

出版社：上海社会科学院出版社

出版年：2017

ISBN：9787552021455

La Perla——Lingerie and Desire

作　者：Isabella Cardinali

出版社：Rizzoli

出版年：2012

ISBN：9780847839162

参考资料 References

拉佩拉

https：//www.globenewswire.com/news-release/2018/08/28/1557607/0/en/Naked-Brand-Group-Limited-Announces-Term-Sheet-for-25-Million-Strategic-Investment-from-Sapinda-Holding-B-V.html

https：//www.rizzoliusa.com/book/9780847839162/

https：//en.wikipedia.org/wiki/La_Perla_（clothing）

https：//www.reuters.com/article/us-laperla-m-a-sapinda/sapinda-buys-lingerie-firm-la-perla-after-fosun-talks-stumble-idUSKCN1GA1NN

https：//www.vogue.co.uk/gallery/la-perla-vintage-campaign-imagery-interview-design-team-nick-tacchi

https：//www.laperla.com/pl/explore/discover/events-news.html

http：//fashiongear.fibre2fashion.com/brand-story/la-perla/history.asp

https：//www.nancymeyer.com/la-perla-a-short-history/825/dept

https：//fashionweekdaily.com/lingerie-legend-inside-la-perlas-haute-history/

https：//www.thedrum.com/news/2017/05/10/la-perla-appoints-threepipe-handle-programmatic-and-retargeting-strategies

https：//www.brandchannel.com/2009/11/09/new-la-perla-brand-structure-less-clothing-less-money/

https：//underlinesmagazine.com/2014/06/26/la-perla-announces-growth-strategy/

https：//www.telegraph.co.uk/fashion/new-york-fashion-week/woman-feeling-confident-comfortable-naomi-campbell-models-whole/

https：//www.hollywoodreporter.com/news/la-perlas-dynasty-tv-cameo-hollywood-ambitions-1104244

https：//www.independent.ie/woman/la-perlas-new-pearls-29794791.html
https：//www.laperla.com/pl/explore/discover/events-news.html
http：//www.luluscouture.com/lulus-fashion/la-perla-unveils-new-strategy/

黛安芬

https：//zh.wikipedia.org/wiki/%E9%BB%9B%E5%AE%89%E8%8A%AC
https：//en.wikipedia.org/wiki/Triumph_International
http：//www.triumph.com/uk/en/7685.html
http：//cn.triumph.com/index.php/shop/brandstory
http：//q.chinasspp.com/1-304017.html
http：//www.chinasspp.com/News/Detail/2017-7-7/385841.html
http：//www.chinasspp.com/News/Detail/2012-11-9/125634.html
http：//www.chinasspp.com/News/Detail/2017-9-22/393317.html
http：//www.chinasspp.com/News/Detail/2018-3-23/408361.html
https：//www.globrand.com/2010/425234.shtml

维多利亚的秘密

https：//en.wikipedia.org/wiki/L_Brands
https：//en.wikipedia.org/wiki/Victoria%27s_Secret
https：//www.statista.com/topics/4819/victoria-s-secret/
http：//www.deliberatemagazine.com/history-victorias-secret/
https：//www.theodysseyonline.com/history-of-victorias-secret
https：//www. huffpost. com / entry / victorias-secret_n_4181683？ guccounter=1&guce_referrer=aHR0cHM6Ly93d3cuZ29vZ2xlLmNvbS8&guce_referrer_sig=AQAAACXGBERLeAHCZllkrg1LtKbE9u-DDiSlupgO7YbcmYgG1CLD2uUKLGGa_QO8utztRolEykRadzF7NlJxsEltbbDOBIZwxVrewazk7JAk4xzfK0CulPE-ckTyJz-YRt2rhNfflUCOyDHEZDws6C3WUzwMo2j7g-AQR7gp63RvnsQju
https：//www.thecut.com/2013/10/victorias-secret-history.html
https：//www. telegraph. co. uk / finance / newsbysector / retailandconsumer / 11267280 / How-Victorias-Secret-became-a-worldwide-phenomenon.html
https：//www.thelist.com/38724/untold-truth-victorias-secret/
https：//www.marketing91.com/marketing-mix-of-victorias-secret/
http：//marketingsmalltalk.blogspot.com/
https：//www.cnbc.com/2019/02/08/victorias-secret-is-retails-latest-fallen-angel.html
https：//www.referralcandy.com/blog/victorias-secret-marketing-strategy/

第七章

配饰品牌

Accessory Brands

第一节

配饰品市场分析

Analysis of Accessories Market

配饰和服装一样，是在人身上穿戴或携带的东西，具有实用性和装饰性。随着时尚观念的变迁，人们对配饰的态度和需求历经演变，如今配饰不再单纯是造型的附属品。近年来，鞋履、珠宝和手袋已成为奢侈品市场增长最快的三个品类，同时硬奢侈品（珠宝和腕表）也在线上销售中表现出强大的增长潜力。

象征强大的社会地位与财富的手袋是众多全球奢侈品公司的立足之本。根据市场调研机构NPD Group发布的2019年第一季度包袋及配饰品类流行趋势报告显示，男女士包袋和配件的销售额同比均呈现下滑趋势。20世纪90年代到21世纪初，Louis Vuitton和Gucci两大品牌共同主导着奢侈品牌手袋市场。而Hermès和Coach则分别垄断着“高端”和“大众”两个细分市场。随着其他高端品牌（如Bottega Veneta，Céline）、高级时装品牌（如Prada，Chanel，Dior，Valentino和Saint Laurent）和轻奢品牌（如Michael Kors，Tory Burch，Kate Spade，Longchamp，Furla）先后进入手袋市场，手袋市场竞争日益激烈。近年来，新款式的手袋日益难以成为“IT Bag”，也少有经典款式的诞生。

纵观鞋履市场近年的业绩表现，普遍仍呈下滑放缓状况，表明产业仍未走出低谷。

当前，我国已转变为全球最大的鞋履消费国，占据内地鞋业市场的品牌大致可区分为主导高档市场的欧美品牌；占有中档市场的中外合资品牌，如百丽（Belle）；低档市场上参差不齐的本地厂商。不断涌现的鞋履品牌以“新”与“小众”为标签，迫使国内的鞋履行业迅速转入革新状态。而随着消费者对运动休闲风格的青睐，高跟鞋品类遇冷，增加运动休闲风格产品线成为诸多鞋履企业的重要措施之一，在营销上也更积极采用社交电商等“新零售”手段，来实现品牌的年轻化。

另外，2018年腕表及珠宝产品的消费总额占中国奢侈品消费总额的22%以上。其中全球制表业的最高标准之一的瑞士钟表牢牢占据中国高端腕表市场。而国产腕表品牌尽管历史积淀相对薄弱，但海鸥、上海和北京等品牌也正积极投入研发和营销，力争在高端腕表市场中占有一席之地。

作为珠宝首饰生产和消费大国，我国珠宝首饰行业市场潜力大，已进入比较平稳的发展时期，国内外品牌在竞争中并存。国内高端市场主要被Tiffany，Cartier，BVLGARI，Van Cleef & Arpels等国际知名珠宝首饰品牌垄断；占据市场主要份额的中高端市场主要有港资品牌的周大福、周生生等和内地品牌的老凤祥、潮宏基、明牌珠宝等。作为主力消费者群体的千禧一代逐渐成为这一市场的指向标，他们往往愿意选择设计独特、价格适中的时尚首饰作为装饰，因此提高产品设计能力是珠宝行业发展的一大趋势，非黄金首饰的市场份额也将得到提升。

As clothing, accessories are worn or carried by people, which are practical and decorative. With the change of fashion concept, people's attitudes and needs for accessories have evolved. In recent years, footwear, jewellery and handbags have become the three fastest-growing categories in the luxury market, while jewelry and watches have also shown strong growth potential in online sales.

Handbags that symbolize strong social status and wealth are the foundation of many global luxury companies. According to the trend report on bags and accessories in the first quarter of 2019 released by the market research organization NPD Group, sales of men's and women's bags and accessories showed a downward trend. From the 1990s to the beginning of the 21st century, Louis Vuitton and Gucci jointly dominated the luxury brand handbag market. Hermès and Coach monopolize the high-end and mass segments with other high-end brands (such as Bottega Veneta, Céline), high fashion brands (such as Prada, Chanel, Dior, Valentino and Saint Laurent) and luxury brands (such as Michael Kors, Tory Burch, Kate Spade, Longchamp, Furla) have entered the handbag market, the competition in the handbag market is increasingly fierce. In recent years, new style handbags have become increasingly difficult to become "IT Bag", and few classic styles have been born.

Looking at the performance of the footwear market in recent years, it is still generally slowing down, indicating that the industry has not yet bottomed out.

At present, China has become the world's largest consumer of footwear. The brands that occupy the mainland footwear market can be roughly divided into: European and American brands that dominate the high-end market; Sino-foreign joint venture brands that have a mid-range market, such as Belle; In the low-end market, there are uneven local manufacturers. The emerging footwear brands are labeled "new" and "niche", forcing the domestic footwear industry to quickly move into innovation. Recently, consumers are more interested in sports and leisure styles, and high-heeled shoes gradually lose their market. Therefore, increasing sports and leisure style products have become one of the important measures for many footwear companies, and adopting social e-commerce in marketing to help the brand rejuvenate.

In addition, the total consumption of watches and jewelry products accounted for more than 22% of China's total luxury consumption in 2018. Swiss watches, one of the highest standards in the global watch industry, firmly occupy the high-end watch market in China. Although the domestic wristwatch brands have a relatively weak historical accumulation, seagull, Shanghai and Beijing are also actively engaged in R&D and marketing, striving for their position in the high-end wristwatch market.

As a large country of jewelry production and consumption, China has great market potential in jewelry industry, and has entered a relatively stable development period. Domestic and foreign brands coexist in the competition. The domestic high-end market is mainly monopolized by Tiffany, Cartier, BVLGARI, Van Cleef&Arpels and other international famous jewelry brands; the middle- and high-end brands that occupy the main market share include Hong Kong funded brands as Zhou Dafu and Zhou Shengsheng and also brands from the mainland as LAO FENGXIANG, CHJ JEWELLERY and MINGR. As the main consumer group, millennials have gradually become the compas of this market. They are often willing to choose fashionable jewelry with unique design and moderate price as decoration. Therefore, improving product design ability is a major trend of jewelry industry development, and the market share of non-gold jewelry will also be increased.

第二节

配饰品牌分析

Analysis of Accessory Brands

宝格丽 BVLGARI

扫一扫

品牌简介

BVLGARI

图7-1 品牌标志

宝格丽是意大利最知名的珠宝品牌之一，其历史可以追溯到1884年，名称出自其创始人银匠索帝里欧·宝格丽的姓氏。该品牌目前隶属于LVMH集团，以高端珠宝闻名，因品质与传统使其许多经典产品备受收藏家和喜爱复古首饰的人们的追捧，特别是Serpenti系列和Tubogas系列。随着产品线不断扩展至腕表、皮具、配饰、香氛和酒店①领域，这个罗马珠宝商如今已成为奢侈品牌的一员。

B. zero 1系列　Serpenti系列　Parentesi系列　Save the Children系列

图7-2 品牌产品系列(1)

① 与万豪国际旗下奢侈品集团成立合资公司，于2001年开发Bulgari Hotels & Resorts。目前已开放米兰(2004年)、巴厘岛(2006年)、伦敦(2012年)、北京(2017年)、迪拜(2017年)和上海(2018)，莫斯科、巴黎和东京将于2020年至2022年间开放。

图7-3 品牌产品系列（2）

品牌战略

宝格丽通过高于其他同类品牌的价格，确立其产品的独家性，比如采取奢侈钟表制造商的惯常做法，推出高价位的限量版系列腕表。同时，与知名人士保持紧密的联系，以提升品牌的世界认知度，包括伊丽莎白·泰勒、卢奇诺·维斯孔蒂以及格蕾丝·凯莉等知名影星都是宝格丽的忠实拥趸。安迪·沃霍尔曾评价道："对我而言，拜访宝格丽的商店就像参观最好的当代艺术展览一样。"

图7-4 第五大道旗舰店门店

宝格丽将数字体验作为品牌的入口点，与实体零售协同发挥作用，并成功利用其独特性树立起强大的社交媒体形象。作为首个宣传“即看即买”的高级腕表品牌，消费者可以通过品牌的微信商店预定商品。此外，与社交媒体意见领袖合作，利用其影响力推动品牌的全渠道购物服务。

宝格丽拥有300余家商店的分销网络，均分布在全球的奢侈品购物区。最大的宝格丽精品店位于东京，面积达940平方米。在一个零售业大规模投资电子商务的年代，宝格丽于2017年在美国第57街和第五大道重新开放旗舰店，使其零售业务翻了一番。品牌的首席执行官让·克里斯托弗·巴宾表示：“当我们谈论奢侈品时，我们更加注重情感消费，尽管数字化也可以实现优质的服务，但最为关键的是品牌想要传达的精神与生活方式，往往需要通过实体店铺呈现。”

品牌历史

1880s—1884年，索帝里欧·宝格丽在西斯廷那大街（Via Sistina）大街开设了第一家精品店，出售银制雕刻品。

1900s—1904年，宝格丽旗舰店在康多提大道（Via Condotti）开业，建立了其作为兼具奢华风格与顶级工艺的珠宝品牌的声誉。

1920s—高级珠宝的设计融合了铂金、钻石与几何风格化的装饰艺术。

1940s—脱离法国珠宝设计的潮流，从希腊、古罗马古典艺术领域汲取灵感，融合意大利文艺复兴美学及19世纪罗马金匠学派风格。

1950s—使用珍稀彩色宝石的大胆配色，并创造了品牌标志性元素——凸圆形宝石。

1970s—电影明星和社交名流的追捧促使品牌开展国际化扩张，在纽约、日内瓦、蒙特卡洛、巴黎等地开设精品店。并于1977年推出首个腕表系列BVLGARI-BVLGARI。

图7-5 Trombino

图7-6 结合黄金材质的Serpenti系列

图7-7 BVLGARI BVLGARI手表

图7-8 第一款花卉胸针En Tremblant

1990s—1993年推出了其第一款香水；1996年推出了首个配饰系列，包括真丝围巾、皮具和眼镜。

2000s—2000年开始积极推动垂直整合计划，包括收购表厂Gerald Genta（尊达表）和Daniel Roth（丹尼尔·罗斯）以及顶级珠宝品牌Crova；2011年，这个家族企业被LVMH集团以60亿美元收购。

BVLGARI

Brand Introduction

BVLGARI is one of Italian most well-known jewellery brands. Its history can be dated back to 1884, and its name comes from the surname of its founder, the silversmith Sotirio Voulgaris (BVLGARI is the voice of Voulgaris). The brand is currently part of the LVMH Group and is known for its high-end jewellery. Its quality and tradition have made many of its classic products sought after by collectors and those who love vintage jewellery, especially the Serpenti and Tubogas collections. With the continuous expansion of the product line, this Roman jewellery brand has now developed into a member of the luxury brands.

Brand Strategy

BVLGARI divides the exclusivity of its products by higher prices than other similar brands, such as the luxury watch manufacturer's usual practice, launching a high-priced limited edition watch. At the same time, maintain close contact with celebrities to enhance the brand's world awareness, including Eliza White Taylor, Lucino Visconti and Grace Kelly, all of which are BVLGARI's Faithful fans. Andy Warhol once said, "For me, calling at Bulgari's shop is like visiting the best exhibition of contemporary art."

BVLGARI uses digital experience as the entry point for the brand, working synergistically with physical retailing, and successfully using its uniqueness to establish a strong social media image. As the first high-end watch brand to promote "See Now, Buy Now", consumers can order the products. It also collaborated with social media influencers, to drive the brand's omni-channel shopping service.

BVLGARI has a distribution network of more than 300 stores, all located in luxury shopping areas around the world. The largest Bulgari boutique is located in Tokyo and covers an area of

940 square meters. In a time when the retail industry invested heavily in e-commerce, BVLGARI reopened its flagship store on 57th Street and Fifth Avenue in the United States in 2017, doubling its retail business. Brand CEO Jean-Christopher Babin said, "When we talk about luxury we talk very much about emotions, no matter how good you are in consumer engagement digitally, eventually the spirit and lifestyle of the brand together with a live boutique is pivotal."

Brand History

1880s—In 1884, Sotrio BVLGARI opened its first boutique on Via Sistina, selling silver carvings.

1900s—In 1904, the BVLGARI flagship store opened on Via Condotti, establishing its reputation as a jewellery brand with a luxurious style and top craftsmanship.

1920s—High jewellery design combines platinum and diamonds with geometric stylized art deco.

1940s—Drawing inspiration from the ancient art realm of Greek and Ancient Rome instead of following the trend of French fewellery desigh, it combines Italian Renaissance aesthetics with the 19th century Roman goldsmith school style.

1950s—Use the bold color of rare colored gemstones and create the brand's signature element—a cabochon.

1970s—The pursuit of movie stars and social celebrities has led to the international expansion of BVLGARI, opening boutiques in New York, Geneva, Monte Carlo, Paris and other places. And in 1977 it launched the first watch collection BVLGARI-BVLGARI.

1990s—In 1993, the first fragrance was launched; in 1996, the first collection of accessories, including silk scarves, leather goods and glasses, was launched.

2000s—In 2000, the vertical integration plan was actively promoted, including the acquisition of the watch factory Gerald Genta and Daniel Roth and the top jewellery brand Crova; in 2011, the family business was acquired by the LVMH group for $6 billion.

卡地亚 Cartier

品牌简介

图7-9 品牌标志

图7-10 历峰集团标志

卡地亚是一个成功融合精致工艺与优雅传统的法国奢侈珠宝品牌，是世界五大珠宝制造商之一。卡地亚于1847年由路易·弗朗西斯·卡地亚（1819—1904）在巴黎创立，1964年之前作为家族企业进行运营，如今隶属于历峰集团①。

图7-11 TRINITY戒指

被威尔士王子爱德华七世指定为“Joaillier des Rois，Roi des Joailliers”（“国王珠宝商，珠宝商之王”）的卡地亚创造了一系列历史性的珠宝和腕表设计。其首次将铂金用于珠宝首饰设计，比如于1925年推出的TRINITY戒指是其简约风格的经典款式之一。同时，该品牌也定义了现代钟表美学标准，区别于当代同业局限于腕表的装饰之美，更专注于尺寸、线条与比例、金属的外型、表壳与表链的连接，突破表盘圆形的传统，如1904年推出的SANTOS-DUMONT腕表②。

图7-12 SANTOS-DUMONT腕表

卡地亚总部位于巴黎，在125个国家开设有200家零售门店。此外，该公司在巴黎、伦敦、纽约和东京设有四家标志性精品店。其历任设计师包括查尔斯·雅克考、路易·约瑟夫·卡地亚以及珍妮·杜桑。

扫一扫

①历峰集团成立于1988年，由南非富翁安顿·鲁伯特（Anton Rupert）创立，是仅次于LVMH的第二大奢侈品集团。

②为巴西飞行先驱阿尔伯特·山度士·杜蒙（Alberto Santos-Dumont）设计的一枚腕表原型。1911年，腕表以Santos为名正式发售，这枚腕表成为现代男士腕表的雏形，凸圆形蓝宝石表冠也成为了卡地亚腕表的特征之一。

图7-13　卡地亚产品系列

卡地亚的珠宝产品主要有戒指、手镯、项链、耳环和胸针等，腕表则细分为男、女士系列和高级珠宝腕表系列，并不断将产品多样化至其他领域，如皮具、香水、眼镜和配件等。

品牌战略

除了拥有精湛的制表工艺、突破性的奢侈珠宝和高端配饰，卡地亚也因受到皇室成员和知名人士的青睐，在国际上吸引了广泛的关注，比如摩纳哥王子雷尼尔与格蕾丝·凯莉的红宝石订婚戒指，以及理查德·伯顿赠予伊丽莎白·泰勒的卡地亚钻石的项链。并且以此为基础，卡地亚始终专注于富裕阶层人士，这确保了其目标的细分市场始终与品牌形象保持一致。而高昂的价格则归因于高品质的材料以及定制服务，也受到产品类型和竞争品牌的驱动。

卡地亚侧重于通过各种渠道不断创新和强化营销策略，战略之一是以故事的形式扩展品牌网络并提高社区的忠诚度，在推出的产品中描绘他们的奢华传统、丰富经验和精致细节等内容。

该品牌将广告投放于国际出版刊物、电视广告等传统平台，也通过Twitter和Instagram等社交媒体以及创建的自有电子杂志，将其品牌形象以专业的内容进行展示，并建立互动以发展各个渠道的潜在客户。

扫一扫

品牌历史

1847—路易·弗朗西斯·卡地亚（Louis-François Cartier）在巴黎蒙特吉尔街29号接管了工匠阿道夫·皮卡（Adolphe Picard）的珠宝工作室。

1874—卡地亚的儿子阿尔弗雷德（Alfred Cartier）接任，将业务扩展至腕表领域。而后直到卡地亚的孙子路易斯、皮埃尔和雅克接管，才成为一家跨国公司，分别在巴黎、伦敦和纽约开展业务。

1988—卡地亚获得了伯爵珠宝和名士手表的多数股权。

1899—路易·卡地亚将品牌总部迁至巴黎和平街（Rue de la Paix）13号，并保留至今。

1904—卡地亚成为西班牙国王阿方索十二世和英国国王爱德华七世的官方供应商，并在伦敦和纽约开设商店。

1909—皮埃尔·卡地亚建立纽约市分公司，并于1917年迁至第五大道653号。

1914—标志性的卡地亚豹（Panthère）图案首次使用，由钻石和黑色玛瑙制成，镶嵌在圆形女士腕表的表盘上。

1933—珍妮·杜桑（Jeanne Toussaint）被任命为Cartier Fine Jewelry的负责人。

1969—推出Love系列手镯。

1972—罗伯特·霍克（Robert Hocq）取得了卡地亚巴黎的所有权，并在接下来的四年内，相继收购了卡地亚伦敦和卡地亚纽约，从而重新统一了卡地亚。

1992—首次进入中国，并于1998年在北京王府井大街开设了第一家中国大陆专卖店。

1993—旺多姆集团（Vendôme）成立，将卡地亚与登喜路、万宝龙、伯爵等奢侈品牌一同纳入旗下。

图7-14 卡地亚豹Panthère图案手表

图7-15 “卡地亚：风格与历史”回顾展

图7-16 “有界之外”展览

2014—在巴黎大皇宫举办主题为“卡地亚：风格与历史”的回顾展。

2019—在中国北京故宫博物院举办了“有界之外”主题展览。

Cartier

Brand Introduction

Cartier is a French luxury jewellery brand that successfully combines exquisite craftsmanship and elegance. It is one of the top five jewellery manufacturers in the world. Founded in Paris in 1847 by Louis-François Cartier (1819—1904) and operated as a family business until 1964, it is now part of the Richemont.

Cartier, appointed by Edward VII, Prince of Wales as “Joaillier des Rois, Roi des Joailliers”, has created a series of historic jewellery and watch designs. For the first time, platinum is used in jewellery design. For example, the TRINITY ring, which was launched in 1925, is one of its classic Concise styles. At the same time, the brand also defines the aesthetic standard of modern watches by focusing on the size, the line and the proportion, the appearance of the metal, and the connection between the case and the bracelet, and breaks through the tradition of the round shape of the dial, such as the SANTOS-DUMONT watch introduced in 1904.

Headquartered in Paris, Cartier has 200 retail stores in 125 countries. In addition, the company has four iconic boutiques in Paris, London, New York and Tokyo. Its successive designers include Charles Jacqueau, Louis-Joseph Cartier, and Jeanne Toussaint.

Cartier’s jewellery products mainly include rings, bracelets, necklaces, earrings and brooches. The watch is subdivided into men’s and women’s collections and high-end jewellery watches, and the products are constantly diversified into other fields such as leather goods, perfumes, glasses, accessories, etc.

Brand Strategy

In addition to its superb watchmaking craftsmanship, luxury jewellery and high-end accessories, Cartier has attracted a lot of attention internationally because of being favored by royalty and celebrities, for example, the Ruby engagement ring of Prince Rainier of Monaco and Grace Kelly, and the Taylor-Burton Diamond that was given by Richard Burton to Elizabeth Taylor. Based on this, Cartier has always focused on the wealthy, which ensures that the target market segment is consistent with the brand image. The high price is attributed to the high quality of materials and customized services, driven by product types and competitive brands as well.

Cartier focuses on continuous innovation and enhancing marketing strategies through a variety of channels. One of the strategies is to expand the brand network and increase the loyalty of the community in the form of stories, depicting their luxury traditions, rich experience and fine details in the launched products.

The brand puts advertisements on traditional platforms such as the international publications and TV commercials. It also displays its brand image with professional content through social media such as Twitter and Instagram, as well as its own e-magazines, and establishes interactions to develop potential customers in various channels.

Brand History

1847—Louis-François Cartier took over the jewelry studio of the craftsman Adolphe Picard at 29 Rue Montorgueil, Paris.

1874—Cartier's son, Alfred Cartier, took it over and expanded its business into the watch industry. And it was not until Cartier's grandsons Louis, Pierre and Jacques took it over that it became a multinational company operated in Paris, London and New York.

1988—Cartier acquired a majority stake in Piaget and Baume & Mercier.

1899—Louis Cartier moved Cartier's headquarter to 13 Rue de la Paix, Paris, which has remained so far.

1904—Cartier became the official supplier of King Alfonso XII of Spain and King Edward VII of England, and opened stores in London and New York.

1909—Pierre Cartier established the New York City branch and moved to No. 653 Fifth Avenue in 1917.

1914—The iconic Panthère was first used, set on the dial of a round ladies watch, made of diamonds and black agate.

1933—Jeanne Toussaint was appointed as the head of Cartier Fine Jewelry.

1969—Launched the Love bracelet.

1972—Robert Hocq took the ownership of Cartier Paris and reunified Cartier in the following four years with the acquisition of Cartier London and Cartier New York.

1992—It entered China for the first time and opened the first mainland China store in Wangfujing Street in Beijing in 1998.

1993—The Vendôme Group was established to incorporate Cartier with luxury brands such as Dunhill, Montblanc and Piaget.

2014—"Cartier: Style and History" was retrospected at the Grand Palais in Paris

2019—The theme exhibition "Beyond Boundaries" was held at the Palace Museum in Beijing, China.

施华洛世奇 Swarovski

品牌简介

1895年，施华洛世奇诞生于奥地利，始终坚持创始人丹尼尔·施华洛世奇[①]（1862—1956）为每个人创造“钻石”的愿景。经过120余年的发展，施华洛世奇已成为国际知名首饰及配饰品牌，并且凭借顶级的水晶切割技术建立起一个价值数十亿美元的公司，在全球近170个国家拥有约2800家门店。

图7-17　施华洛世奇品牌logo

作为全球最大的切割水晶产品制造商，施华洛世奇以其仿水晶首饰而闻名，包括项链、耳环、手链、戒指和胸针等，也相继推出腕表、装饰摆件，以及太阳眼镜、发饰、手袋等时尚配饰。除了业务量最高的仿水晶业务部门外，施华洛世奇集团旗下还包括：

Tyrolit（1919）-世界领先的黏合磨削、切割、锯切、钻孔和修整工具制造商之一，以及建筑行业工具和机器的系统供应商。

Optik（1949）-开发和制造市场上高精度的远程光学仪器，如双筒望远镜、定位镜、步枪瞄准镜和光电仪器等。

Swareflex（1950）-开发和生产反射光学元件，用于道路安全和光导。

品牌战略

施华洛世奇作为全球首屈一指的精确切割仿水晶制造商，通过其出色的营销策略，不断扩展到珠宝和时装领域，瞄准更广泛的受众。

与社交媒体影响者合作是其成功的策略之一，包括邀请模特米兰达·可儿、卡莉·克劳斯担任品牌形象大使，以及赞助时尚博主Melissa Koh（其Instagram帐户上拥有大约

① 丹尼尔·施华洛世奇（1862—1956）出生于波希米亚北部（现捷克共和国），年轻时在其父亲的小型玻璃厂学习并掌握了玻璃切割技术。

图7-18 施华洛世奇Swarovski品牌广告

234000名粉丝）的婚礼等，以更具创意与现代性的基调展现品牌内容，吸引年轻消费群体。同时，该品牌也致力于成为领先的时尚品牌，与香奈儿、迪奥和维多利亚的秘密等品牌维持长期的合作关系。

施华洛世奇密切关注零售体验，结合口碑传播和数字互动，开展迎合时下潮流且具有针对性的营销活动。通过数字化建立更广泛的网络，以在线对话推动线下店铺销售，比如联合新加坡IH Digital发布情人节宣传视频，激励线上用户将施华洛世奇作为其礼物的首选。另外，其还于2018年在伦敦牛津街推出数字零售技术的新店铺“先行者”Forerunner，使用AR试穿技术和交互式自拍墙等数字功能，旨在增加互动和停留时间。获得成功后，2019年在中国成都的远洋太古里购物中心开设了第二家概念店。

图7-19 与维多利亚的秘密合作产品

品牌历史

1892—丹尼尔·施华洛世奇发明的切割含铅玻璃水晶的电动切割打磨机器获得专利。

1895—施华洛世奇在阿尔芒·柯斯曼和弗朗茨·魏斯的资助下，创立A. Kosman, Daniel Swartz&Co.（K.S. &Co）。

图7-20 1956年施华洛世奇与克里斯汀·迪奥合作创新的水晶涂层耳环

1899—将雪绒花作为其徽标的元素，并将业务扩展到法国。

1956—与克里斯汀·迪奥（Christian Dior）合作创新的水晶涂层。

1962—玛丽莲·梦露穿着贴满10,000个施华洛世奇水晶的连衣裙为美国总统约翰·肯尼迪(John F. Kennedy)献唱。

图7-21 1962年玛丽莲·梦露穿着贴满施华洛世奇水晶的连衣裙献唱

1974—开发了Hotfix技术，允许将晶体直接固定在衣服和织物上。

1977—进入美国珠宝市场。

1989—其标志从雪绒花变为天鹅。

1995—知名的多媒体艺术家Andre Heller设计名为“Kristallwelten”（水晶世界）的互动体验。

图7-22 1995年知名媒体艺术家Andre Heller设计的水晶世界

图7-23 2008年“水晶森林”的门店形象设计

2007—推出了高级定制水晶配饰系列Atelier Swarovski，并与时尚、珠宝和建筑领域的人士合作推出创新设计，包括Karl Lagerfeld, Maison Martin Margiela, Viktor & Rolf和Joseph Altuzarra等。

2008—“水晶森林”的门店形象设计应用于世界各地的商店中。

Swarovski

Brand Introduction

In 1895, Swarovski was born in Austria and always adhered to the vision of its founder Daniel Swarovski (1862—1956) to create a “diamond” for everyone. After more than 120 years of development, Swarovski has become an internationally renowned jewellery and accessories brand, and has built a multi-billion dollar company with top-quality crystal cutting technology, with approximately 2,800 stores in nearly 170 countries.

As the world's largest manufacturer of crystal cutting, Swarovski is known for its imitated crystal jewellery, including necklaces, earrings, bracelets, rings and brooches, as well as watches, decorative ornaments, and fashion accessories like sunglasses, hair accessories and handbags. In addition to the most business-oriented crystal imitated business unit, the Swarovski Group also includes:

Tyrdit (1919) - One of the world's leading manufacturers of bonded grinding, cutting, sawing, drilling and dressing tools, as well as a system supplier of tools and machines for the construction industry.

Optik(1949)-Develop and manufacture high-precision remote optical instruments such as binoculars, spotting scopes, rifle scopes and photoelectric instruments.

Swareflex(1950)-Develop and produce the reflective optics for road safety and light guides.

Brand Strategy

As the world's leading manufacturer of precision-cut imitated crystals, Swarovski continues to expand into the jewellery and fashion sector with its marketing strategy to reach a wider audience.

Collaborating with social media influencers is one of its successful strategies, including inviting models Miranda Kerr and Karlie Kloss as the brand ambassadors, and sponsoring the fashion blogger Melissa Koh's wedding, etc. The tone of creativity and modernity reveals brand content and appeals to young consumers. At the same time, the brand is also committed to becoming a leading fashion brand, maintaining long-term cooperative relationships with brands such as Chanel, Christian Dior and Victoria's Secret.

Swarovski pays close attention to the retail experience, combining word-of-mouth communication and digital interaction to develop targeted marketing campaigns that cater to current trends. It digitally build a broader network and promote offline store sales through online conversations, such as the launch of Valentine's Day promotional videos with IH Digital of Singapore, to encourage online users to choose Swarovski as the preferred choice. In addition, in 2018, the new store "Forerunner", which launched digital retail technology in Oxford Street, London, used AR try-on technology and interactive self-portrait wall to increase interactions. After the success, in 2019, the second concept store was opened at Sino-Ocean Taikoo Li in Chengdu, China.

Brand History

1892—Daniel Swarovski patented the machine for perfectly cutting jewelry stones.

1895—Swarovski founded A. Kosman, Daniel Swartz & Co. (K.S. & Co) with the funding from Armand Kosman and Franz Weis.

1899—Used edelweiss as an element of its logo and extend the business to France.

1956—Collaborated with Christian Dior, creating an innovative crystal coating "Aurora Bo - realis Effect".

1962—Marilyn Monroe sang to President John F. Kennedy in a dress covered in 10,000 Swarovski crystals.

1974—The Hotfix technology was developed to allow the crystal to be attached directly to clothing and fabric.

1977—Entered the US jewelry market.

1989—Its logo was changed from edelweiss to swan.

1995—The well-known multimedia artist Andre Heller designed the interactive experi - ence called "Kristallwelten".

2007—Introduced the high-end custom crystal accessories Atelier Swarovski, and collab - orated with people in the fashion, jewelry and construction sectors to launch innovative de - signs, including Karl Lagerfeld, Maison Martin Margiela, Viktor & Rolf and Joseph Altuzarra.

2008—"Crystal Forest"interior design was implemented in stores worldwide.

蒂芙尼 Tiffany & Co.

品牌简介

扫一扫

TIFFANY & CO.

图7-24　蒂芙尼品牌logo

蒂芙尼是最具标志性的奢侈珠宝品牌之一，其总部位于美国纽约。以1837年查尔斯·刘易斯·蒂芙尼和约翰·B.扬成立的文具饰品店为起点，蒂芙尼以其创新设计与精致匠心，逐渐演化为象征美国设计的知名品牌，蒂芙尼蓝色礼盒和六爪镶嵌钻戒已成为其经典标志。

图7-25　蒂芙尼产品系列

蒂芙尼以珠宝、钻石首饰和纯银制品而闻名。其于1951年制定了925纯银标准，并在1867年的巴黎世界博览会上获得优质银器奖。除了永久展览于第五大道旗舰店重达287.42克拉的“蒂芙尼传奇黄钻”外，蒂芙尼还先后发现并推出了kunzite紫锂辉石（1903）、摩根石（1910）、坦桑石（1968）和沙弗莱宝石（1974）。同时，蒂芙尼被委任制作多个赛事的奖杯，包括NFL超级碗奖杯和NBA总冠军奖杯等。

该品牌出售品种繁多且设计独特的个人配件、定制产品及手工制品，包括高级珠宝、婚戒、腕表、家居用品、香水和皮具等。

品牌战略

蒂芙尼以其强大而积极的促销政策创造了广泛的品牌影响力。1845年的“蒂芙尼蓝皮书”，作为其首个产品邮购目录就是广告策略的一部分，该目录的订阅人数在1994年达到了1500万。此外，蒂芙尼还在众多平台上进行广告投放，包括传统纸质出版物，如《名利场》杂志；还有新兴的移动端软件，纽约时报的App中就曾出现过免费下载蒂芙尼应用程序的广告窗口。

蒂芙尼也使用社交媒体平台与客户直接联系，其Facebook和Twitter帐户分别拥有1000万和160万粉丝，官方网站详尽地提供了品牌各方面的信息。该品牌最近推出Engagement Ring Finder移动应用程序是其制订的在线营销策略，以突破在实体店购买订婚戒指的局限，目的在于将消费者的购物情感和体验带入数字时代。

品牌历史

1837—首家蒂芙尼门店在纽约开业。区别于同时代的其他商店，蒂芙尼明码标价且只接受现金支付。

1845—发布美国境内首个邮购目录，被称为“蒂芙尼蓝皮书”。

1886—推出Tiffany Setting六爪镶嵌钻戒，成为日后熟知的订婚戒指。

1902—查尔斯·刘易斯·蒂芙尼（Charles Lewis Tiffany）的儿子路易斯·康福特·蒂芙尼（Louis Comfort Tiffany）成为首位设计总监。

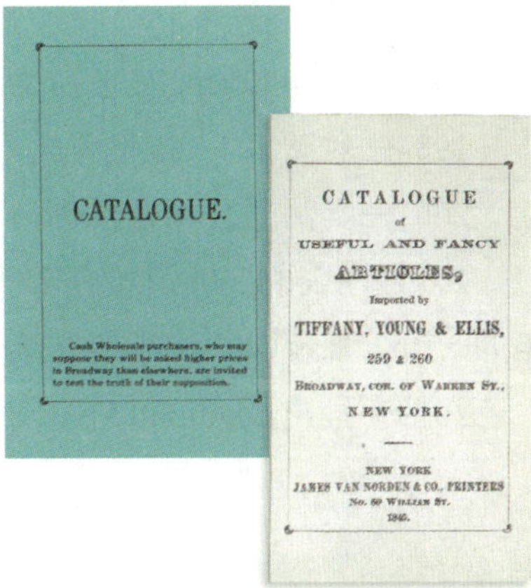

图7-26 蒂芙尼蓝皮书

图7-27　Tiffany Setting六爪镶嵌钻戒

图7-28　《蒂芙尼的早餐》剧照

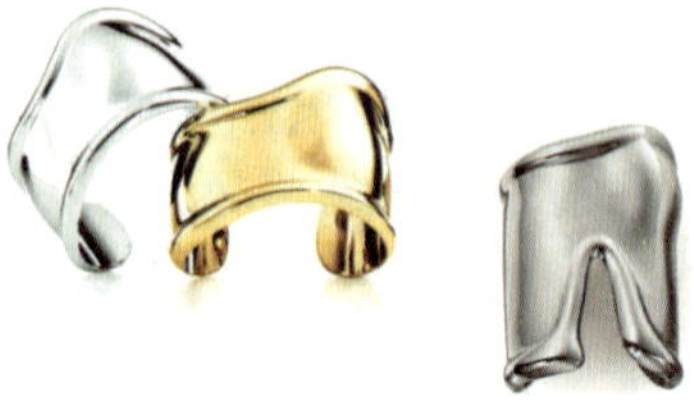

图7-29　Elsa Peretti代表作

1956—设计师Jean Schlumberger加入蒂芙尼。

1961—蒂芙尼在奥黛丽·赫本主演的《蒂芙尼的早餐》中首次亮相大银幕。

1974—Elsa Peretti加入蒂芙尼，融入雕塑般的美感与现代性。

1978—蒂芙尼公司以约1.04亿美元的股票出售给雅芳产品公司。

图7-30　蒂芙尼香水系列

1979—John Loring被任命为设计总监，塑造了其随后四十年的设计传承。

1984—雅芳以1.355亿美元现金将蒂芙尼卖给了威廉·R.钱宁领导的投资集团。

2001—与潘通公司合作创造了“1837蓝”，以致敬标志性的蒂芙尼蓝色调。

2017—Reed Krakoff被任命为蒂芙尼艺术总监，并推出家居精品系列和香水系列；同年The Blue Box Café咖啡店在第五大道开业。

2019—推出Diamond Source Initiative计划，提供开采钻石的出处信息。

Tiffany & Co.

Brand Introduction

Tiffany & Co. (commonly known as Tiffany), based in New York, USA, is one of the most iconic luxury jewellery brands. Starting with the stationery store established by Charles Lewis Tiffany and John B. Young in 1837, Tiffany has evolved into a well-known brand of American design with its innovative design and exquisite craftsmanship. The Tiffany Blue Box and The Tiffany Six-Prong Ring have become its classic symbol.

Tiffany is known for its jewellery, diamond and sterling silver products. It was the first American company to adopt the British silver standard of using only metal that was 92% pure in 1951. In addition to the permanent exhibition of the 287.42-carat Tiffany Legendary Yellow Diamond on the Fifth Avenue flagship store, Tiffany has also discovered and launched kunzite, the purple spodumene (1903), Morganite (1910), Tanzanite (1968) and Shafley Gems (1974). At the same time, Tiffany has been commissioned to produce trophies for multiple events, including the NFL Super Bowl and the NBA Championship Trophy.

It sells a wide range of uniquely designed personal, custom and handmade products, including fine jewellery, wedding rings, watches, household items, perfumes and leather goods.

Brand Strategy

Tiffany's strong and aggressive promotional policies are used to create a wide range of brand influences. The "Tiffany Blue Book" of 1845, whose first mail-order catalogue was part of the advertising strategy, reached 15 million subscribers in 1994. In addition, Tiffany also advertises in many places, including magazines such as *Vanity Fair* and *New York Times*, as well as online platforms such as the Tiffany app ad banner downloaded for free in the mobile app of New York Times .

Tiffany also uses the social media platform to directly contact customers. Its Facebook and Twitter accounts have 10 million and 1.6 million fans respectively, and the official website provides detailed information on all aspects of the brand. The launching of Engagement Ring Finder mobile app is an online marketing strategy to break through the limitations of buying engagement rings in off-line stores, with the goal of bringing consumers' shopping sentiments and experiences into the digital age.

Brand History

1837—The first Tiffany store opened in New York. Different from other stores of the same generation, Tiffany marked the price clearly and only accepts cash.

1845—The first mail-order catalogue in the United States was published, known as the "Tiffany Blue Book".

1886—Introduced the Tiffany Six-Prong Ring, becoming an engagement ring that is well known later.

1902—Louis Comfort Tiffany, the son of Charles Lewis Tiffany, became the first design director.

1956—Designer Jean Schlumberger joined Tiffany.

1961—Tiffany debuted on the big screen in *Breakfast at Tiffany's* starring Audrey Hepburn.

1974—Elsa Peretti joined Tiffany and incorporates sculptural beauty and modernity.

1978—Tiffany & Co. sold the company to Avon Products with approximately $104 million in stock.

1979—John Loring was appointed as the design director, shaping the design for the next forty years.

1984—Avon sold Tiffany to the investment group led by William R. Chaney for $135.5 million in cash.

2001—In cooperation with Pantone, it created "1837 Blue" to pay tribute to the iconic Tiffany Blue color.

2017—Reed Krakoff was appointed as the Art Director of Tiffany. It launched collections of home collections and fragrances, the Blue Box Café opening its flagship store on Fifth Avenue in the same year.

2019—Launched of the Diamond Source Initiative program, providing the provenance information of diamond mining.

爱马仕 Hermès

品牌简介

爱马仕（Hermès）是法国著名奢侈品牌，由蒂埃里·爱马仕（1801—1878）成立于1837年的马具制作工作室发展而来。该工作室位于巴黎的林荫大道（Grands Boulevards），致力于为欧洲贵族提供服务。预见到汽车技术的发展，爱马仕开始将事业的重心转移到皮夹及包袋的生产，并且凭借其精湛的工艺和卓越的品质，不断推出独特的奢华产品，保持以产品为中心的高端市场定位的同时，加强了品牌的差异化。

图7-31 品牌logo

皮具和马术用品是爱马仕如今最主要的业务，其他产品类别还包括成衣、丝巾配饰、首饰、钟表、香水和鞋履等。另外，该集团旗下还拥有多个子品牌，如图7-32可见。

作为家族企业，自成立以来爱马仕家族始终保持对品牌业务的经营与维护，并严格控制分销和特许经营权，通过全球311家门店进行产品的销售，其中207家由该公司直接拥有和经营。

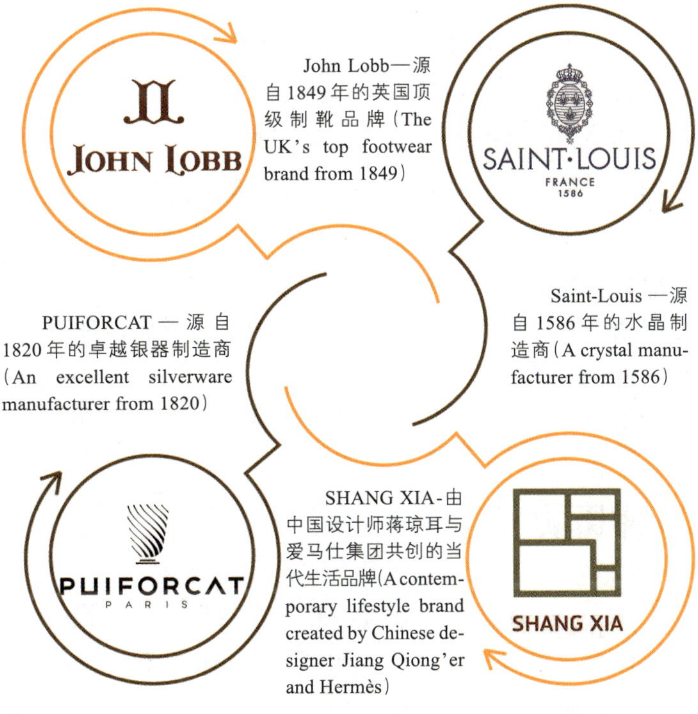

图7-32 爱马仕品牌一览表

品牌战略

爱马仕前首席执行官帕特里克·托马斯曾评论说："奢侈品行业建立在一个悖论上：品牌越是受欢迎，销售的越多；但销售的越多，它就会变得不太理想。"他的评论完全体现了爱马仕这一品牌所遵循的排他性和稀缺性战略。爱马仕始终坚守超豪华细分市场，而非大众奢侈品市场，其产品和服务只为极少数人提供且不易获得，推出限量版和限制其产品在其商店中的分销是其举措之一，比如购买经典铂金包Birkin必须进行预订且须排队等候。

图7-33 爱马仕线上商店界面

如今爱马仕已经创造了60亿美元的业务，但并未设立营销部门，而是聘请专业团队进行媒体管理和创意活动策划，且其营销支出低于行业标准。其品牌传播和营销策略始终与公司的传统和排他性原则保持一致，并非将直接销售产品作为推广目的。该公司致力于赞助与公司形象和传统密切相关的活动，比如赞助世界各地众多赛马赛事，展示其精致皮革产品及其与马术运动的历史渊源，以在目标消费者群体中创造知名度。

除了在电视、平面广告、在线广告等方面投入大量资金，推广不同的系列外，爱马仕还积极使用内容营销，利用社交媒体的力量，比如近期推出的在线弹出式虚拟商店，专门用于销售品牌的围巾类产品，展示了600多种爱马仕标志性丝巾模型，同时提供在线点击购买服务。

品牌历史

1837—蒂埃里·爱马仕在巴黎的林荫大道开设了马具工作室。

1880—爱马仕的儿子查尔斯-埃米尔·爱马仕接管了工作室，并将商店搬至巴黎的圣路易斯堡街24号，至今仍然是品牌的全球总部。

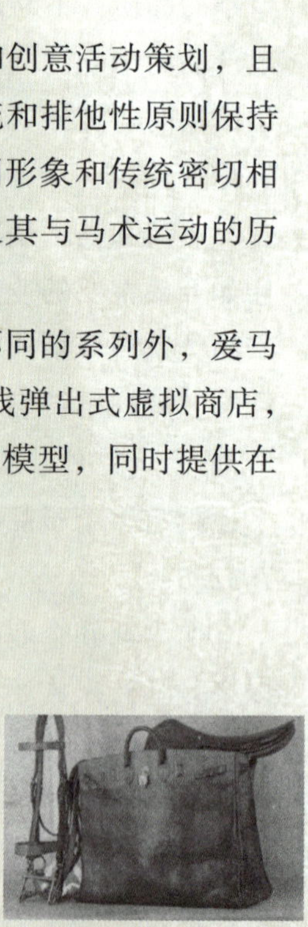

图7-34 爱马仕
Haut a courroies bag

1900—推出Haut a courroies bag，是其最古老的包型，可供骑手携带马鞍或其他随身用品。

1918—推出了第一款带拉链的皮革高尔夫夹克，为当时的威尔士亲王制作。

1927—推出首款手表。随后积极拓展其产品线，并在美国纽约开设第一家海外专卖店。

图7-35 Apple Watch Hermès系列

1937—爱马仕推出的丝巾随着杰奎琳·肯尼迪等名人的使用而备受瞩目。

1950s—香水部门成立，并开始使用马车标志和经典橙色礼盒。

1970s—建立手表子公司La Montre Hermès，并与英国制鞋品牌John Lobb签订协议以扩大该品牌的分销范围。

图7-36 爱马仕经典橙色礼盒

1980s—收购了Puiforcat，Saint Louis和Perigord等餐具制造商。

1997—进入中国并迅速将其网络扩展到覆盖中国15个城市的22家门店。

1999—爱马仕购买了Jean-Paul Gaultier时装店35%的股份。

2012—合作推出中国奢侈品牌“上下”。

2015—与美国科技公司Apple合作推出Apple Watch Hermès系列。

扫一扫

经典包袋

图7-37 爱马仕凯莉包

图7-38 爱马仕康康包

1935—凯莉包，起初被称为Sac a Depach，这一款原为狩猎者设计的马鞍袋，因摩纳哥王妃葛莉丝·凯莉的使用成为爱马仕皮具系列中的常青树。其皮革材质超过30种，其售价从7500美元至25000美元不等。

1959—康康包，由设计师凯瑟琳·柴利勒以其女儿康斯坦茨（Constance）的名字命名，使用了醒目的H形金属配件。

1984—铂金包，这款手提包以英国歌手简·柏金命名，其售价是7500美元。

图7-39 爱马仕铂金包

Hermès

Brand Introduction

Hermès is a famous French luxury brand, developed from a harness production studio which established by Thierry Hermès(1801–1878)in 1837 in Grands Boulevards, Paris, which is dedicated to serving European nobility. Foreseeing the development of automotive technology, Hermès began to shift the focus of its business to the production of wallets and bags, and with its exquisite craftsmanship and excellent quality, it constantly launched unique luxury products to maintain a high-end market positioning centered on products while strengthening brand differentiation.

Leather goods and equestrian supplies are Hermès's main business nowadays. Other product categories include ready-to-wear, silk scarves, jewelry, watches, perfumes and shoes. In addition, the group also has multiple sub–brands.

As a family business, the Hermès family has always maintained its operation and maintenance of the brand business since its inception, strictly controlled distribution and franchise rights, and sold its products through 311 stores worldwide, 207 of which are directly owned and operated by the company.

Brand Strategy

Former CEO Patrick Thomas once commented, "The luxury industry is built on a paradox: the more desirable the brand becomes, the more it sells; but the more it sells, the less desirable it becomes." His comment entirely encapsulates the strategy of exclusivity and scarcity that Hermès follows for its brand. Hermès has always adhered to the ultra–luxury segment market insted of the mass luxury market. Its products and services are only available to very few people and are not readily available. It is one of the initiatives to launch limited editions and limit the distribution of their products in their stores, for example, the classic Birkin must be booked before buying and consumers must queue up.

Today, Hermès has established a $6 billion business, but has not set up a marketing department. Instead, it hires a professional team to conduct media management and event planning, and its marketing expenses are lower than industry standards. Its brand communication and marketing strategy are consistent with the company's tradition and exclusivity principles, and it do not treat direct sales of products as promotional purposes. The company is committed to sponsoring events that are closely related to the company's image and tradition, such as sponsoring numerous horse racing events around the world, showcasing its fine leather products and its historical origins with equestrian sports to create its popularity in the target consumer community.

In addition to investing heavily in TV, print advertising, online advertising, etc., to promot the different product series, it also actively uses content marketing to harness the power of social media, such as the recently launched online pop-up virtual store, which is dedicated to scarves, containing more than 600 Hermès iconic silk scarves and offering an online click-to-buy service.

Brand History

1837—Thierry Hermès opened a harness studio on the Grands Boulevards in Paris.

1880—Hermès's son Charles-Émile Hermès took over the studio and moved the store to 24 Rue Faubourg Saint-Honore, Paris, and it remains its global headquarters up to now.

1900—Introduced the Haut a courroies bag, the oldest bag type for riders to carry saddles or other personal belongings.

1918—Launched the first leather golf jacket with a zipper for the Prince of Wales.

1927—Launched the first watch. Subsequently, it actively expanded its product line and opened its first overseas specialty store in New York, USA.

1937—The scarves launched by Hermès have attracted attention with the use of celebrities such as Jacqueline Kennedy.

1950s—The perfume department was established and began to use the logo, a Duc carriage with horse, and the classic orange gift box.

1970s—Established watch subsidiary La Montre Hermès and signed an agreement with British shoe brand John Lobb to expand the brand's distribution.

1980s—Purchased tableware manufacturers such as Puiforcat, Saint Louis and Perigord.

1997—Entered China and quickly expanded its network to cover 22 stores in 15 cities across China.

1999—Hermès purchased a 35% stake in the Jean-Paul Gaultier boutique.

2012—Cooperated to launch Chinese luxury brands "Shang Xia".

2015—Cooperated with American technology company Apple to launch the Apple Watch Hermès.

Classic Bags

1935—Kelly Bag, formerly known as Sac a Depach, is a saddle bag originally designed for hunters, and has become a classic design in the Hermès leather collection due to the use of Grace Kelly, the Princess of Monaco. Its leather material is available in over 30 options, which range in price from $7,500 to $25,000.

1959—Constance bag, with a H-shaped fastenethe, is named after Constance, the daughter of designer Catherine Chaillet.

1984—Birkin, named after the British singer Jane Birkin, starts at $7,500.

路易·威登 Louis Vuitton

“每天，全球各地的宾客都会踏入精品店，找寻一些只有Louis Vuitton才能呈现的独特佳作。正是这种激情促使Louis Vuitton不断开拓，将品牌创始人最初的创业之旅转变为一段辉煌的冒险征程，时至今日，这段传奇仍在继续，并且每日都在不断发展。”

——麦克·伯尔克，路易·威登首席执行官

品牌简介

路易·威登始于旅行的理念，由路易·威登先生(Louis Vuitton Matellier)[①]于1854年在巴黎创立，被视为奢侈品中最有价值的品牌之一。现隶属于奢侈品酩悦·轩尼诗-路易·威登集团（Louis Vuitton Moët Hennessy，即LVMH），总部位于法国巴黎香榭丽舍大道。该品牌在全球60多个国家开展业务，开设500余家门店，包括洛杉矶、迪拜、拉斯维加斯、纽约、巴黎和东京等城市。

图7-40 路易·威登品牌logo

品牌自创立之初便不断发展箱包制造这一主业，并同时拓展皮具、锁具和板箱制造等辅助工艺。于1997年开始相继推出女士与男士系列，正式成为一个“时尚品牌”，广泛涉及皮具、成衣、配饰、鞋履、腕表和珠宝等多个领域。现任设计团队集结了女装创意总监Nicolas Ghesquière、男装创意总监Virgil Abloh和珠宝腕表艺术总监Francesca Amfitheatrof。

除了路易·威登经典的标志性印花Monogram和Damier帆布系列外，品牌发展历史上相继推出的产品或产品系列还包括：

扫一扫

① Louis Vuitton Matellier(1821—1892)出生于法国。1837年，16岁的路易·威登成为Monsieur Marechal工坊的一名硬箱工匠，仅在几年内，凭借其创新工艺在巴黎业界赢得了声誉。

1924—Keepall，轻型防水旅行箱包
1932—Noé 手提袋，用于携带香槟
1934—Alma 阿尔玛包，最初为可可·香奈儿女士设计
1966—Papillon 手袋由 Henri Racamier 设计
1985—第一个皮革系列 Epi 系列问世
1993—采用黑色真皮 Taiga 系列箱包

图7-41　经典产品1

图7-42 经典产品2

品牌战略

路易威登不断呈上升趋势的盈利能力，一方面在于该品牌始终致力于提升其实力，推出个性化和定制产品设计的同时，还预留生产材料以便为客户提供修护产品服务，获得客户忠诚度。另一方面则来自其有效的营销计划，在Vogue，Elle和InStyle等时尚杂志投放商业平面广告，邀请Jennifer Lopez，Kate Moss，Scarlett Johansson和Uma Thurman

等知名演员出任形象大使并参演广告，并且积极参与大型体育赛事的赞助。

图7-43　路易·威登与Supreme合作产品

路易·威登营销策略的独特之处还在于其并没有将奢侈品与排他性等同起来。通过其传承的独特美学，借助社交资源的凝聚力和互联性，鼓励大众熟悉品牌及其故事，为目标客户创造吸引力，提升参与度和引导其做出购买决策。路易·威登拥有多个社交媒体账户，包括Facebook，Twitter，Instagram，Pinterest和YouTube，发布的内容包括时装发布会、广告活动、促销活动、商店开业以及穿戴其产品的知名博主的相关信息。基于此，路易·威登利用互联网流量，发布互动活动以实现最佳目标：让人们感受到与品牌的联系。

路易·威登鲜明的品牌形象源于其自身发展中实现的长期愿景，坚持标志性系列的开发和更新，比如Monogram经典产品和旅行艺术理念等。同时，品牌与知名艺术家开展合作推出限量版系列，如与Jeff Koons，Takashi Murakami和Pharrell Williams等合作；与美国街头品牌Supreme合作，在世界各主要城市的快闪商店发布产品；开发运动鞋等现代产品。这些举措并未稀释品牌，而是有助于实现多元化发展，并有效地与年轻的消费者建立联系。路易·威登仍被视为世界上最负盛名的奢侈品牌。

近年来，路易·威登一直在积极升级其为中国消费者提供的产品与服务，从降低大陆价格到扩大其在中国的电子商务范围等方面不断升级，如在2012年成为首个开设微信服务账户的奢侈品牌。为与本土目标受众建立情感联系，除了邀请中国明星作为形象大使外，还于2018年在上海展览中心举办由Olivier Saillard策划的《飞行 航行 旅行——路易·威登》展览，追溯品牌自1854年创立至今的辉煌历史。

图7-44　路易·威登运动鞋

图7-45　“飞行 航行 旅行——路易·威登”展览

品牌历史

1854——路易·威登在法国巴黎的卡普西尼街创立了路易·威登品牌。

1858——路易·威登对当时凸面的行李箱进行改良，推出 Trianon Trunk，一款便于叠放的平顶箱。

1876——路易·威登开发了条纹图案帆布 Rayée Canvas。

1888——路易·威登的儿子乔治·威登(Georges Vuitton)推出棋盘格图案帆布 Damier Canvas。

1892——乔治·威登接管公司，旨在将路易·威登发展为全球品牌，开始推出手提包产品，并发行了第一份产品名录。

1893——路易·威登参加在美国芝加哥举办的世界博览会，正式登陆美国。

1896——路易·威登正式推出了具有品牌标识功能的帆布设计——LV Monogram 帆布。

1946——为了抵制第二次世界大战后经济萧条的局面，路易·威登开始涉足箱包设计外其他领域的投资。

1987——路易·威登公司和轩尼诗公司合并组成酩悦·轩尼诗－路易·威登集团，正式成为跨越箱包、名酒的奢侈品牌。

1992——路易·威登在北京开设第一家分店。

1997——品牌新任创意总监马克·雅克布斯推出首个女装成衣系列。

2013——尼古拉·盖斯奇埃尔开始担任路易·威登的创意总监。

图7-46 Trianon Trunk 平顶箱

图7-47 Damier Canvas 印花

图7-48 Monogram 印花

Louis Vuitton

“Each day, all over the world, our customers enter our stores in search of something truly extraordinary, something that Louis Vuitton has a unique ability to offer. This enthusiasm inspires Louis Vuitton to constantly go further, transforming its founders’ initial journey into a great adventure that continues and gains momentum every day.”

——Michael Burke, CEO of Louis Vuitton

Brand Introduction

Louis Vuitton, beginning with the philosophy of travel, was found by Louis Vuitton Matellier in Paris in 1854 and was considered one of the most valuable brands in luxury. Now it is part of Louis Vuitton Moët Hennessy (LVMH), headquartering in Avenue des Champs-Elysées, Paris. The brand operates in more than 60 countries around the world, opening more than 500 stores, including Los Angeles, Dubai, Las Vegas, New York, Paris and Tokyo.

Since its inception, the brand has continued to develop the main business of luggage manufacturing, and at the same time has expanded the auxiliary processes such as leather goods, locks and crates. Since 1997, the women's and men's collections have been launched, and it has officially become a "fashion brand", covering a wide range of fields including leather goods, ready-to-wear, accessories, shoes, watches and jewelry. The current design team has assembled women's creative director Nicolas Ghesquièire, menswear creative director Virgil Abloh and jewelry-watch art director Francesca Amfitheatrof.

Brand Strategy

Louis Vuitton continues to show an upward trend in profitability. On the one hand, the brand is always striving to enhance its strength, launching personalized and customized product designs, while also reserving production materials to provide customers with repair services to obtain customer loyalty. On the other hand, it comes from its effective marketing plan, launching commercial print ads in fashion magazines such as Vogue, Elle and InStyle, and inviting well-known actors such as Jennifer Lopez, Kate Moss, Scarlett Johansson and Uma Thurman to serve as the ambassadors and participate in campagin. In addition, Louis Vuitton actively participates in sponsorship of major sports events.

Louis Vuitton's marketing strategy is unique in that it does not equate luxury with exclusivity. Through its unique aesthetics, cohesiveness and interconnectivity of social resources, the public is encouraged to become familiar with the brand. It creates attractiveness to target coustomers, enhance their participation and guide the purchasing decisions. Louis Vuitton has multiple social media accounts, including Facebook, Twitter, Instagram, Pinterest and YouTube, and publishes content including the information of fashion shows, advertising campaigns, promotions, store openings, and well-known bloggers who wear their products. Based on this, it use Internet traffic to publish interactive activities to achieve the best goal: to make people feel connected with the brand.

Louis Vuitton's distinctive brand image stems from its long-term vision of its own development, adhering to the development and renewal of iconic collections such as Monogram classics and travel art concepts. At the same time, it cooperated with famous artists to launch limited edition series, such as Jeff Koons, Takashi Murakami and Pharrell Williams; in cooperation with American street brand Supreme, it released products in flash stores in major cities around the world; it developed modern products such as sports shoes. These initiatives do not dilute the brand, but help to achieve diversification and effectively connect with young consumers. Louis Vuitton is still considered to be the most prestigious luxury brand in the world.

In recent years, Louis Vuitton has been actively upgrading its products and services for Chinese consumers, from lowering mainland prices to expanding its e-commerce coverage in China, such as becoming the first luxury brand to open a WeChat service account in 2012. In order to establish emotional connections with local target audiences, in addition to inviting Chinese stars as the ambassadors, in 2018, at the Shanghai Exhibition Center, "VOLEZ VOGUEZ VOYAGEZ—Louis Vuitton" curated by Olivier Saillard was held to show its glorious history since 1854.

Brand History

1854—Louis Vuitton Malletier founded Louis Vuitton on Rue Neuve des Capucines in Paris, France.

1858—Louis Vuitton improved the convex luggage at the time and launched the Trianon Trunk, a flat-top box that is easy to stack.

1876—Louis Vuitton Introduced the striped pattern Rayée Canvas.

1888—Louis Vuitton's son, George Vuitton, introduced the checkerboad pattern Damier Canvas.

1892—George Vuitton took over the company, aiming to develop Louis Vuitton into a global brand, launching handbags and its first product list.

1893—Louis Vuitton participated in the World Expo held in Chicago, USA, officially landing in the United States.

1896—Louis Vuitton officially launched the canvas design with brand marking function, the LV Monogram canvas.

1946—In order to resist the economic depression after the Second World War, Louis Vuitton began to invest in other areas outside the design of luggage.

1987—Louis Vuitton and Hennessy merge to form Louis Vuitton Moët Hennessy, officially becoming a luxury brand that covers bags and wines.

1992—Louis Vuitton opened its first branch in Beijing.

1997—New creative director Marc Jacobs launched the first women's ready-to-wear collection.

2013—Nicolas Ghesquière became the creative director of Louis Vuitton.

克里斯提·鲁布托 Christian Louboutin

扫一扫

品牌简介

克里斯提·鲁布托（Christian Louboutin）是最具辨识度的鞋履奢侈品牌之一，1992年在法国巴黎创立。该品牌以采用红色鞋底而闻名，成功地将曾经被忽视的鞋底设计转变为标志性的象征。如今，克里斯提·鲁布托在全球超过35个国家约150家百货商店和自有品牌精品店出售其鞋履，年销售量超过一百万双。其产品也可通过其官方网站和Net-a-Porter等线上高端零售商进行购买。

2012年，克里斯提·鲁布托第一家男士鞋履商店于纽约开业，以推出一系列男式鞋履来拓展其产品线。同时，品牌开始进军包袋市场，还于2012年推出奢侈品美妆系列，包括指甲油（2012）、口红（2015）、香水（2016）等产品。

图7-49 品牌logo

图7-50 奢侈品美妆系列

图7-51 男式鞋履

图7-52 产品系列

品牌战略

从经典设计到装饰铆钉的高跟鞋，克里斯提·鲁布托的系列鞋履收获了麦当娜、妮可·基德曼、迪塔·冯·蒂斯和布莱克·莱弗利等一众名人粉丝。从红毯到晚宴活动，其鞋履已成为奢侈品的代名词。同时，与流行文化保持联系，如2012年受邀为迪士尼电影《灰姑娘》设计限量发行的水晶鞋，以及2017年为电影《星球大战：最后绝地武士》打造的特别鞋履。

图7-53 《星球大战：最后绝地武士》特别鞋履

图7-54 克里斯提·鲁布托香港限定概念店

克里斯提·鲁布托开展活跃的数字化活动。其精心策划的品牌社交账户Instagram通过发布优质内容，吸引超过1200万粉丝，发起的#LouboutinWorld#话题使其在2015年赢得了Footwear News的年度营销大奖。此外，Louboutinize于2012年推出的跨媒体应用程序，可以让用户快速查找商店，观看品牌视频和产品系列，并鼓励用户加上#Louboutinize标签，把Louboutinize内的照片分享至Facebook，Instagram和Twitter等社交媒体平台。同时，Louboutin也注重提升消费者线下的购物体验，比如2019年3月，在香港开设独家限定概念店以庆祝Run Loubi Run系列登陆亚洲，其整体红色的设计与创意互动装置，充分体现了品牌的创意世界。

品牌创始人

鞋履设计师克里斯提·鲁布托于1963年出生在法国巴黎。他的设计使得高跟鞋在20世纪90年代和21世纪初再次流行，他相信他设计的高跟鞋“能使女性看起来更加性感与美丽，并且能够尽可能拉长其腿部线条”。

图7-55 克里斯提·鲁布托

鲁布托于1982年开始从事鞋履设计，并以自由设计师的身份先后为香奈儿、伊夫·圣罗兰和罗杰·维维尔工作。20世纪90年代初，他创立了属于自己的高端鞋履品牌，于1992年在法国巴黎开设了第一家鞋店。品牌的首批顾客之一是摩纳哥的卡罗琳公主，她对鲁布托高跟鞋的公开赞美极大地提升了品牌的知名度。1993年，鲁布托将红色鞋底引入其鞋履设计中，成功开辟了该品牌在高端制鞋行业的独特利基市场。如今，具有闪亮的红漆鞋底的女士极细高跟鞋Sammy Red Soled Shoes已成为该品牌的经典。

Christian Louboutin

Brand Introduction

Christian Louboutin is one of the most recognizable footwear luxury brands, founded in 1992 in Paris, France. The brand is known for its red soles, which has successfully transformed sole design once neglected into a symbol. Today, Christian Louboutin sells its shoes in about 150 department stores and private label boutiques in over 35 countries around the world, selling more than one million pairs a year. Its products are also available through its official website and online high-end retailers such as Net-a-Porter.

In 2012, Christian Louboutin's first men's footwear store opened in New York to expand its product line. At the same time, the brand began to enter the bag market, and in 2012 launched the luxury beauty collection, including nail polish (2012), lipstick (2015), perfume (2016) and other products.

Brand Strategy

From classic design to decorative studded high heels, Christian Louboutin's shoes has won celebrity fans such as Madonna, Nicole Kidman, Dita Von Teese and Blake Lively. From the red carpet to the dinner event, its shoes have become synonymous with luxury goods. At the same time, it keeps in touch with popular culture, such as the limited edition crystal shoes designed for the Disney movie *Cinderella* in 2012, and the special shoes for the movie *Star*

Wars: The Last Jedi in 2017.

Christian Louboutin conducts an active digital campaign. His well-planned brand social account, Instagram, has attracted more than 12 million fans by publishing premium content, and the "#LouboutinWorld" launched in 2015 has won Footwear News' annual marketing award. In addition, the cross-media app launched in 2012 allows users to quickly find stores, watch branded videos and product lines, and encourage users to add "#Louboutinize" tags to share photos from Louboutinize to social media like Facebook, Instagram and Twitter. At the same time, Louboutin also focuses on improving the offline shopping experience of consumers. For example, in March 2019, an exclusive limited concept store was opened in Hong Kong to celebrate the Run Loubi Run collection landing in Asia, with its overall red design and creative interaction device, which fully reflect the creativity of the brand.

Brand Founder

Footwear designer Christian Louboutin was born in Paris, France, in 1963. His design made high heels popular again in the 1990s and the early 2000s. The designer believes that his shoes have the ability to "make a woman look sexy and beautiful, and to make her legs look as long as possible."

Louboutin began working on footwear design in 1982 and worked as a freelance designer for Chanel, Yves Saint Laurent and Roger Vivier. In the early 1990s, he founded his own high-end footwear brand and opened his first shoe store in Paris, France, in 1992. One of the brand's first customers is Princess Caroline of Monaco, and her public praise of Louboutin high heels has greatly enhanced the brand's popularity. In 1993, the red sole was introduced into its shoe design, which successfully opened up the brand's unique niche market in the high-end footwear industry. Today, Sammy Red Soled Shoes, a women's stiletto heel with a shiny red lacquered sole, has become the brand's classic.

周仰杰 Jimmy Choo

品牌简介

周仰杰是一家英国奢侈配饰品牌，源于由高级制鞋师周仰杰先生于20世纪90年代初创立的私人订制鞋业务。凭借其性感剪裁、时尚设计与出色的意大利工艺，周仰杰首个设计系列成功赢得一众名流顾客的青睐，从位于伦敦的小型创业公司逐渐发展为全球性品牌。该品牌如今隶属于时尚奢侈品集团卡普里①。周仰杰先生的侄女桑德拉·周自1996年加入东区设计工作室以来，担任品牌的创意总监；前路威酩轩集团的执行官皮埃尔·丹尼斯则于2012年被任命为该品牌首席执行官。

JIMMY CHOO

图7-56 品牌logo

周仰杰涉及较为全面的奢侈配饰品牌业务，以女鞋为核心产品，并同时推出手袋、小皮具、丝巾、太阳镜、眼镜、皮带、香水和男鞋等产品。周仰杰在全球共开设150多家专卖店，同时亦在世界各地知名百货公司及品牌专卖店内设有销售点。

图7-57 周仰杰 Jimmy Choo 产品系列

① Capri Holdings Limited，前身为 Michael Kors Holdings Limited。

品牌战略

图7-58　维多利亚·贝克汉姆穿周仰杰女鞋露面

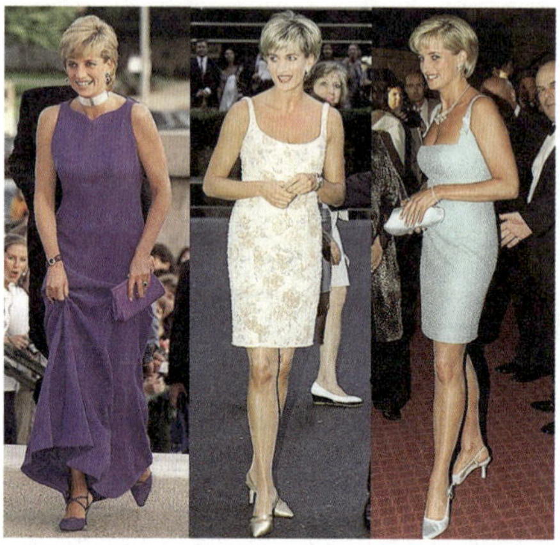

图7-59　戴安娜王妃穿周仰杰女鞋露面

以创立和发展遍布全球的奢侈品业务为目标，周仰杰已发展成一个从名流到皇室，由音乐人至国家元首都推崇的时尚标志。成立之初，其顾客已是来自世界各地上层社会的名流。作为名人时尚服装造型的先驱之一，周仰杰是第一批率先将华丽鞋履和手袋引进好莱坞的品牌之一，茱莉亚·罗伯茨（Julia Roberts）、麦当娜（Madonna）和维多利亚·贝克汉姆（Victoria Beckham）都曾将周仰杰作为红毯鞋履的首选。

图7-60　宋茜与周仰杰店合作胶囊系列

正由于深受名人喜爱与推崇，品牌积极扩展产品种类、销售管道及分店版图，其业务得以快速发展。第一家周仰杰店于1996年在伦敦莫特科姆街开业。两年后其销售网络扩展至美国，于纽约及比弗利山庄开设分店。此后，该品牌继续在全球范围扩展，并于世界各地著名奢侈品购物中心如伦敦的斯隆街和邦德街、巴黎的蒙田大道、罗马的康多提大道等地开设分店。2011年起，周仰杰开始发展其在亚洲的业务。2018年，中国女艺人宋茜成为周仰杰亚太地区代言人，并于2019年推出合作胶囊系列，在中国内地和香港地区限量发售。

周仰杰将创造体验型消费作为营销策略之一，以引导顾客接受其品牌理念，适应千禧一代以及其他潜在目标消费群的期望和要求。无论在实体零售店、在线商店，还是社交媒体活动，周仰杰都通过故事来传达其主张，比如邀请著名摄影师马里奥·特斯蒂诺、彼得·林德伯格、史帝文·梅西、克雷格·迈克迪恩及摄影师组合伊内兹和维努德等操刀拍摄的一辑品牌形象广告大片，以充满戏剧的效果诠释其独特品牌形象。

扫一扫

图7-61 品牌形象广告大片

品牌创始人

图7-62 Jimmy Choo Couture

周仰杰，品牌的联合创始人，于1948年11月15日出生在马来西亚槟城的一个鞋匠世家，在其11岁时制作了他生平的第一双鞋。

周仰杰以优异成绩毕业于英国伦敦考德维纳学院（现为伦敦时装学院的一部分）后，在伦敦北部哈克尼开设了他的第一家店。1988年，时尚杂志*Vogue*史无前例地用了8页版面介绍周仰杰的手工女装鞋，让周仰杰名声大噪。1990年之后，周仰杰为戴安娜王妃制作了无数双鞋子，其名声得到了更大的提升。1996年，周仰杰与《时尚》杂志编辑塔玛拉·梅隆共同创立了Jimmy Choo Ltd.，并开设精品鞋店，设计和销售工厂量产的女士鞋履。2002年，周仰杰脱售了他手上所有的Jimmy Choo Ltd.股份，继续专心于他的高档女士鞋履设计。目前Jimmy Choo Couture的鞋子是世界上最昂贵的鞋子，仅限在伦敦的康诺特街预约定制；其拥护者包括各国王室、影视明星、政商名流等。

周仰杰获得了多项荣誉，包括2002年的大英帝国勋章（OBE），以表彰他对英国时装业的贡献。

Jimmy Choo

Brand Introduction

Jimmy Choo is a British luxury accessories brand, originated from the private custom shoe business founded by senior shoemaker Jimmy Choo in the early 1990s. With its sexy tailoring, stylish design and outstanding Italian craftsmanship, Jimmy Choo's first design collection has won the favor of multitudinous celebrity customers and has grown from a small London-based startup to a global brand. The brand is now part of the fashion luxury group Capri Holdings Limited. Sandra Choi, the niece of Jimmy Choo, has been the creative director of the brand since joining the East-Area Design Studio in 1996; former LVMH group executive Pierre Dennis was appointed CEO of the brand in 2012.

Jimmy Choo is involved in a more comprehensive luxury accessories brand business. With women's shoes as the core product, it launches handbags, small leather goods, scarves, sunglasses, glasses, belts, perfumes and men's shoes and other products. It has opened more than 150 specialty stores around the world, and has retail stores in well-known department stores and brand stores around the world.

Brand Strategy

With the goal of creating and developing a global luxury goods business, Jimmy Choo has developed into a fashion symbol from celebrities to royalty, from musicians to heads of state. At the beginning of its establishment, its customers have been celebrities from the upper class in the world. And as one of the pioneers of celebrity fashion brand, Jimmy Choo is the first to introduce gorgeous shoes and handbags to Hollywood. Julia Roberts, Madonna Ciccone and Victoria Beckham have chosen Jimmy Choo as the first choice for red carpet shoes.

Due to the popularity and respect of celebrities, the brand has actively expanded its product range, sales pipeline and store layout, and its business has developed rapidly. The first Jimmy Choo store opened in 1996 on Motcomb Street in London. Two years later, the sales network was extended to the United States, opening branches in New York and Beverly Hills. Hereafter, Jimmy Choo continued to expand globally and opened stores in prestigious luxury shopping center around the world such as Sloane Street and Bond Street in London, Avenue Montaigne in Paris, and Via Condotti in Rome. From 2011, Jimmy Choo began to develop its business in Asia. In 2018, Chinese female artist Song Qian became Jimmy Choo spokesperson in the Asia-Pacific region and it launched a collection of cooperative capsules in 2019, which were sold in limited quantities in mainland China and Hong Kong.

Jimmy Choo creates experiential consumption as one of the marketing strategies to guide customers to embrace their brand philosophy, and adapt to the expectations and requirements of millennials and other potential target consumers. Whether in physical retail stores, online stores, or social media events, Jimmy Choo uses stories to convey his ideas, such as inviting famous photographers Mario Testino, Peter Lindbergh, Steven Meisel, Craig McDean, and photographers Inez and Vinoodh to shoot advertisements to express its unique brand image with dramatic effects.

Brand Founder

Jimmy Choo, co-founder of the brand, was born on November 15, 1948 in a shoemaker family in Penang, Malaysia. At the age of 11, he produced his first pair of shoes.

After graduating with honors at Cordwainers Technical College (now part of the London College of Fashion), Jimmy Choo opened his first store in Hackney, North London. In 1988, fashion magazine *Vogue* unprecedentedly used an eight-page layout to introduce his handmade women's shoes, which made him famous. After 1990, Jimmy Choo made countless pairs of shoes for Princess Diana, and his reputation has been greatly enhanced. In 1996, Jimmy Choo co-founded Jimmy Choo Ltd. with Tamara Mellon, editor of *Fashion* magazine, and opened a boutique shoe store to design and sell mass-produced women's shoes. In 2002, Jimmy Choo sold all his shares and continued to concentrate on his high-end women's shoes Jimmy Choo Couture. Jimmy Choo Couture's shoes are currently the most expensive shoes in the world. They are only available for appointment at Connaught Street in London; their supporters include the royal family, movie stars, and political and business celebrities.

Jimmy Choo has received a number of honors, including the 2002 Order of the British Empire (OBE), in recognition of his contribution to the fashion industry in the UK.

菲拉格慕 Salvatore Ferragamo

扫一扫

品牌简介

图7-63 菲拉格慕品牌logo

菲拉格慕是意大利奢侈品牌，由鞋履设计师萨尔瓦多·菲拉格慕（1898—1960）创立于1927年。该公司为菲拉格慕家族所有，总部自1938年以来一直位于佛罗伦萨市中心的中世纪斯皮尼大宅。2018年，菲拉格慕任命Micaela Le Divelec Lemmi（1998—2018年任职于古驰）为品牌首席执行官；2019年，Paul Andrew（2016年加入集团）被任命为品牌创意总监。

菲拉格慕以女士鞋履为起点并将其作为发展的重点，兼具经典设计与突出风格，注重高品质的材料和提升舒适感。继承品牌传统的同时，将对细节的关注和对工艺的坚持扩展到更广泛的商品开发，包括包袋（1949）、丝巾（1955）、手表（2008）、眼镜（1998）、香水（1997）和男女士成衣系列（1965/1970）等。发展至今，菲拉格慕已成为一个国际品牌，在世界各地的主要城市均设有店铺。

1995年落成于佛罗伦萨的萨尔瓦多·菲拉格慕博物馆，记录了该品牌创始人菲拉格慕的创意设计和精湛技艺。值得一提的是，菲拉格慕拥有制鞋业内最多的发明专利，曾在1929年至1960年间共获得368项专利。

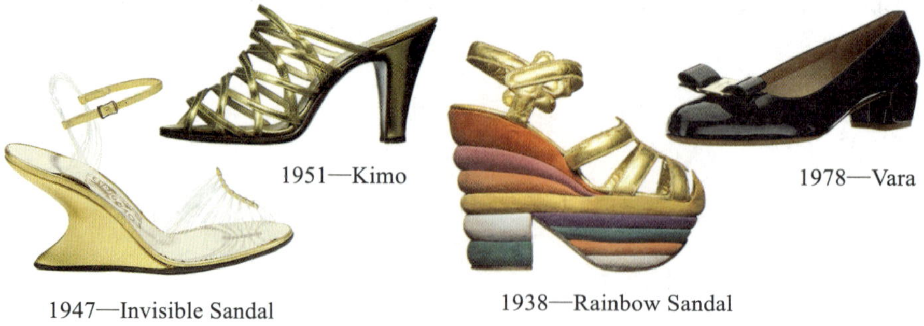

图7-64 菲拉格慕经典产品

品牌战略

20世纪50年代，菲拉格慕的名字是高品质、奢华的象征，其多年来的客户包括Audrey Hepburn，Greta Garbo，Paulette Goddard，Sophia Loren和Marilyn Monroe等。随着相继在伦敦和罗马开设商店，菲拉格慕采用现代商业营销策略，比如与未来主义艺术家合作推出广告，将其业务扩展到约700名专业工匠的规模，每天生产350双手工鞋。

为适应社会变革，重振其影响力，菲拉格慕致力于在传统设计、创新和趋势之间取得平衡。一方面，它将传统的标签作为其数字化演变的焦点，在传承品牌核心的基础上来多样化其产品，如经典产品Vara芭蕾平底鞋和印花真丝围巾，以及推出以插图叙述其品牌历史的Instagram计划。另一方面，菲拉格慕重新规划其设计和沟通策略。该品牌重新推出电子商务平台，并通过社交平台，与世界性影响者合作以开展数字营销活动，推广该品牌除鞋履之外的产品类别，努力建立新的品牌经典并重振其现有产品。比如，Rosie Huntington-Whiteley、Kendall Jenner和Lily Aldridge等超模分享其与Sofia手提包的合影。针对发展最快的中国市场则利用微信实施有针对性的数字化举措。

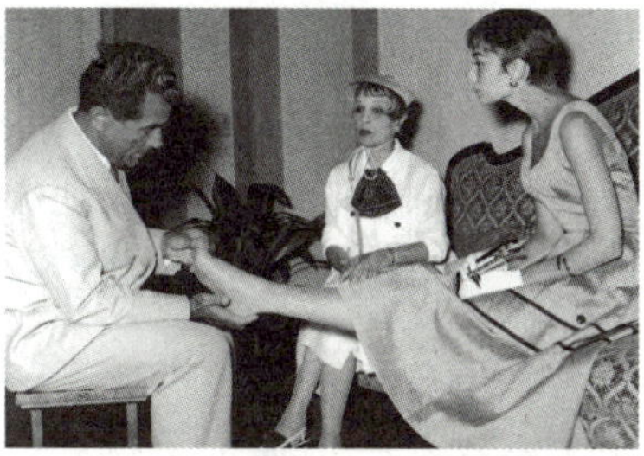

图7-65 奥黛丽赫本与菲拉格慕

图7-66 Kendall Jenner与Sofia手提包合影

扫一扫

品牌创始人

萨尔瓦多·菲拉格慕于1898年出生在意大利Bonito。从意大利南部移民至美国后，他于1919年开始在加利福尼亚州修理和定制鞋履。1923年，菲拉格慕在拉斯帕尔马斯大道开始经营一家好莱坞鞋店，为Joan Crawford和Gloria Swanson等电影明星以及电影制作鞋子，这促成了菲拉格慕成功的开端。与此同时，他在洛杉矶大学学习人体解剖学、化学和数学，以解决身体重

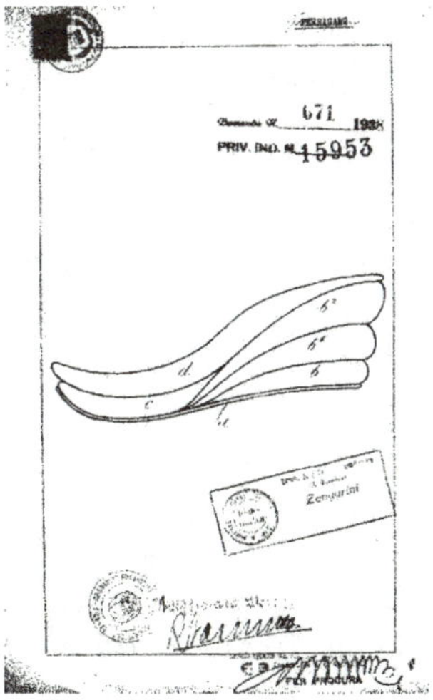

图7-67 软木楔形鞋跟设计图

量在足弓上的分布问题，最终成功研发了内部钢支撑shank，并获得了专利。这种支撑使鞋子变得更轻但耐用，也能在不牺牲鞋履定制质量的前提下实现批量生产。

1927年，菲拉格慕回到佛罗伦萨创立同名品牌，开始为女性设计时尚鞋履。作为时尚史上第一项专利的发明者，菲拉格慕创新了许多鞋履的设计，例如1938年推出的软木楔形鞋跟；"二战"期间，面对材料的缺乏，他选择了更便宜的材料，如使用经典的佛罗伦萨蕾丝、纸、树皮、椰叶纤维、大麻、鱼皮和玻璃纸来替代柔软的真皮材质；战后，又发明了使用尼龙或合成椰叶纤维的制鞋技术。

Salvatore Ferragamo

Brand Introduction

Salvatore Ferragamo is an Italian luxury brand founded in 1927 by shoe designer Salvatore Ferragamo (1898—1960). The company is owned by the Ferragamo family and has been headquartered in Palazzo Spini Feroni in Florence since 1938. In 2018, Ferragamo appointed Micaela Le Divelec Lemmi, who worked at Gucci from 1998 to 2018, as CEO of the brand; in 2019, Paul Andrew was appointed as the brand creative director, who joined the group in 2016.

Ferragamo takes the women's shoes as the starting point and as the focus of development, combining classic design with outstanding style, focusing on high-quality materials and comfort. Inheriting the brand tradition, it extends the attention to detail and the persistence of craftsmanship to a wider range of product development, including bags (1949), silk scarves (1955), watches (2008), glasses (1998), perfumes (1997) and RTW collection (1965) and so on. Since its inception, it has become an international brand with stores in major cities around the world.

The Salvatore Ferragamo Museum in Florence, completed in 1995, records the creative design and exquisite craftsmanship of the brand's founder. It is worth mentioning that Ferragamo has the largest number of invention patents in the footwear industry. It has obtained 368 patents from 1929 to 1960.

Brand Strategy

In the 1950s, Ferragamo was a symbol of high quality and luxury. Its clients over the years include Audrey Hepburn, Greta Garbo, Paulette Goddard, Sophia Loren and Marilyn Monroe.

With the opening of stores in London and Rome, Ferragamo adopted modern commercial marketing strategies. For example, collaborting with futuristic artists to launch advertising, Ferragamo expands its business to approximately 700 professional craftsmen, producing 350 pairs of handmade shoes each day.

To adapt to social change and reinvigorate its influence, Ferragamo is committed to striking a balance among traditional design, innovation and trends. On the one hand, it regards the traditional label as the focus of its digital evolution, diversifying its products on the basis of inheriting the core of the brand, such as the classic Vara ballet flats and printed silk scarves, and introduces the Instagram plan to elucidate its brand history with illustrates. On the other hand, Ferragamo re-planned its design and communication strategies. The brand relaunched the e-commerce platform and partnered with world influencers to develop digital marketing campaigns, promote product categories aside from the brand's footwear, and strive to build new brand classics and reinvigorate existing products. For example, supermodels such as Rosie Huntington-Whiteley, Kendall Jenner and Lily Aldridge share photos with their Sofia handbags. For the fastest growing Chinese market, it use WeChat to implement targeted digital initiatives.

Brand Founder

Salvatore Ferragamo was born in Bonito, Italy, in 1898. After immigrating to the United States from southern Italy, he began repairing and customizing shoes in California in 1919. In 1923, Ferragamo started a Hollywood shoe store on Las Palmas Avenue, making shoes for film stars such as Joan Crawford and Gloria Swanson and films, which led to the beginning of Ferragamo's success. At the same time, he studied human anatomy, chemistry, and mathematics at the University of Los Angeles to find a solution to the problem of body weight distribution on the arch. The internal steel support shank was successfully developed and patented. This makes the shoes lighter and more durable, and can also be mass-produced without sacrificing the custom quality of the shoes.

In 1927, Salvatore returned to Florence to create the eponymous brand and began to design fashionable shoes for women. As the inventor of the first patent in fashion history, Ferragamo has innovated many shoe designs, such as the cork wedge heel introduced in 1938; during World War II, he chose cheaper materials in the face of lack of materials, such as classic Florence lace, paper, bark, coir, marijuana, fish skin and cellophane instead of soft leather material; after the war, he invented the use of nylon or synthetic coconut fiber technology.

浪琴 Longines

品牌简介

浪琴是一家瑞士奢侈手表制造商，其总部设在瑞士圣耶米，由奥古斯特·阿加西于1832年创立，如今隶属于斯沃琪集团①。浪琴表历史悠久，其双翼沙漏徽标至今仍具有强大的品牌标识作用，也是全球首个进行商标注册的手表品牌。浪琴在全球150多个国家开展业务，其首家精品店位于悉尼的皮特街（Pitt Street）。

图7-68 浪琴品牌logo

自1999年以来，浪琴将“优雅态度，真我个性”作为品牌理念，进行多个类别腕表的开发。除了优雅系列（ELEGANCE）、制表传统系列（WATCHMAKING TRADITION）、马术系列（EQUESTRIAN）、运动系列（SPORT）外，还推出了经典复刻系列（HERITAGE），以彰显品牌的经典恒久与历史传承。

图7-69 浪琴经典产品

① 1985年，海耶克先生在对ASUAG和SSIH进行了历时四年多的重组后，最终促成两家钟表公司合并成立斯沃琪集团。如今，斯沃琪集团被认为是“世界顶级成表制造商”，自行生产机械表和石英表的零部件，独立进行产品的设计、生产及分销业务，同时拥有庞大的精品店网络和零售商网络。作为全球唯一一家利用大市场战略占领多个细分市场的制表商，斯沃琪为不同品味、不同经济阶层的顾客制造腕表，旗下拥有众多腕表品牌，其中包括斯沃琪（Swatch）、宝玑（Breguet）、欧米茄（OMEGA）、浪琴（Longines）、雷达（Rado）、天梭（Tissot）、美度（Mido）、汉米尔顿（Hamilton）等。

品牌战略

图7-70 加入斯沃琪集团

图7-71 浪琴表博物馆开幕

浪琴将自身定位为高级腕表品牌，通过口号“优雅是一种态度”来传达其品牌定位，致力于生产销售传统、优雅且兼具性能的产品，同时提供具有价值的客户服务，包括售前服务和零部件维修等。与零售商的关系是浪琴产品分销的重要组成部分，除了特许经营的零售店铺，也可以通过其官方网站及其他电子商务网站在线选购浪琴表。浪琴表新的市场也因此得到有效拓展。

浪琴表与全球多项体育赛事开展合作，加强了其优雅、精准的品牌定位，利用自身卓越可靠的专业技术，曾为众多体育项目提供计时装置，参与国际级别的体操、高山滑雪及射箭赛事。值得一提的是，该品牌参与马术运动的历史可追溯至一个多世纪以前，如今已成为众多著名平地赛马与马术障碍比赛赞助商。

广告视频也是其营销策略的一部分。这些短片围绕品牌精心打造腕表的故事，增强了消费者的体验，并通过使用YouTube等社交媒体，使品牌知名度得以提升。浪琴也积极运用“名人效应”，指定知名演员和体育明星作为其品牌大使以体现其腕表的优雅和高性能，其中包括演员凯特·温斯莱特、西蒙贝克，体操运动员朱利亚·斯泰因博格（Giulia Steingruber）、马术运动员珍·理查德（Jane Richard）等。

图7-72 浪琴中国区形象代言人彭于晏

品牌历史

1832——奥古斯特·阿加西（Auguste Agassiz）与拉伊格尔·亨利（Raiguel Henri）、弗洛里安·莫雷尔（Florian Morel）共同创办了Raiguel Jeune＆Cie钟表行，生产并销售怀表。

1852——阿加西的侄子，拥有经济学教育背景的欧内斯特·法兰西昂逐渐取得了家族企业的管理权。

图7-73　创始人奥古斯特·阿加西

1867——坐落在Es Longines的浪琴表工厂在法兰西昂的主持下落成，其生产的首款机芯20A在同年的巴黎国际博览会上荣获大奖。

1878——浪琴表在计时及测时方面研发生产了首款装置——计时机芯20H。自此浪琴表以其精确计时的秒表，开始在马术运动中建立起声誉。

图7-74　欧内斯特·法兰西昂

1889——法兰西昂为企业采取了一系列保护举措，包括将浪琴表的名称在联邦知识产权局进行商标注册。

1905——推出了第一款男士腕表。

图7-75　浪琴商标注册

1916——打破机芯的固有形状，推出一系列装配在腕表之上的椭圆形或方形机芯。

1931——与飞行员查尔斯·A.林德伯格合作，以1927年创作的威姆士（Weems）表款为基础，推出运用六分仪与航海历的航空腕表the Lindbergh Hour Angle watch。

图7-76　椭圆形机芯

1945——推出首款自动上链机芯22A。

1954——开发出首款石英表——Chronocinégines计时秒表装置。

1979——推出厚度仅为1.98毫米的石英腕表（金叶）。

图7-77　航空腕表

图7-78　Chronocin é gines计时秒表装置

图7-79　浪琴金叶石英腕表

图7-80　悉尼的皮特街浪琴精品店

1983-加入瑞士微电子和钟表公司（SMH），即今日的斯沃琪集团。

1992-浪琴表博物馆开幕，以追溯公司的发展历程。

Longines

Brand Introduction

Longines is a Swiss luxury watch manufacturer headquartered in Saint-Imier, Switzerland. It was founded in 1832 by Auguste Agassiz and is now part of the Swatch Group. Longines has a long history, and its double-wing hourglass logo still has a strong brand identity as the world's first watch brand for trademark registration. Longines operates in more than 150 countries around the world, and its first boutique is located in Pitt Street, Sydney.

Since 1999, Longines has developed "Elegance is an attitude" as a brand concept to develop watches of various categories. In addition to ELEGANCE, WATCHMAKING TRADITION, EQUESTRIAN and SPORT, it has also launched HERITAGE to highlight the brand's classic long-lasting and historical heritage.

Brand Strategy

Longines positions itself as a premium watch brand. Conveying its brand positioning through the slogan "Elegance is an attitude", Longines producing and selling traditional, elegant and high-performance products, while providing valuable customer service, including pre-sales services, parts repairs, etc. The relationship with retailers is an important part of Longines' product distribution. In addition to franchised retail stores, Longines can also be purchased online through its official website and other e-commerce sites. The new market for Longines has been expanded.

Longines has cooperated with many sports events around the world to strengthen its elegant and precise brand positioning. With its excellent and reliable professional technology, it has provided timing devices for many sports events, participating in international gymnastics, alpine skiing and archery competitions. It is worth mentioning that its participation in equestrian sports can be traced back to more than a century ago, and it has now become a sponsor of show-jumping, flat racing, endurance and eventing competitions.

Advertising videos are also part of their marketing strategy. These short films recreate the story of meticulously creating the wrist watch around the brand, enhance the consumer experience, and increase brand awareness through the use of social media such as YouTube. Longines also actively uses the "Celebrity Effect", designating well-known actors and sports stars as its brand ambassadors to reflect the elegance and high performance of its watches, for example, actress Kate Winslet, actor Simon Baker, gymnast Giulia Steingruber and equestrian Jane Richard.

Brand History

1832—Auguste Agassiz with Raiguel Henri and Florian Morel co-founded Raiguel Jeune & Cie watch-shop to produce and sell pocket watches.

1852—Agassiz's nephew, Ernest Francillon, who has an economics education background, gradually gained management of the family business.

1867—The Longines factory in Es Longines was inaugurated by Ernest Francillon, and its first movement, the 20A, won an award at the Universal Exhibition in Paris in 1867.

1878—Longines produced the first chronograph movement, the 20H calibre. Since then, Longines has established a reputation in equestrian sports for its precise timekeeping stopwatch.

1889—Francillon took measures to protect his business. From 1880, the brand name was filed with the Federal Office of Intellectual Property, while the logo was registered.

1905—Launched the first men's watch.

1916—The company began to develop shaped movements and produce a range of oval and rectangular calibres for wristwatches

1931—Working with pilot Charles A. Lindbergh, launched a navigational instrument, the Lindbergh Hour Angle watch, used in conjunction with a sextant and a nautical almanac, based on the model Weems created in 1927.

1945—Launched its first self-winding movement, the patented calibre 22A.

1954—Developed its first quartz clock—the timekeeping instrument, Chronocinégines.

1979—Presented a quartz watch that is only 1.98 mm thick, called Feuille d'Ork.

1983—Longines became part of Société Suisse de Microélectronique et d'Horlogerie (SMH), now renamed Swatch Group.

1992—The Longines Museum opened with a gallery retracing the company's history.

劳力士 Rolex

品牌简介

劳力士是瑞士奢华手表生产商，前身为由德国人汉斯·威尔司多夫（Hans Wilsdorf）与英国人阿尔弗雷德·戴维斯（Alfred Davis）1905年创立于英国伦敦的威尔司多夫·戴维斯（Wilsdorf and Davis）。自20世纪机械表时代开始，劳力士就已是全球手表业的翘楚。时至今日，凭借其超卓的工艺、创新技术和经典设计，劳力士依旧是奢侈品腕表市场的领跑者。

图7-81　劳力士最初使用的标志是一个五指伸开的手掌，寓意其产品完全靠手工精制，后来逐渐演变为现在人们所熟知的皇冠，展现着劳力士在制表业的领先地位

劳力士公司及其子公司帝舵[①]设计、制造、分销以及保养劳力士及帝陀品牌的腕表。该品牌的总部位于瑞士日内瓦，并在近100个国家拥有28家分支机构和4000名制表师，腕表年产量达到约100万只。劳力士的大多数手表为瑞士制造，在全球范围内通过自有商店、多品牌商店、电子商务网站和授权经销商等优质渠道分销其手表和配件，以保持其高端价值。

品牌战略

劳力士始终致力于将自身打造为奢侈品牌，凭借其象征性地位和其产品的差异化而广受欢迎。劳力士坚守产品质量，并注重细节，每一只劳力士手表往往由经过一系列严格质量检查的组件经手工组装而成。并且劳力士针对不同客户群设计特定的产品，例如劳力士游艇大师（Rolex Yacht-master），是拥有游艇并定期航行的客户的理想选择。

---

①帝舵于1946年开始设计、制造和销售手表，是劳力士创始人汉斯·威尔司多夫为拓展市场、增加销量而推出的普及版“劳力士”。帝陀表的标志采用英国都铎王朝时期玫瑰战争的标志，经过修改发展为盾牌状。(Montres Tudor S.A. began to design, manufacture and sell watches in 1946. It is the popular version of Rolex launched by Rolex founders Hans Wilsdorf to expand the market and increase sales. The logo of the Tudor used the logo of the Rose War during the Tudor dynasty in the United Kingdom and was modified to a shield.)

因此，劳力士将手表与特定的高端运动或活动联系起来，将手表作为专用产品推广给每个消费者。超过一世纪以来，劳力士腕表伴随世界各地的探险家探索世界之巅与海洋最深处。现在，劳力士全力支持高尔夫球、航海、网球、赛车及马术盛事，并为全球文化、科学及探险领域带来独特且持续的贡献。其于2019年推出的“保护地球，恒动不息”计划，旨在进一步加强对探险家的长期支持，合力保护环境。

扫一扫

品牌历史

1905—阿尔弗雷德·戴维斯和汉斯·威尔斯多夫在英国伦敦成立了威尔司多夫·戴维斯公司（Wilsdorf and Davis），从事钟表分销。

1908—正式注册“劳力士（Rolex）”作为其手表的品牌名。

1910—劳力士手表成为世界上第一款获得瑞士计时精度证书的腕表。

1914—伦敦基尤天文台授予劳力士手表A级精密证书。

1915—将公司更名为劳力士手表有限公司。

1920—在瑞士日内瓦将公司更名为劳力士制表公司，而后公司名最终演变为劳力士公司。

1926—推出世界上第一款防水腕表劳力士蚝式腕表。

1931—推出第一款自动腕表劳力士蚝式恒动腕表。

1945—推出第一款带有日历的防水手表日志型。（图7-82）

1953—推出Submariner，防水深度达100米。（图7-83）

1955—推出GMT-Master，适应航空公司飞行员的特殊需求。（图7-84）

1956—推出星期日历型Day-Date，第一款可同时显示日历及星期功能的手表。（图7-85）

图7-82

防水手表日志型

图7-83

Submariner

图7-84

GMT-Master

图7-85

Day-Date

1956——推出Milgauss，具备防御1000高斯磁场干扰的能力。（图7-86）

1963——推出新一代计时码表Cosmograph Daytona，防水且表围上有一个测速刻度，用于计算平均速度。（图7-87）

1985——成为第一个使用904L钢材制表的品牌。904L钢常用于高科技、航天及化工等行业，具有优异的抗蚀性能，自2018年起被称为蚝式钢“Oystersteel”。

2005——由劳力士研发并获得专利的Cerachrom外圈，可确保在最极端的环境下维持腕表的外观与功能。

2008——推出防水3900米的Deep Sea Sea-Dweller，专为极端水下探险而设计。（图7-88）

2012——推出蚝式恒动Oyster Perpetual Sky-Dweller，提供了直观读取的双时区，以及一个名为Saros的年度日历。（图7-89）

图7-86
Milgauss

图7-87
Cosmograph Daytona

图7-88
Deep Sea Sea-Dweller

图7-89
Oyster Perpetual Sky-Dweller

Rolex

Brand Introduction

Rolex is a Swiss luxury watch manufacturer, formerly known as Wilsdorf and Davis, founded by the German Hans Wilsdorf and the British Alfred Davis in 1905 in London, England. Since the mechanical watch era in the 20th century, Rolex has been the leader in the global watch industry. Today, with its superior craftsmanship, innovative technology and classic design, Rolex remains a leading player in the luxury watch market.

Rolex and its subsidiary, Montres Tudor S. A., design, manufacture, distribute and maintain Rolex and Tudor watches. Headquartered in Geneva, Switzerland, the brand has 28 branches and 4, 000 watchmakers in nearly 100 countries, with an annual production of approximately 1 million watches. Most of Rolex watches are made in Switzerland. Rolex maintained its high-end value by distributing their watches and accessories through quality channels such as their own stores, multi-brand stores, e-commerce sites and authorized dealers worldwide.

Brand Strategy

Rolex has always been committed to building itself into a luxury brand, which is popular for its symbolic status and differentiation of its products. Rolex adheres to product quality and pays attention to detail. Each Rolex watch is often assembled by hand through a series of strict quality inspection components. And Rolex designs specific products for different customer groups, such as the Rolex Yacht-master, which is ideal for customers who have a yacht and sail regularly.

Therefore, Rolex associates watches with specific high-end sports or activities and promotes watches as a dedicated product to each consumer. For more than a century, Rolex watches have explored the world's top and benthos with explorers from around the world. Now, Rolex is fully committed to golf, sailing, tennis, racing and equestrian events, and brings unique and continuous contributions to the global culture, science and adventure. The Perpetual Planet program, launched in 2019, aims to further strengthen long-term support for explorers and work together to protect the environment.

Brand History

1905—Alfred Davis and Hans Wilsdorf founded Willsdorf and Davis in London, England, for watch distribution.

1908—It officially registered "Rolex" as the brand name of its watch.

1910—The Rolex watch became the world's first watch to obtain the Swiss Chronograph Accuracy Certificate.

1914—The Kew Observatory in London awarded the Rolex Watch Class A Precision Certificate.

1915—It changed the company name to Rolex Watch Co. Ltd.

1920—In Geneva, Switzerland, the company was renamed to Montres Rolex S.A., and the company name eventually evolved into Rolex S.A.

1926—Rolex launched the world's first waterproof watch Rolex Oyster.

1931—Rolex launched the first automatic watch Rolex Oyster Perpetual.

1945—Rolex launched the first waterproof watch log with calendar Date Just.

1953—Rolex launched Submariner, which is waterproof for 100m underwater.

1955—Rolex launched GMT-Master to meet the special needs of airline pilots.

1956—Rolex launched the Day-Date, the first watch that displays both calendar and the day of week.

1956—Rolex launched Milgauss with the ability to withstand 1000 gauss magnetic field interference.

1963—Rolex launched a new generation of chronograph Cosmograph Daytona which is waterproof and has a speed scale on the bezel for calculating the average speed.

1985—Rolex became the first brand to use 904L steel watchmaking. 904L steel is commonly used in high-tech, aerospace and chemical industries, and has excellent corrosion resistance. It has been called "Oystersteel" since 2018.

2005—Developed and patented by Rolex, the Cerachrom outer ring ensures the appearance and function of the watch in the most extreme environments.

2008—What Rolex launched is waterproof for 3, 900m underwater, Deep Sea Sea-Dweller, designed for extreme underwater adventures.

2012—Rolex launched the Oyster Perpetual Sky-Dweller, which offers a dual time zone for intuitive reading and an annual calendar called Saros.

百达翡丽 Patek Philippe

扫一扫

品牌简介

百达翡丽（Patek Philippe）是一家瑞士日内瓦独立家族制表企业，从1839年成立以来始终保持着不间断的制表历史，自主设计研发机芯和钟表，包括构造复杂的机械机芯和石英表。1932年后，其一直为瑞士的斯登家族所有。

百达翡丽被广泛认为是世界上最负盛名的奢侈钟表品牌之一，也是精密机械钟表的领先制造商，对制表业做出了巨大贡献，先后获得了100多项专利。如：

1845—无匙上弦和手动设定系统

1868—第一款瑞士腕表

1925—首款万年历腕表

1933—“格雷夫斯”超级复杂功能怀表

1949—Gyromax平衡摆轮

1956—世界上第一个全电子钟

1989—Calibre 89配备33项复杂功能

其经典产品/产品系列包括：

PATEK PHILIPPE
GENEVE

图7-90　百达翡丽品牌logo[①]

图7-91　日内瓦百达翡丽博物馆

Calatrava（1932）　Perpetual calendar（1941）　Golden Ellipse（1968）　Nautilus（1976）　Gondolo（1993）　Aquanaut（1997）　Twenty-4（1999）　Star Caliber2000（2000）

图7-92　百达翡丽产品图片

① 百达翡丽著名的Calatrava十字星标志：Calatrava的名字源自一支成立于12世纪末的西班牙骑士团，该标志象征着独立勇敢的骑士精神；百合花纹样则表达其出众工艺和超凡设计的初衷。

百达翡丽在全球拥有400余个零售点，在亚洲、欧洲、北美和大洋洲均设有分销中心，为确保其提供的服务能够最大程度地满足客户的预期，其经销网络经过甄别筛选，并提供最高水准的售后服务。其于2001年在日内瓦Plainpalais区开设的百达翡丽博物馆则对不同时期的各种制表艺术杰作进行展示。

扫一扫

品牌战略

1996年百达翡丽推出“Generations”活动时，引入了其经典广告标语之一：“没有人能够真正拥有一块百达翡丽，你只不过在为下一代保管它。”这并非纯粹将产品作为导向来激发收藏家的热情，而是将品牌塑造为生活方式的选择，以体现其所遵循的传统感。除了由几代工匠的精湛技艺和艺术天赋创造的，兼具美学设计和机械精度的高级钟表，百达翡丽还通过其设于日内瓦罗纳大街（rue du Rhône）、巴黎芳登广场（Place Vendme）和伦敦邦德街（Bond Street）的沙龙呈现品牌的个性风格及设计作品，为客户提供品牌体验和情感价值。

图7-93　百达翡丽沙龙图片

百达翡丽所采用的稀缺原则，是其成为客户心目中的顶尖品牌的策略之一。除了推出限量发售的产品外，其手表都是直接销售给客户。并且每个腕表的生产，包括多达1200个步骤的手工制作与组装，都被严格要求以高超的工艺水准完成。因此，其手表售价是奢侈腕表领域的最高价格，单价往往不低于20000美元。同时，百达翡丽无需邀请知名人士为其代言，其自身所拥有的客户不乏贵族、政界人士和著名艺术家，如维多利亚女王、伊丽莎白二世女王、玛丽·居里、阿尔伯特·爱因斯坦、约翰·肯尼迪等等，足以在全世界范围内为其进行广告宣传，以吸引其目标消费群体。

品牌历史

1839—波兰制表师安东尼·百达与他的合作伙伴弗朗索瓦·沙柏在日内瓦成立了Patek，Czapek＆Cie钟表公司并开始制作怀表。

1844—让·阿德里安·翡丽凭借无匙上弦和手动设定系统在巴黎工业博览会上荣获

铜奖。

1851—公司更名为Patek，Philippe & Cie-Fabricants à Genève。在同年的伦敦世博会期间，其首款无匙怀表得到了维多利亚女王的青睐。

图7-94　女伯爵科索维茨瑞士腕表

1868—百达翡丽为匈牙利的女伯爵科索维茨创造了第一款瑞士腕表。

1910—百达翡丽打造出“雷盖尔公爵”西敏寺钟声怀表。

图7-95　“雷盖尔公爵”西敏寺钟声怀表

1927—杰姆斯·沃德·帕卡德收到他定制的百达翡丽天文怀表“帕卡德”。

1932—斯登兄弟投资收购Patek，Philippe&Cie。

1935—百达翡丽进入美国市场。

1962—百达翡丽的陀飞轮机芯在日内瓦天文台精准时计大赛中刷新了机械腕表的走时精度世界纪录。

1996—百达翡丽迁入位于日内瓦普朗莱乌特（Plan-les-Ouates）工业区的全新工坊。

2006—罗纳大街整饰一新的日内瓦百达翡丽沙龙隆重开幕。

2014—为庆祝175周年，百达翡丽推出一系列全新纪念表款。

图7-96　百达翡丽天文怀表“帕卡德”

图7-97　175周年系列全新纪念表款

Patek Philippe

Brand Introduction

Patek Philippe is an independent family watchmaking company in Geneva，Switzerland.

Since its establishment in 1839, it has maintained an uninterrupted history of watchmaking, independently designing and developing movements and watches, including the Complex-Structured mechanical movements and quartz watches. After 1932, it was owned by the Swiss Stern family.

Widely regarded as one of the world's most prestigious luxury watch brands and a leading manufacturer of precision mechanical watches, Patek Philippe has made great contributions to the watchmaking and has won more than 100 patents. Such as:

1845—Keyless winding and hand-setting system

1868—First Swiss wristwatch

1925—First wristwatch with perpetual calendar

1933—"Graves" supercomplication pocket watch

1949—Gyromax balance

1956—The first all-electronic clock

1989—The Calibre 89 with 33 complex functions

Patek Philippe has more than 400 retail stores around the world, with distribution centers in Asia, Europe, North America and Oceania. To ensure that its services meet customer expectations to the fullest extent, its distribution network is screened and provides customer service of the highest standards. The Patek Philippe Museum, which opened in 2001 in the Plainpalais district of Geneva, presents a collection of masterpieces of various watchmaking art in different periods.

Brand Strategy

In 1996, when launching the "Generations" event, Patek Philippe introduced one of its classic advertising slogans: "You never actually own a Patek Philippe. You merely look after it for the next generation." This is not a purely product-oriented approach to stimulating collectors' enthusiasm, but rather shaping the brand as a lifestyle choice to reflect the traditional sense. In addition to the high-end timepieces with both aesthetic design and mechanical precision created by the craftsmanship of several generations and artistic talents, Patek Philippe also presents its branded personality and timepieces through its salons at Rhone Street in Geneva, Place Fontaine in Paris and Bond Street in London, providing customers with brand experience and emotional value.

Patek Philippe's scarcity principle is one of its strategies to become a top brand in the minds of its customers. In addition to the launch of limited-edition products, its watches are sold directly to customers. And the production of each watch, including the handcrafting and assembly of up to 1,200 steps, is strictly required to be of a high level of craftsmanship. Therefore, the price of the watch is the highest in the field of luxury watches, and the unit price is often no less than 20,000 US dollars. At the same time, Patek Philippe does not need to invite celebrities to endorse it. Its clients include nobility, politicians and famous artists such as Queen Victoria, Queen Elizabeth II, Mary Curie, Albert Einstein, and John Kennedy, who are enough to advertise around the world to attract its target consumer groups.

Brand History

1839—Patek, Czapek & Cie was founded by the Polish watchmaker Antoine Norbert de Patek and his partner François Czapek and began to produce pocket watch.

1844—Jean Adrien Philippe obtained a bronze medal for his keyless winding and hand-setting system at the Industrial Exposition in Paris.

1851—The name of the company was changed to Patek, Philippe & Cie-Fabricants à Genève. And its first keyless watch was admired by Queen Victoria during The Great Exhibition in London in the same year.

1868—Patek Philippe created the first Swiss wristwatch for Countess Koscowicz of Hungary.

1910—Patek Philippe created the "Duke of Regla" Westminster chime pocket watch.

1927—James Ward Packard received his customized Patek Philippe astronomical pocket watch, "Packard".

1932—Brothers Jean and Charles Henri Stern invested in and purchased Patek, Philippe&Cie.

1935—Patek Philippe entered the US market.

1962—A Patek Philippe tourbillon movement bettered the world timekeeping precision record for a mechanical watch, at the Geneva Observatory.

1996—Patek Philippe moved into a new production facility in Plan-les-Ouates, Geneva.

2006—The renovated rue du Rhône salons in Geneva opened grandly.

2014—The 175th anniversary is marked with a new collection of commemorative watches.

第三节

本章讨论与阅读推荐

Discussion and Reading Recommendation

本章讨论

1. 请结合本章内容分析传统奢侈品牌（如LV）如何通过引入街头潮牌元素、借助明星效应，获得新的增长动力。

2. 尝试说明奢侈鞋履品牌应如何摆脱过度依赖经典款式、产品结构单一的局面。

3. 对于诸多高端腕表和珠宝等“硬奢侈品”来说，是否有必要开辟在线渠道作为品牌的增长点?

Discussion

1. Please analyze the contents of this chapter: How Could the traditional luxury brands (such as Louis Vuitton) gain new growth momentum by introducing street fashion elements and using the star effect?

2. Try to explain how luxury footwear brands should get rid of the situation of over-reliance on classic styles and single product structure.

3. For many “hard luxury goods” such as high-end watches and jewellery, is it necessary to open up online channels as a growth point for brands?

阅读推荐 Reading recommendation

《奢侈品之王》

作　者：［法］埃里·鲁迪埃（Airy Boutier）

出版社：中信出版社

译　者：岳瑞 / 张雪 / 刘倩

出版年：2013

ISBN：9787508637853

《卡地亚珍宝艺术》

作　者：故宫博物院编

出版社：紫禁城出版社

出版年：2009

ISBN：9787800478598

The Towering World of Jimmy Choo ——A Story of Power，Profits and the Pursuit of the Perfect Shoe

作　者：Lauren Goldstein Crowe / Sagra Maceira de Rosen

出版社：Bloomsbury Publishing PLC

出版年：2009

ISBN：9781408802151

参考资料 References

宝格丽

https：//en.wikipedia.org/wiki/Bulgari

http：//igem.ly/e/2643/fc4M1v

https：//www.mbaskool.com/marketing-mix/products/17351-bvlgari.html

https：//economia. uniroma2. it / master-science / ba / announcement / 2-816 / bulgari-marketing-sales-study-case#.XQJm0xYzYdU

https：//www. forbes. com / sites / rebeccasuhrawardi / 2017 / 10 / 20 / bulgari-ceo-talks-retail-strategy-and-the-opening-of-their-fifth-avenue-flagship/#32e2bb376837

https：//journal.hautehorlogerie.org/en/bulgari-a-leading-brand-in-digital/
https：//journal.hautehorlogerie.org/en/bulgari-a-leading-brand-in-digital/
https：//blog.usantiqueshows.com/2015/02/13/7-things-you-should-know-about-bulgari/
https：//translate.google.com/translate？ hl=zh-CN&sl=en&u=https：//www.truefacet.com/guide/beginning-brand-bvlgari/&prev=search

卡地亚

https：//ja.wikipedia.org/wiki/%E3%82%AB%E3%83%AB%E3%83%86%E3%82%A3%E3%82%A8
https：//www.invaluable.com/blog/cartier-collectors-guide/
https：//timeandtidewatches.com/insight-the-100-year-history-of-the-cartier-tank-and-people-who-made-it-famous/
https：//www.richemont.com/group/history-including-significant-investments-and-divestments.html
https：//www.vogue.com/article/a-look-at-the-cartier-style-and-history-retrospective-at-the-grand-palais-in-paris
https：//medium.com/@acoterof/cartier-king-of-jewelers-f52b078ae267
https：//daxueconsulting.com/market-strategy-cartier-in-china/
https：//jingdaily.com/cartier-culture-china/
https：//www.marketing91.com/marketing-mix-cartier-cartier-marketing-mix/
https：//www.koganpage.com/article/cartier-case-study-how-to-retain-relevance-in-luxury-marketing
https：//www.mbaskool.com/marketing-mix/products/16813-cartier.html
https：//www.hautehorlogerie.org/en/brands/brand/h/cartier/
https：//blog.theluxurycloset.com/2017/07/13/a-history-of-cartier/

施华洛世奇

https：//www.harmanbeads.com/history-of-swarovski
https：//www.jewelrysupply.com/120-years-of-swarovski-crystal
https：//www.savoirflair.com/fashion/93344/a-brief-history-of-swarovski
https：//www.savoirflair.com/fashion/93344/a-brief-history-of-swarovski
https：//en.wikipedia.org/wiki/Swarovski
https：//www.swarovskigroup.com/S/world_of_swarovski/optik.html
https：//www.8ways.ch/en/digital-news/secrets-swarovskis-marketing-strategy
https：//www.dmnews.com/marketing-channels/social/news/13055420/swarovskis-wordofmouth-strategy-sparkles
https：//www.ihdigital.com/digital-marketing-swarovski/
https：//econsultancy.com/how-swarovski-is-using-influencers-experiences-to-modernise-its-brand-for-millennials/

蒂芙尼

https：//en.wikipedia.org/wiki/Tiffany_%26_Co.

http：//www.thejewelleryeditor.com/jewellery/article/the-history-of-tiffany-tiffanys/
https：//www.truefacet.com/guide/history-tiffany/
https：//www.tiffany.cn/world-of-tiffany/the-world-of-tiffany-timeline/
https：//www.marketing91.com/marketing-mix-of-tiffany-company/
https：//etaileast.wbresearch.com/tiffany-co-diamond-digital-marketing-strategy-ty-u
https：//www.referralcandy.com/blog/tiffany-marketing-strategy/
https：//www.cmdsonline.com/blog/the-looking-glass/3-digital-marketing-lessons-brands-learn-tiffany-co/
https：//www.mbaskool.com/marketing-mix/products/17449-tiffany.html

爱马仕

https：//zh.wikipedia.org/wiki/%E6%84%9B%E9%A6%AC%E4%BB%95
https：//www.hermes.cn/cn/zh/
https：//baghunter.com/blogs/insights/hermes-brand-history-timeline
https：//www.bagsofluxury.com/guides/the-history-of-hermes/
https：//martinroll.com/resources/articles/strategy/hermes-the-strategy-behind-the-global-luxury-success/
https：//www.businessoffashion.com/articles/professional/hermes-anti-marketing-marketing
https：//www.ukessays.com/essays/marketing/hermes-analysis-in-business-marketing-essay.php
http：//www.reuters.com/article/idUSTRE5572K820090608
http：//www.iasdr2009.org/ap/Papers/Orally%20Presented%20Papers/Design%20Management/Luxury%20Brand%20Strategy%20of%20Louis%20Vuitton.pdf
https：//zh.wikipedia.org/wiki/%E5%87%B1%E8%8E%89%E5%8C%85
https：//zh.wikipedia.org/wiki/%E6%9F%8F%E9%87%91%E5%8C%85

路易·威登

https：//www.askattest.com/blog/news-and-trends/how-louis-vuitton-are-killing-it-on-social-media-awr
https：//www.luxurysociety.com/en/articles/2018/05/louis-vuitton-art-top-luxury-brand-maintenance-and-success/
https：//medium.com/global-luxury-goods-management/pros-and-cons-of-louis-vuittons-social-media-marketing-fe334cd9bee1
https：//www.ukessays.com/essays/marketing/louis-vuitton-becoming-successful-in-the-luxury-market-marketing-essay.php
https：//www.catawiki.com/stories/4913-the-secret-behind-the-success-of-louis-vuitton
https：//gfluence.com/expensive-taste-louis-vuitton-become-1-luxury-brand-china/
https：//jingdaily.com/louis-vuitton-digital-china/
https：//www.talkwalker.com/industry-research/retail/louis-vuitton-social-media-analytics
https：//www.marketing-etudiant.fr/marques/louis-vuitton-marketing.html
https：//www.theatlantic.com/business/archive/2011/05/branding-louis-vuitton-behind-the-worlds-most-famous-luxury-label/238746/
https：//en.wikipedia.org/wiki/Louis_Vuitton
https：//www.lvmh.cn/
https：//wiki.mbalib.com/wiki/LV

https：//en.wikipedia.org/wiki/Louis_Vuitton_（designer）
https：//thehandbagspa.com/blog/history-of-louis-vuitton/

克里斯提·鲁布托

https：//www.catawiki.com/stories/4533-the-secret-behind-the-red-soles-of-christian-louboutin
https：//www.glamour.com/story/the-true-story-of-how-christia
https：//blog.theluxurycloset.com/2017/07/13/christian-louboutin-history/
https：//didyouknowfashion.com/history-of-christian-louboutin/
https：//en.wikipedia.org/wiki/Christian_Louboutin&prev=search
https：//www. uselessdaily. com / fashion / christian-louboutin-25-interesting-facts-about-the-designer-and-his-shoes/&prev=search
http：//asia. christianlouboutin. com / cn_sc / news / cn_sc_innovation-meets-imagination-christian-louboutin-unveils-one-of-a-kind-collaboration-with-disney-studios-and-lucasfilm-for-star-wars-the-last-jedi/
http：//asia.christianlouboutin.com/cn_sc/news/cn_sc_naples/
http：//asia.christianlouboutin.com/cn_sc/news/cn_sc_zap-power-up-with-louboutinize/
https：//www.referralcandy.com/blog/louboutin-marketing-strategy/
https：//chelsealaurensmith.wordpress.com/2013/04/14/louboutins-brand-strategy-more-than-remarkable-its-trademarkable/
http：//www.redhotmarketingblender.com/2012/11/the-louboutin-brand-experience-flirting-with-your-feet/
https：//www.thebrandingjournal.com/2014/08/christian-louboutin-enters-make-industry-nail-polish-line/
https：//www.academia.edu/26277625/Assignment_Marketing_mix_tactics_for_achieving_Christian_Louboutin_shoes_positioning

周仰杰

https：//zh.wikipedia.org/wiki/%E5%91%A8%E4%BB%B0%E6%9D%B0
https：//en.wikipedia.org/wiki/Jimmy_Choo
https：//www.biography.com/fashion-designer/jimmy-choo
https：//www.jimmychoo.cn/about-us
https：//baike.baidu.com/item/Jimmy%20Choo/1699730？ fr=aladdin
https：//en.wikipedia.org/wiki/Jimmy_Choo_Ltd&prev=search
http：//fernfortuniversity.com/hbr/marketing/strategy/13808-jimmy-choo.php&prev=search
http：//jimmychooanalysis.blogspot.com/2014/12/brand-strategy.html
https：//www.vogue.co.uk/article/jimmy-choo-strategy-plans
https：//www. thedrum. com / news / 2016 / 05 / 12 / why-jimmy-choo-using-experiences-help-reach-luxury-shoppers
https：//www.forbes.com/sites/msolomon/2017/08/15/luxury-lineage-a-brief-history-of-jimmy-choo/
https：//blog.theluxurycloset.com/2017/09/04/history-jimmy-choo/&prev=search
https：//didyouknowfashion.com/history-of-jimmy-choo/#google_vignette

菲拉格慕

https：//en.m.wikipedia.org/wiki/Salvatore_Ferragamo
https：//ouahh.wordpress.com/2014/05/10/salvatore-ferragamo-branding-strategy/
https：//www.launchmetrics.com/resources/blog/digital-evolution-luxury-fashion
https：//www.forbes.com/sites/marioabad/2019/02/25/salvatore-ferragamo-sale-rumors/#201f916a9227
https：//fashionunited.uk/news/people/riccardo-vannetti
https：//www.nytimes.com/2010/11/09/fashion/09iht-rferr.html
https：//blog.theluxurycloset.com/2017/09/04/history-salvatore-ferragamo/
http：//www.catwalkyourself.com/fashion-biographies/salvatore-ferragamo/
https：//www.massaboutique.eu/the-brand/salvatore-ferragamo/
http：//www.afashionhistory.com/fashion-exhibition/walking-through-the-history-of-ferragamos-shoes/
https：//www.ferragamo.cn/

浪琴

https：//en.wikipedia.org/wiki/Longines
https：//www.longines.cn/company/presentation/longines
https：//www.chronext.com/guide/longines
https：//wornandwound.com/182-years-long-meadows-history-longines/
http：//swisswatchguy.blogspot.com/2008/03/from-ebauches-sa-to-eta-sa-75-years-of_15.html
http：//www.fundinguniverse.com/company-histories/the-swatch-group-sa-history/
http：//www.longines.com/company/history/19
https：//www.mbaskool.com/marketing-mix/products/17359-longines.html
https：//www.marketingmag.com.au/hubs-c/luxurious-but-functional-longines-brand-profile/
https：//www.forbes.com/sites/arianarockefeller/2017/09/14/longines-vice-president-juan-carlos-capelli-on-luxury-timing-and-equestrian-sport/#4d6b09c11e95

劳力士

http：//www.rolex.cn/about-rolex-watches/materials.html
https：//www.rolex.org/perpetual
https：//zh.wikipedia.org/wiki/%E5%8A%B3%E5%8A%9B%E5%A3%AB
https：//www.marketing91.com/marketing-strategy-rolex/
https：//www.marketing91.com/marketing-mix-of-rolex/
https：//www.marketing91.com/swot-analysis-of-rolex/
https：//www.rolex.com/about-rolex-watches/rolex-history/1905-1919.html
https：//zh.wikipedia.org/wiki/%E5%B8%9D%E8%88%B5

百达翡丽

https：//en.m.wikipedia.org/wiki/Patek_Philippe_SA

https：//www. studocu. com / en-au / document / national-economics-university / marketing-essential / essays / marketing-strategy-of-patek-philippe/3903661/view

https：//www.bartleby.com/essay/Patek-Philippe-Marketing-P3X8BY8KD6VS

http：//watchonado.com.au/patek-philippe-marketing-masters/

https：//www.randstad.com/workforce-insights/employer-branding/case-study-employer-branding-at-patek-philippe/

https：//www. europastar. com / magazine / features / 1004088464-business-strategies-patek-philippe-is-investing.html

https：//jingdaily.com/luxury-watchmaker-patek-philippe-china-market/

https：//deployant.com/history-at-a-glance-the-story-of-patek-philippe/

https：//www.patek.com

图书在版编目（CIP）数据

时尚品牌解析：英、汉 / 郑喆编著. — 杭州：浙江工商大学出版社，2020.4（2024.7 重印）

ISBN 978-7-5178-3580-6

Ⅰ. ①时… Ⅱ. ①郑… Ⅲ. ①服装－品牌－介绍－世界－英、汉 Ⅳ. ①F768.3

中国版本图书馆CIP数据核字（2019）第257680号

时尚品牌解析（双语）

SHISHANG PINPAI JIEXI（SHUANGYU）

郑 喆 编著

责任编辑 王黎明

封面设计 潘 洋

责任印制 包建辉

出版发行 浙江工商大学出版社

（杭州市教工路198号 邮政编码310012）

（E-mail：zjgsupress@163.com）

（网址：http://www.zjgsupress.com）

电话：0571-88904980，88831806（传真）

排　　版 杭州红羽文化创意有限公司

印　　刷 杭州宏雅印刷有限公司

开　　本 787 mm×1092 mm 1/16

印　　张 14.5

字　　数 368千

版 印 次 2020年4月第1版 2024年7月第3次印刷

书　　号 ISBN 978-7-5178-3580-6

定　　价 78.00元